Global Development and the Environment Series

Series Editors
Richard M. Auty and Robert B. Potter

Water and the Quest for Sustainable Development
in the Ganges Valley

Water and the Quest for Sustainable Development in the Ganges Valley

Edited by

G.P. Chapman and M. Thompson

MANSELL

First published in 1995 by
Mansell Publishing Limited, *A Cassell Imprint*
Villiers House, 41/47 Strand, London WC2N 5JE, England
387 Park Avenue South, New York, NY 10016-8810, USA

British Library Cataloguing-in-Publication Data
A catalogue record for this book is available from the British Library.

ISBN 0-7201-2191-4

Library of Congress Cataloging-in-Publication Data
Chapman, Graham.
    Water and the quest for sustainable development in the Ganges
valley / G.P. Chapman and M. Thompson.
        p.   cm. — (Global development and the environment series)
    Includes bibliographical references.
    ISBN 0-7201-2191-4 : $60.00
    1. Sustainable development—India.   2. Water—India.
3. Environmental policy—India.   4. India—Economic
conditions—1947–   I. Thompson, M. (Michael). 1937–   .   II. Title.
III. Series: Global development and the environment.
HC435.2.C474 1995
333.91′62′09541—dc20   94–18515
                                                                    CIP

Typeset by Litho Link Ltd, Welshpool, Powys, Wales

Printed and bound in Great Britain by Biddles Ltd, Guildford
and King's Lynn

Contents

Part III Midstream

Part IV Downstream

Part V Conclusions

Contributors

Sara Ahmed
Institute of Rural Management, PO Box 60, Anand 388001, Gujurat, India

Graham Chapman
Professor, Department of Geography, University of Lancaster, Lancaster
LA1 4YB, UK

Thomas Hofer
Institute of Geography, Universitat Bern, CH-3012 Bern, Hallerstrasse 12,
Switzerland

Shahnaz Huq-Hussain
Department of Geography, University of Dhaka, Dhaka, Bangladesh

V.K. Kumra
Department of Geography, Banaras Hindu University, Varanasi 221005,
India

Bruno Messerli
Professor, Universitat Bern, Institute of Geography, CH-3012 Bern,
Hallerstrasse 12, Switzerland

K.B. Sajjadur Rasheed
Professor, Department of Geography, University of Dhaka, Dhaka,
Bangladesh

Michael Thompson
The Musgrave Institute, 52 Northolme Road, London N5 2UX, UK

John Thornes
Professor, Department of Geography, King's College, Strand, London
WC2R 2LS, UK

Kegan Wu
Department of Geography, King's College, Strand, London WC2R 2LS, UK

Foreword

The principal aim of the Global Development and the Environment series is to provide an outlet for scholarly work covering important aspects of Third World development and change. The series is aimed at a multi-disciplinary audience and it is intended that the issues covered will be treated from a variety of different disciplinary perspectives – economic, social and political, historical and environmental among them. At the same time, we are aware of the need to achieve balance with respect to the various regions of the Third World that are covered by volumes in the series, not least because of the striking heterogeneity that is so characteristic of the nations that make up what we refer to in shorthand terms as the 'developing world'. In essence, we are seeking to promote the publication of works that deal in a rigorous manner with Third World themes and issues that are of topical interest and pressing social importance.

One important objective of the series is to encourage new and bold perspectives on development problems and issues. A second key objective is to develop inter-country comparisons that achieve balanced coverage of the principal regions of the world. It is hoped that such inter-country comparisons will shed new light on the ways in which differing social, cultural, economic, political, ecological and natural resource systems condition responses to global processes of change.

The series is thereby built around two closely related themes: globalization and environmental change. Globalization is a major trend affecting contemporary Third World countries. It is reflected in the diffusion of capital and technology, the evolution of new production systems and the spread of Western life-styles among elites and other groups. It is also witnessed in the increasing importance of multinational corporations. Yet it is clear that the processes of global restructuring and change are affecting various regions and nations at different rates and in a variety of different ways. For example, large income gaps have opened up within countries of Latin America and the Caribbean, while pressures on resources vary markedly among the various rural areas of Sub-Saharan Africa. Similarly, rates of economic growth have diverged sharply in East Asia. It is clear that patterns of production are becoming increasingly heterogeneous when viewed at the international level, while patterns of consumption and associated aspirations are frequently converging on what might be described as a global norm. However, such patterns of consumption are likely to be found to be strongly differentiated when they are examined in different groups and areas at the local scale.

Environmental change is strongly affected by the globalization of development, whether through the clearance and destruction of rain-forests, the occurrence of industrial accidents, the despoliation of attractive environments, indigenous cultures and socio-economic landscapes by the demands of international tourism, or the consequences of global warming for sustainable patterns of development and resource use. The examination of the interacting socio-political and environmental causes of these problems, and practical responses, stands as a further major theme of the series.

The present volume, jointly edited by Professor Graham Chapman and Dr Michael Thompson, fits well the the aims and remit of the Global Development and the Environment Series. In examining hydrological issues in the Ganges Valley, the book focuses on the complex relations which exist between environmental sustainability, development and poverty, and in so doing, ranges widely – and in places most provocatively – over both the human and physical environmental circumstances of the Ganges Valley. The editors have adopted a bold attitude towards some of the contradictions which exist between the chapters, and we feel sure that the volume will stimulate much-needed debate on some of the key issues which affect the relationships between environment and development.

Preface

The origins of this book lie in concern for the issues surrounding environment and development – or, as we would prefer, development and environment. To that end the India Development Group (UK) together with the Centre for South Asian Studies at the School of Oriental and African Studies held a conference in London on 'Environmental Problems in the Ganges–Brahmaputra Basins', an area which contains 10 per cent of the human race, and many of its poorest members. We could have held a conference on any South Asian geographical region – e.g. certain of the states of northern India, or the whole of India – but it seemed to us that in some ways these major river systems defined areas of interest in which many of the problems were interrelated. The extent to which this is true is nevertheless something of a surprise. The environmental problems of these basins are thought to include deforestation, soil erosion, soil degradation, sedimentation, floods, droughts, water and air pollution, loss of biodiversity, and a host of others. The extent to which, and the manner in which these are real and interrelated problems is examined in this book.

The defining characteristic of a river basin is of course water, and the movement of water. But even then the degree of centrality of water as the connecting thread between these problems has again been something of a surprise – indeed, in the list above only two items, air pollution and some kinds of loss of biodiversity, are not directly connected with water (although indirectly even these sometimes are). That is why the title of the book is no longer the same as the title of the conference.

There is no way in an area so vast and so diverse that we could produce a definitive account of water and its role in development and environmental issues. Instead, what we have tried to do is illustrate the many different approaches that different experts from both the physical sciences and the social sciences take in understanding how society and water interact, and how water and landscape interact. Although the book cannot be comprehensive, we feel that by consulting all the chapters a reader will come away with a much enhanced understanding of this region and the complexity of its dependence on what is, together with air, the most basic of life-sustaining elements. The fact that this complexity leads to contradictory but equally valid viewpoints is to be expected: and to help handle these contradictions Michael Thompson has provided a chapter on uncertainty and conflicting certainty.

We wish to thank the contributors, and many other persons, for their help – amongst these we single out Surur Hoda, Chairman of the India Development Group, Peter Robb, at the time of the conference Chairman of the Centre for South Asian Studies, Catherine Lawrence and Claire Ivison for their excellent cartography, Charlotte Reisch for her dextrous typing, and Jane Greenwood for putting the book through press.

Glossary

-ji	See Gangaji.
aman	The main monsoon season (Bengal).
aus	An early crop season at the beginning of the monsoon (Bengal).
Banares	Older spelling of Varanasi.
Banarasis	Inhabitant of Varanasi.
Benares	Older spelling of Varanasi.
bari	An unirrigated terrace in Nepal, usually sloping slightly downwards for surface drainage.
bastee	An informal slum squatter settlement, usually illegally occupying land.
BJP	Bharatiya Janata Party (Indian People's Party) – a Hindu fundamentalist party.
BOD	Biological oxygen demand – the amount of oxygen that would be used by micro-organisms to decompose organic material within a sample of water. The greater the BOD, the greater the pollution level.
boro	Usually of rice, in Bengal, which is grown in winter when elsewhere in Northern India other crops are grown.
bund	A bank around a field to retain water.
bustee	See bastee.
caste	An endogamous marriage group; or a class of such groups deemed to be of the same social status.
char	Land newly deposited by a river; usually sandy.
chawr	See char.
clastic	A sedimentary rock composed of mineral fragments – to be distinguished from igneous rock and organic rock such as coal or chalk.
clay	A very fine-grained sediment.
COD	Chemical oxygen demand – the oxygen required to break down all organic matter in water, by chemical action as well as micro-organisms.

crore	Indian decimal quantity = 100 lakhs, or in Western terminology 10 million. Note that Indian spaces therefore occur differently. 1 crore = 1 00 00 000.
dhobi	Washing. A dhobi-wallah is a washerman.
DO	Dissolved oxygen. In healthy water this is enough to meet BOD and also the demands of aquatic life such as fish.
doab	Interfluve – literally 'two rivers'. If not otherwise indicated, the Doab refers to the Yamuna–Ganges interfluve.
evapo-transpiration	The moisture lost to the atmosphere from a vegetated surface, both from direct evaporation and also from plant transpiration.
fault	A major fracture line in a geological structure between two rock masses which may move relative to each other.
Gangaji	Ganga enobled by suffix -ji, indicating holiness, esteem, sanctity.
ghat	A hill, escarpment, slope, bank. In this book it mostly means the steps down a river bank.
glacial outburst	Glaciers can dam meltwater near their snouts. These lakes may drain suddenly if the snout breaks or the depth of water floats the snout.
hydel	Hydroelectricity.
IAS	Indian Administrative Service – the successor to the Indian Civil Service.
Infiltration	The penetration of surface water directly into the soil.
INTACH	Indian National Trust for Art and Cultural Heritage.
KGGSS	Kashi Ganga Ghat Sudhir Samiti.
kharif	The main monsoon season in northern India (except Bengal, see aus and aman).
khet	A terrace which has a bund and is level, so that it can be irrigated or can retain rainwater.
KOE	Kilos of oil equivalent.
KTST	Kashi Tirth Sudhir Trust.
kumba	A vase or water vessel. A vase accompanies statues of the Goddess Ganga, and partly represents the formlessness of God alongside the form of the river.

kumbh mela	A major Hindu festival celebrated every three years rotating between Allahabad, Haridwar (both on the Ganges) and Ujjain and Nasik. The Mela at Allahabad is most significant.
lakh	Indian decimal quantity – 100 000. See crore.
matric suction	Negative pore water pressure, likely to induce capillary action.
MLA	Member of the State Legislative Assembly (state-level parliament).
Neotectonic	Recent tectonic.
NGO	Non-governmental organization, e.g. development charity.
PCB	Pollution Control Board.
piezometric surface	Ground water table if the water is unconstrained by overlying impermeable rock.
platy clay	Clay with flat particles.
pore air pressure	Air pressure in soil spaces.
pore water pressure	Water pressure in soil spaces.
puddling	The churning of soil and water in a paddy field prior to transplanting seedlings, which can then be pushed in by hand.
PWD	Public Works Department.
rabi	The winter crop season when temperatures are cooler.
riser	The steep front to a terrace.
rotational	Of a land slip where the back part of the slip moves down further than the front, so that a level surface ends by sloping backwards into the hill slope.
run-of-the-river	An irrigation or power system that relies on river flow without storage – i.e. no dams to supplement low flows.
saprolites	Weathered rock which is *in situ*.
sediment delivery ratio	The ratio of total erosion in a basin to the amount that is transported out – typically only a small part, since much of the eroded material will be deposited elsewhere within the basin.
seismic	Of shock waves in the rocks caused by earthquakes.
shear strength	Level of resistance before a sudden shearing breakage.
tectonic	Mass movement of a regional geological structure, e.g. uplift.

tensiometer	An instrument for measuring the soil's power of suction for absorbing water.
throughflow	Subsurface water that flows down a slope but within the soil. To be distinguished from water which infiltrates vertically into the ground water table.
usar	Northern Indian local term for land which is unusable due to waterlogging and salinity. Occurs naturally as well as a result of mismanagement.
Varanasi	See Banares.

PART I

Introduction

1

The Ganges and Brahmaputra Basins

Graham P. Chapman

Introduction

The Ganges and Brahmaputra are not just two of the mightiest rivers on earth, but they drain two basins of extraordinary variation in every sense – in altitude, in climate, in flora, in fauna and in the density of human settlement – and they are finally confluent in the world's largest and most active delta in Bengal. Nearly 500 million people live here: that is to say, 10 per cent of the human race inhabit this river system, the vast majority of them in the Ganges basin. This 10 per cent includes at least 30 per cent of the world's poorest 1 billion people – the poorest farmers and labourers of Nepal, Bhutan and Uttar Pradesh, and the poor of West Bengal and Bangladesh. Quite obviously for these people, and even for those in the comparatively wealthier sections of society, the key issue is one of development – achieving an adequate material standard of life, and hopefully too a political system that is representative and which guarantees civil liberties.

But even the simple facts as just stated would imply that there are great strains on resources in this region. Since the whole basin is still 80 per cent rural, a population of small farmers will put pressure on land and every imaginable rural resource – and above all demand more water for irrigation of every kind. Since the basin already has 100 million urban inhabitants, likely to grow to 450 million in the next 40 years, the cities will demand an ever-increasing supply of water and power, and they will discharge ever-increasing amounts of waste. Since the climate is so seasonal, with nearly all the precipitation in a three-month monsoon period, and with many tributaries drying up during the winter and hot season, the problems of storing water to provide a constant year-round flow become overwhelming.

Table 1.1 Current and projected total population and level of urbanization for the Ganges and lower Brahmaputra basins

	Total population 1991 '000's	% Urban population 1991	Annual % growth of population 1981–1991	% Population below poverty line (India only)	Projections 2011		Projections 2031	
					Total population	% Urban	Total population	Urban
Ganges hills								
UP Hills*	5 900.9	21.6	2.0		8 763.7	31.5	13 015.4	41.0
Himachal Pradesh	5 111.1	8.7	1.8	19.1	7 277.8	16.2	10 363.0	24.9
Nepal	19 379	8	2.6		32 084.2	18.8	53 119.3	31.3
	30 391	**10.8**	**2.3**		**48 125.7**	**20.7**	**76 497.7**	**32.1**
Ganges plains								
Delhi	9 370.4	89.9	4.2	15.8	15 155.5	91.2	24 512.2	92.3
Chandigarh	640.7	89.7	3.6		1 039.4	91.0	1 686.1	92.2
Bihar	86 338.8	13.2	2.1	47.9	131 197.7	23.1	199 363.9	33.6
Harvana	16 317.7	24.8	2.4	17.2	25 907.9	36.3	41 134.3	46.8
UP Plains	133 130	19.8	2.3	42.9	208 967.1	31.1	328 004.2	41.9
	245 798	**20.7**	**2.3**		**382 267.6**	**31.2**	**594 700.7**	**41.7**
Brahmaputra hills								
Arunachai Pradesh	858.4	12.2	3.1	12.3	1 572.0	26.6	2 878.8	41.3
Manipur	1 826.7	27.7	2.5	37.3	3 001.3	39.8	4 931.2	50.5
Megha	1 760.6	18.7	2.8		3 039.2	32.3	5 246.4	45.0
Mizoram	686.2	46.2	3.4		1 314.5	58.5	2 518.0	67.9
Naga	1 215.6	17.3	4.6		2 949.3	38.9	7 155.4	56.9
Sikkim	405.5	9.1	2.5		662.5	20.0	1 082.3	32.2
Bhutan	1 476	4	2.3		2 325.7	11.6	3 664.7	22.2
	8 229	**19**	**3.0**		**14 864.4**	**33.0**	**27 476.7**	**47.3**
Brahmaputra plains								
Assam	22 294.6	11.1	2.1	38.0	33 939.4	20.7	51 666.5	31.2
Bengal Delta								
Tripura	2 744.8	15.3	3.0	47.4	4 958.6	29.7	8 958.0	43.8
West Bengal	67 982.7	27.4	2.2	48.1	105 094.1	38.1	162 464.5	47.8
Bangladesh	107 993	15.7	1.9		155 549.6	24.6	224 048.7	33.8
	178 720.5	**20.1**	**2.0**		**265 602.3**	**30.0**	**395 471.2**	**39.5**
South Asian Ganges–Brahmaputra Basin	**485 433.1**	**19.4**		**36.9****	**744 799.4**	**29.7**	**1 145 812.8**	**39.9**

Sources: Census of India, 1991, Muthiah (1987), and Encyclopaedia Britannica (1992).
*Districts of UP included in Hills:
Uttar Khashi; Dehradun; Almora; Chamoli; Garhwal; Nainital; Terhi Garhwal; Poithoragarh

Because the basins are politically divided between five sovereign states, each jealous of its rights, a co-ordinated response to the growing problems of the area is currently impossible to achieve.

That there are problems would appear to be self-evident, yet there is little agreement within the political community or even within the scientific community as to what they are. For many of the major issues, good and reliable data for decision-making simply do not exist. Neither will such data ever exist – since it is impossible in real time to record by census, by satellite or by other means 'everything relevant' that is going on, even if the concept of 'everything relevant' could ever be defined. Part of this book is about the problems of decision-making when what is known is, firstly, hardly anything, and secondly, contradictory or unreliable.

Then there is the question of sustainability – a word added by reflex to any contemporary development objective, a word in grave danger of losing all meaning, if it has not already done so through endless mantra-like recitation. The usual definition of sustainability is 'development that meets the needs of the present without compromising the ability of future generations to meet their own needs' (World Commission on Environment and Development). The problems of operationalizing this definition are immediate. It assumes that the twin goals are reconcilable, without proof. It also makes a distinction between present and future which on close examination is seen to be untenable. The present embodies the future – indeed in a sense there is no 'present' but only the future, and the past. Those who are presently in abject poverty – hundreds of millions in the river basins we survey here – will not have had their present needs met by tomorrow. What we have to do now is admit that the future demands of those presently alive will escalate, and that if we attempt to meet them, then by accepting them as a justified present liability, we may compromise the ability of future generations to meet their demands. And this argument can be made tomorrow and every day afterwards – so that we will always be able to justify the demands of the present.

If one looks at the issue less philosophically and more pragmatically, there can be other surprises. The extent of current poverty in India is recorded by the number of people living below the official poverty line. In 1983–1984 37 per cent of the population was recorded as living below this very low and basic standard (see Table 1.1). In Bihar the figure was nearly as high as 50 per cent, and in Uttar Pradesh 45 per cent. The Government has admitted that in the short term there is very little it can do for many of these people. On the surface this might look like abandoning hopes that present needs can be satisfied, and to that extent the reduced consumption of the present may save resources for future generations. However, there are many studies which suggest that poverty and low levels of consumption may be linked to particularly destructive and wasteful use of the environment. Anyone who has watched children lopping branches off trees and women scraping grass roots up with a small trowel, to bundle up and take home to feed the family goats, will recognize how this can happen. This reinforces a view taken by Sundaram (1993) that operationally what is important is not to demonstrate sustainability, but to make sure that what is unsustainable is avoided. The practices just described can lead to loss of vegetation cover and soil loss, and to that extent are explicitly unsustainable.

Throughout this book we will look implicitly at unsustainable practices, and from time to time explicitly so. We do not do so from every possible angle. We say little about urban pollution – indeed, nothing about air pollution and acid rain. We say little about what is explicitly sustainable – nothing about, for example, low external input agriculture. Such issues are of great importance – but here, for the sake of this one volume, we concentrate on that most basic of resources, water, in many of its manifestations in this region. Water is implicated in erosion, sedimentation, irrigation, flooding and drowning (crops as well as people), quenching thirst, hygiene, power generation, cooling, manufacturing, and fishing, amongst other things, and therefore hardly surprisingly it is deeply implicated in politics, religion and art as well. All these manifestations of water are interconnected in the physical and mental landscapes of the Ganges valley, one of the demographically most significant river basins of the planet. It is also a river basin subject to rapid rates of environmental change – and it is to these background geological and geographical dynamics that we turn next.

The Geological and Geomorphological Background

Although we know so little about the area, we know enough at least to sketch a backdrop against which to understand the kinds of forces at work in the environment, and, critically, the scale of these forces. Roughly speaking, there are three major regions to consider. These are: (1) the Deccan block, the northern front of which forms the southern catchments of the Ganges; (2) the riverine sedimentary plains of the Ganges in Uttar Pradesh, Bihar and West Bengal, and the sedimentary plains of the Brahmaputra in Assam and Bangladesh; and (3) the Himalayas. The first region, the Deccan block, is normally considered a not very dynamic environment, being an old part of Gondwanaland which has ancient and stable slopes. It is not considered a seismic risk zone, despite the unpredicted and catastrophic earthquake of September 1993. But the other two regions are some of the most dynamic environments on earth, with massive rates of change and massive movements of material. We have to start with this as the backdrop to this book.

Current knowledge is fairly conclusive about the fact that the earth's land masses were originally in two pan-continents: northern Laurasia, which comprised North America and the main European, former Soviet

Asian and Chinese land mass; and southern Gondwanaland, comprising South America, Africa, India, Antarctica, and Australia (King, 1983). Between the two was the middle Tethys Sea, whose remnants now include the Mediterranean and Caspian. Beneath these pan-continents were (and are) a series of plates, which have moved apart from each other. Laurasia has split into two, opening the North Atlantic; and Gondwanaland has split into several pieces in a process which is ongoing. These parts have been moving relative to each other for more than 1000 million years, and at various times parts of Africa have ground into the southern flank of Europe. About 200 Ma (million years ago) the Indian Deccan block broke off from southern Africa, and drifted across the Arabian sea (and therefore for a long time was a very large island); and then about 80 Ma it first

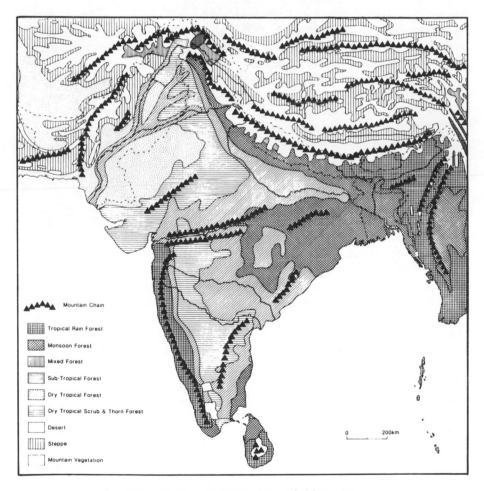

Figure 1.1 The physical background of South Asia.

pushed into the southern fringe of Laurasia, denting what was a fairly straight line between the straits of Hormuz and southern Malaya.

Part of the result of this denting has been the folding and uplifting of the mountain rim on all landward sides of South Asia – from the northwest frontier through the high Himalayas to the Burmese border. The aptness of calling India and South Asia a subcontinent, of dwelling on its distinctiveness as another world separate from the rest of Asia, is immediately apparent.

This contact zone and that of adjacent East Asia is the most powerful and most recent of continent-to-continent collisions. The thrusting has resulted in part of the India plate pushing under the Tibetan plate in what is known as a subduction zone, and the result includes both a trough (the Ganges–Brahmaputra plains) and the Himalayan mountains. Not everything is known about the complex processes involved, but the following are facts: the Deccan block is still pushing at the Tibetan plateau at a rate of about 5 cm/year (Tapponnier *et al.*, 1986, p. 116); the Himalayas are uplifting at the rates of between 1 and 9 cm/year (Ives and Messerli, 1989, p.98); and inevitably this is a very active zone both for seismic (earthquake) and tectonic (mass land displacement) activity. The earliest stages of Himalayan uplift are dated at about 70 Ma, and some of the more recent uplifting of Tibet and the Himalayas towards current heights is within the last 600 000 years, and therefore within the Pleistocene, and the uplifting of the fore ranges such as the Mahabharat began 200 000 years ago – so recently in terms of earth history, that if the earth has existed for one *year*, this event started in the last 23 *minutes*.

Given that this has happened in an area of extremely high rainfall, and that some of the rock lifted and exposed has been comparatively young sediment from the Tethys sea bed, it is not surprising that the Himalayas are suspected of having the highest natural denudation rate in the world (Ives and Messerli, 1989, p. 96f). It is of course this denudation that has deposited the great alluvial plains, in places on top of marine sediments, which are quoted as being 5000 m thick (Ives and Messerli, 1989, p. 21) and more than a mile deep (Michel, 1967, p. 30) with respect to the Indus basin. The sediment pouring into the Bay of Bengal has built the current visible delta, but sedimentation from the Ganges–Brahmaputra continues into the bay for a further 2000 nautical miles (King, 1983, p. 119): the current delta is a little like the proverbial iceberg, nine-tenths hidden, and the actual point at which land crawls out of the sea almost arbitrary.

Inland equivalents of the delta are the alluvial fans at the foot of the mountains, across which the rivers migrate as they drop their loads. The Kosi has migrated 100 km west in 250 years (Ives and Messerli, 1989, p. 140), and the Tista has behaved similarly (see below): the Beas (Indus basin) was captured by the Chenab in 1790 (Buckley, quoted in Michel, 1967, p. 48). Since the British arrived in Bengal and founded Calcutta

(1670s) it has become evident that there is a long-term shift of the discharge from the western to the eastern distributaries. The Hooghly has accordingly lost discharge and become more heavily silted, a point of great importance in the relations between India and Bangladesh, to which we will return in later chapters.

The Climatic Background

The pre-eminent climatic feature of the region is the monsoon. The word monsoon, derived from the Arabic for 'season', normally refers to any constant wind in any region where there are seasonal changes in such winds. There are thus actually two monsoons in India – the advancing southerlies, southwesterlies and southeasterlies of June to September, which bring heavy rain, and the retreating monsoon of October and November. The advancing monsoon comes from the Arabian Sea and Indian Ocean, and carries a very heavy moisture load. The retreating monsoon comes from the landmass, and has very little moisture, although some is again picked up in the Bay of Bengal and precipitated over Tamil Nadu in southern India in October, November and December, to give that small area a very distinctive rainfall regime.

Although a full and detailed explanation of the monsoon has yet to be developed, enough is known of the major factors to provide an adequate understanding for the purposes of this book. The major factors are the Himalayan and other mountain systems which block India off from the rest of Asia, the seasonal movement of the inter-tropical zone of convergence, the position of the subtropical (not polar-front) jet stream, and seasonal changes in temperature and pressure near ground level.

To take the last first, it was long thought that as temperatures rose very high from March onwards in Punjab (both Pakistani and Indian) and the Ganges valley, and atmospheric pressure fell, then the subcontinent modelled seasonally the local daily phenomenon felt by many coasts, of a sea breeze by day, and a land breeze by night. In both cases the winds would blow from the cooler and higher pressure zone to the hotter and lower pressure zone. The problem with this as a simple theory was that it failed to explain why the onset of the monsoon should be so late and so sudden – like an annual seasonal switch being thrown.

There are two latitudional belts that are of most concern here. The first is the subtropical jet stream which occurs in the upper air above the anticyclones where descending air dries out the desert belts of the northern hemisphere – the Sahara, the Mexican etc. Then south of this there is the inter-tropical zone of convergence, which on average is situated over the equator, but which goes south of the equator in the northern winter, to return north of the equator in the northern summer. It seems that during the winter months the massive height and breadth of the Himalayas and

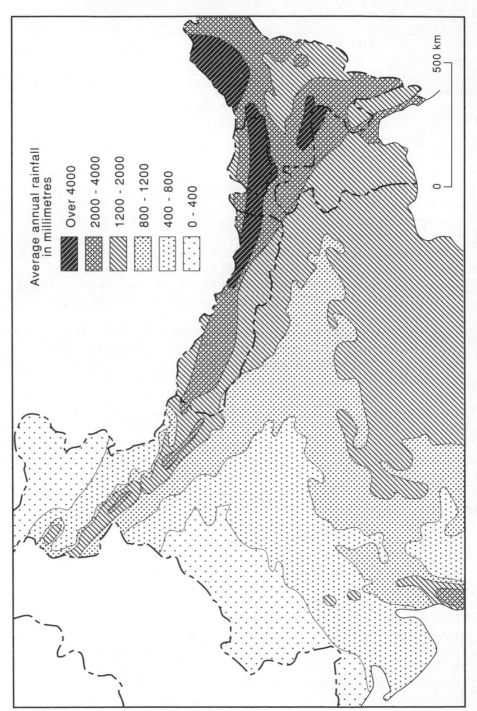

Figure 1.2 Average annual precipitation in northern South Asia.

Average annual rainfall
in millimetres

Over 4000

2000 - 4000

1200 - 2000

800 - 1200

400 - 800

0 - 400

500 km

0

the Tibetan plateau cause the subtropical jet stream to move south of the mountains, possibly further south than it would otherwise be, and it 'locks' south of the mountains. As the northern summer progresses, the movement north of the inter-tropical zone of convergence is delayed by the continuation of the jet stream south of the Himalayas. Only in late May does the northward march of the climatic belts shift the sources of the jet stream west of India far enough for the stream suddenly to switch to the north of Tibet. When this happens the surface winds respond to the trough of low pressure over the Ganges valley, and the monsoon starts.

The winds track northeast from the Arabian sea, and then move north into Bengal and Assam. But a considerable part is deflected northwest by the mountain wall of the Himalayas, to turn west and north up the Ganges valley, finally reaching the northwest frontier of Pakistan. In general terms this means that rainfall ought to be heavier in Bengal near the sea than further up in the Ganges valley – and this indeed is the case. It further explains why Cherrapunji in Meghalaya is the wettest place on earth. It also means that most rainfall occurs in just a few short months.

There are of course many complicating factors. Although the lower and more southerly ranges of the Himalayas get extremely heavy rainfall, at higher altitudes, which means further north as well, the precipitation may be reduced by rain-shadow effects. In many higher valleys it is actually very low, and parts of the Tibetan plateau are meteorological deserts. This means some of these mountain arid areas are very fragile and sensitive environments. Finally, of course, at high altitudes it is not rainfall but snowfall, accumulating in the largest area and number of glaciers outside of the polar circles. Rainfall from winter westerlies is possible, but it is only in the mountains of the north and west that there is a winter maximum.

In general, then, there is heavy precipitation on the mountain fronts, poorer precipitation in the large catchments beyond, quite heavy precipitation in Bengal, but sparser and less reliable rainfall the further north and west one traverses up the plains. The maps depicting the onset and retreat of the monsoon (Figures 1.3 and 1.4) also show how the length of the rains varies from five months in the east to three in the west.

It is usual to think of the year as having three climatic seasons: the monsoon, which is the rainy period, and during which the kharif crops are grown; winter, which is cooler and may have a few showers, and during which the diurnal range of temperature is maximized between cold nights and warm days, and the rabi crops are grown; and the hot season. During the hot season, which peaks somewhere around May–June, temperatures in the western parts of the plains may reach 46°C. At such a temperature and with low humidity the potential evapotranspiration is enormous. Thus the dormant period for deciduous trees and grasses is the hot season, not the cold season as in higher latitudes. It is also the dormant time for farming, as desiccation of the crops is almost instantaneous. In fact, for all

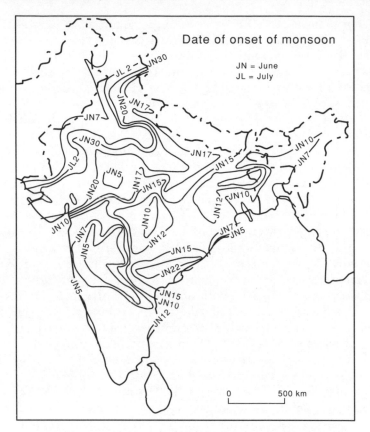

Figure 1.3 Date of onset of monsoon. *Source:* Chatterjee (1953).

the non-monsoon period of winter and the hot season – therefore up to nine months in the western plain – evapotranspiration exceeds precipitation by a wide margin. This means that vegetation will only grow in these two seasons to the extent that temperatures are not too high, that there is some retained soil moisture, or that irrigation is provided.

The natural vegetation of most of the area is forest, different kinds of tropical deciduous forests reflecting the different precipitation regimes on the plains and ultimately degenerating into semi-arid scrub in the far northwestern plains. In the lower mountains evergreen shrubs and trees predominate. In the higher mountains there are some fragile grasslands. The natural vegetation of the area would also include pockets of non-forest: in some areas of the Terai (immediate foreland plains of the Himalayas, mostly in Nepal) extensive tall grasslands do still exist, often associated with sandy tracts and sometimes with waterlogging.

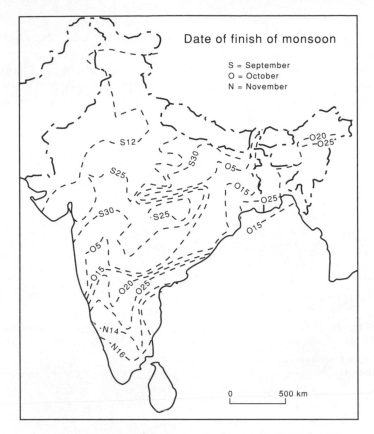

Date of finish of monsoon

S = September
O = October
N = November

Figure 1.4 Date of retreat of monsoon. *Source:* Chatterjee (1953).

Early Settlement: of Gods and Society

The Ganges plains are the heartland of Hinduism – one of the older of the world's religions – if that inappropriate Western word can be so lightly applied to the varieties and complexities of ways of life, beliefs, rituals and philosophies of northern India. The actual word is, curiously, derived from the Indus, that river by which and beyond which lived the people who became known to the outside world as (H)Indus. The origins of Hinduism are closely tied up with waves of Indo-Aryan settlers from central Asia and Iran who swept into India from the northwest through such passes as the Khyber from about 1500 BC. Before the Aryans agriculture had already been established in South Asia, in for example the Harappan civilization of the Punjab and Indus, whose greatest glory was Monhenjo-daro. Although initially the Aryans were a pastoral people, they too adopted agriculture and a more settled way of life, subjugating the indigenous population. They were bolstered by the traditions of their oral history as recorded in the Vedas (the 'Truth' or 'Knowledge', the sacred hymns of the Aryans *very roughly* analogous to the Jewish psalms and the Old Testament), and for a while the view was held that they absorbed little of the extant culture of the area. But it now seems likely that even such important Hindu gods as Shiva and perhaps such common Hindu practices as phallus worship, and certainly the technology of the ox-cart, were adopted from their predecessors.

We have some idea of these early times because the priestly caste of the Hindus, the Brahmans, have jealously guarded the Vedas since these early invasions. There are four sets – the oldest, known as the Rig-veda, was composed about the time of their first arrival in the Punjab. From it we can get an idea of the geography of the land of the Sapta-Sindhu (they recognized seven (sapta) rivers in the Indus where now we know five, Punjab meaning Panch (five) ab (river)). It was a land of cold winters and hot summers, and unreliable rain which could fall in either winter or summer.

South lay the land of Vitra – the land of drought – the present lower Indus Valley and the Thar Desert. To the east lay the land of both Vitra and Indra – drought and rain, the monsoon lands of the Ganges basin. The Aryans pushed east into this land of Vitra and Indra and intermarried with the indigenous Dasyus (Dravidian people), but also treated them as beneath and below them. From this comes the beginning of a caste system. In India sometimes the word *varna* is used instead of caste, and it means 'colour'. They also began to adopt the ways of the agriculturalists of the plains, in the days of the Rig-veda cultivating barley in the Punjab, and later in the Ganges lowlands to the east and south both wheat and of course rice. By about 500 BC society had evolved enough for urban centres to develop at different locations up and down the Ganges and its tributaries. It was not an easy task to tame the landscape. The tropical deciduous forests (losing their leaves in the hot dry season), thick with teak, sal, simul and sisoo, and in Bengal with bamboo thickets as well, were stocked with a fearsome fauna, of tigers, elephants (often more dangerous), snakes and boars, and disease. The forest demons were not far from the early wooden stockades.

From the Vedas, Saxena (1968) has been able to sketch a convincing picture of the contemporary agriculture, and for the author of this chapter one of the exciting details is to learn that it was already organized according to the *nakshatra* (literally 'asterisms'), an astronomical calendar of 24 divisions (as opposed to our 12 months). Farmers were enjoined to sow in Rohini, exactly as even now in Bihar farmers use the same calendar and still sow in Rohini. We can also learn how the geography and environment was seen from the Puranas (literally 'old' or 'ancient'), a set of folk histories and of genealogies (many invented or 'improved') of the early kings. The Puranas were transmitted, and therefore presumably adorned, orally for many centuries, and were only recorded in script at various dates between 500 BC and AD 500. The first king of India was Manu Svayambhu (the self-born Manu), born directly from Brahma, the god of all, and she/he was hermaphroditic. From him there sprang a line of descendants who gave the earth its name, and cleared the forests, cultivated the land, and introduced commerce and cattle breeding. But the most famous Manu was the tenth, who was warned by the God Vishnu of a great flood that was to come. Manu built a boat to carry his family and the seven sages to safety, and the boat was towed by Vishnu, who had taken the form of a fish, to a high mountain, where they waited till the floods subsided and Manu's family could repeople the earth. From his hermaphroditic son there issued the two lines of descent, the Lunar and the Solar, which included the names of all the kings until the Epic Age, so that the list finally fits with Rama the hero of the Ramayana who lived at Ayodhya, by the Gaghara River, a north bank tributary of the Ganges.

Much as the Vedas do, the Puranas contain much geographical information (Singh, 1972), much of it fascinating. The world is like a lotus (as one version depicts it) with at the centre the great Mount Meru, and around it the eight petals of the eight lands of the world, one of which, to the south, is Bharat (India). On the summit of Meru is the vast city of Brahma, enclosed by the Ganges. The river issues from the foot of Vishnu above, washes the lunar orb and falls here from the sky, encircles the city and then divides into four mighty rivers flowing in four directions, north, east, south and west. These are the Sita, the Alakananda, the Chaksu and the Bhadra. The first flows east through the country of Bhadrasva to the ocean, and the Alakananda flows south to Bharat, and then divides into seven and flows to the sea. The Chaksu flows west, and the Bhadra north across Uttarakaru to the northern sea. The Sita has been identified with the Yarkand, the Chaksu with the Oxus, and the Bhadrasva with the Indus certainly, and perhaps the Indus and Ganges. The last is unidentified. The rivers flow through regions whose people are described and named. Obviously identification becomes even more tenuous here, but clearly some haunting early memory survives.

There are two major possibilities for the location of Mt Meru. In one account it could have been in the Pamirs or Kashmir, the pivot of Asia, where Tibet, India, (former Soviet) Central Asia and Afghanistan grasp each other. From this mountain stronghold the rivers flow in many directions to many seas, some inland, like the Aral Sea. The Aryans came from somewhere beyond the Oxus and crossed it on their way to India. It is a curious river dribbling to the Aral Sea, but it crops up in many stories of the Aryans themselves, the Persians, and the Bactrian Greeks. In another account Meru is the revered mountain of Kailas(h) in southern Tibet near Lake Manasowar (literally 'the lake of the mind'), near the sources of the Brahmaputra-Tsang-po, the Indus, the Sutlej and the Kali rivers. Until the early nineteenth century it was thought that the Ganges itself flowed from here too.

What is clearly of most importance is not the exact accuracy of the memory found in the Puranas, but the deeply ingrained memory of an origin near these life-giving rivers, which spout from the home of the gods where the great snows fall from the sky. These memories are part of the history and mythology of Hinduism, part of the blend of legend and reality, and reach into our own age. No wonder Mother Ganges is still holy, that the source of the Ganges near Badrinath is a pilgrimage shrine of great importance, that others make the even more epic pilgrimage to Mt Kailas itself, and that the Himalayas are revered even by the people of the plains who may never make the journey and may never see them. Ganges water is renowned amongst Hindus for its purity – and also of course for its purifying powers. Ganges water is used for oblations and celebrations, such as at weddings, when even those in the far south may pay substantial money for water to be brought in containers for their rituals. Some of the holiest cities of Hinduism lie on its banks. At Hardwar the river debouches from the hills onto the plains. At Allahabad the confluence with the Yamuna is especially holy. All Hindus would wish, if they could, to die within the city of Varanasi and be cremated at the ghats by the river, for their ashes to be scattered straight into the river. Although a bathe at any time is purifying, there are particular times when it is more auspicious to do so. The great religious festival known as the Kumbh Mela takes place every three years, rotating around the towns of Haridwar, Allahabad, Ujjain and Nasik (the latter two are outside the Ganges basin). During the auspicious month of the 1989 Kumbh Mela, 30 million pilgrims came to Allahabad (Encyclopaedia Britannica, 1990, p. 315), a city whose normal population is about 1 million. At daybreak on 6 February, 15 million people managed to bathe at this most auspicious hour. (The construction of the temporary township and the movement of people to the river ghats was a stupendous feat of organization by the Indian authorities.) Taking either figure, this must be the greatest number of people ever gathered together at one place on earth for one purpose. It is clearly difficult to overstate the significance the Ganges has for Hindus.

Hinduism is unlike Christianity and Islam in many ways, and in this context in one particularly important respect. There is only one Brahma, one force, god, consciousness, call it what you will, in the universe, in everything, and everything is a fraction of that force. Brahma has different aspects represented by different gods and avatars (incarnations – not necessarily human). As Vishnu the Creator he created the whole world together. There is no garden of Eden. Man was not placed in creation last with the authority to gain dominion over it. And as well as Vishnu, there is Shiva the Destroyer.

Brahma wakes and sleeps, and the universe goes through cycles of recreation and collapse. Order is born out of chaos, to collapse into chaos again. In all there is a struggle between creation and destruction, and both are necessary. They are two aspects that are split apart as order is created, and re-unite as disorder is re-established. It is a cosmology which fits the modern scientific ideas of the big bang and the (possible) retraction of the universe back to a singularity. It also fits the uplift of the Himalayas and the erosion of the slopes, and the shifting rivers of Bengal, eroding land from one place and creating new land elsewhere. In Hinduism the different stages of the cycle chaos–order–chaos are given different names. We are currently in the last quarter, i.e. the last stages of the descent back into chaos, when Shiva has the upper hand. This is the Kaliyuga, the black universe. In the 1960s, when the resurgent West was imbued still with the optimism of 'progress' and before the environmental crisis and burgeoning world population had given people pause for thought, in India it was nevertheless recognized that the Kaliyuga was on us. Dams break, rivers flood, cars and buses crash, malaria strikes, industry pollutes; and that is the way things are.

The Political Geography of the Ganges–Brahmaputra Basin

Historically, the dominant or major power base of South Asia has always been somewhere in the Ganges valley, where population was densest, communication easiest, and the taxation of sedentary agriculture possible to sustain a ruling elite and its armed forces. The capitals of early Hindu and Buddhist empires were mostly in the eastern part – often somewhere near Patna in Bihar. The Islamic empires that followed concentrated their imperial capitals in the western parts – particularly at Delhi and Agra, though for them the taxation of agricultural and other wealth in Bihar and Bengal was of as much importance as before.

Muslim influences reached India through Arab traders in Sind and in Bengal, and through the teachings of wandering Muslim saints or mystics, known as Sufis, not unlike the wandering Christian monks who took Christianity to Ireland and Scotland. But when Islam came in force, literally, when the first of the successful Muslim invasions burst into India through the northwest in the twelfth century, it brought something radically different to anything India had encountered before. The Guhrids established in northern India an Empire (or more correctly a confederacy), acknowledged by the Khalif of Baghdad as the Sultanate of Delhi. Therefore, very rapidly after its establishment in India, Islam was known to be precisely that – Islam-in-India, and not simply an extension of Islam in general. This was the beginning of 600 years of Muslim domination, the second part, after the sultanate, generally being known as the Mogul Empire.

This Islam was iconoclastic, and brought destruction to many Hindu temples, and the forcible conversion of some subjects. Other subjects voluntarily chose the new religion, and this was particularly true of the untouchables and low-caste people, perhaps attracted by the doctrine of the equality of man. Mass conversion of lower castes seems to have been greatest, for reasons which are not clear but may have been connected with Arab seafarers, in East Bengal. The distribution of Muslims in South Asia therefore mostly reflected and still reflects majority areas in the Indus valley, contiguous with the Middle East, and in East Bengal. These are roughly the areas of contemporary Pakistan and Bangladesh.

Following the Mogul Empire, the British extended their dominion over India from the mid-eighteenth century onwards. Their first territorial acquisition was the delta of Bengal, an area which they could penetrate with their large ships and their heavy armaments. Calcutta became the capital of Bengal Province, and then of the whole of India. It became the major port and the metropolitan heart of Bengal, with extensive jute industries buying jute mostly from the farms of East Bengal. It was a classic city–hinterland relationship. But the seafaring British who had established a new port as a new capital moved the central government to New Delhi in 1911 in emulation of the Moguls, in effect proclaiming their inheritance of the land empire, even though their penetration had begun from the sea.

British power had extended into indirect domination in Kashmir, and direct domination in much of the mountain regions of Uttar Pradesh and Himachal Pradesh. But Nepal, a kingdom forged out of 50 principalities established by Hindu warlords escaping Muslim domination in the plains, maintained its independence. At this stage it is well to reflect on certain recurring patterns on the map. The territorial organization of the Mogul and British empires both essentially treated Bengal as one united province (with one language even if two religions), and other areas recognized today as states were also recognized as provinces (Bihar and Uttar Pradesh) under central power. But modern Assam and the modern-day states of the Brahmaputra valley never came under a central Gangetic authority, even though there was strong Hindu influence in the valley of Assam itself, until annexation by the British. Lower Assam was incorporated as part of British India only in 1832, and Upper Assam only in 1873. The hill areas were and are dominated by numerous tribes, many of them with animist faiths at the time of annexation. Many have since adopted Christianity under the influence of missionaries. The area as a whole remains culturally very distinct from 'mainstream' India.

The nationalist movements of South Asia wrested sovereignty from the British in August 1947; or, Britain granted independence to India and Pakistan in August 1947. Either way, essentially both Indian nationalists and the British hoped to establish democratic and representative self-government in the successor states. But in achieving this goal the genie of communal identity had been let out of the bottle. The Muslims of India

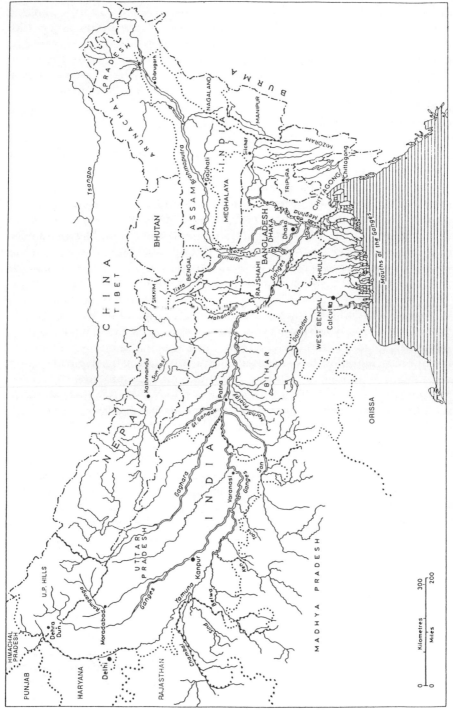

Figure 1.5 The Ganges–Brahmaputra basin and political divisions.

demanded and ultimately achieved their own state, Pakistan, created in two 'wings'. West Pakistan incorporated most of the Indus valley. East Pakistan was created by dividing Bengal in a way which made no sense on any grounds other than to give self-determination to the two religious communities – but even then the new boundary did not succeed as well as it could have done if that was the priority aim. The union of the two Pakistans lasted only 24 years, before East Pakistan broke away to become the sovereign state of Bangladesh in 1971.

This history has therefore produced under the modern system of sovereign states, recognized through the UN, the five states of the Ganges–Brahmaputra basins. India is the dominant power in both basins, but India is only connected by a narrow neck of land with Assam, and the people of Assam and the northeastern hill states have often been in violent conflict with the power of Delhi, and there are strong secessionist movements. Bhutan, a Buddhist kingdom by background, has maintained its independence, but is heavily influenced by India, and the same can be said of Nepal, though both countries can play China off against India. China is the dominant power of the upper Brahmaputra/Tsang-Po, in Tibet, but the restoration of Tibet's independence cannot be ruled out.

The infrastructure and urban hierarchy of Bangladesh have grown so that now it is clearly a separate spatial economy centred on Dhaka. Nepal is religiously mixed, with Buddhism being stronger in the higher valleys. But continuous migration has confused the picture and caused further, often violent, reaction. Nepalese Hindu migrants in Bhutan are now the subject of internal pressure and reaction from the Bhutanese. Bangladeshi illegal migration into Assam caused violent backlashes and massacres in the mid-1980s. And many Hindus over the years have fled from Bangladesh to India during periods of disturbance.

Although in this book we concentrate on considering resource issues, it is worth remembering that there are many other tensions between the sovereign states, and that even the definition of these states could change – although the diplomatic consensus of the members of the UN is that it is not 'correct' in this day and age to admit that territorial redefinition and the establishment of new statehoods is a solution to ethnic and communal tension, and the quest for minority rights.

River Discharges

All freshwater resources at the surface start as rain or snow, and some of what falls will end up as surface discharge, in well-defined drainage channels. But there are many routes for water to take once it has fallen. Figure 1.6 shows how precipitation ground water, surface flow, evapo-transpiration, extraction for urban and rural use, and recycling, among other paths, interrelate in the Indian context. This ought to be quite

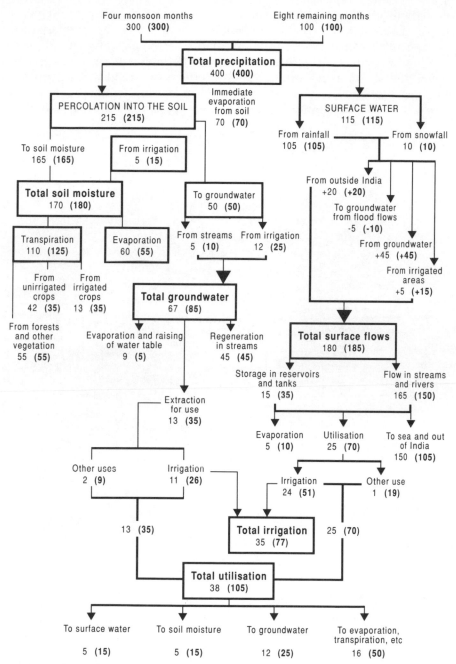

Four monsoon months
300 (**300**)

Eight remaining months
100 (**100**)

Total precipitation
400 (**400**)

PERCOLATION INTO THE SOIL
215 (**215**)

Immediate evaporation from soil
70 (**70**)

SURFACE WATER
115 (**115**)

From rainfall
105 (**105**)

From snowfall
10 (**10**)

To soil moisture
165 (**165**)

From irrigation
5 (**15**)

To groundwater
50 (**50**)

From outside India
+20 (**+20**)

To groundwater from flood flows
-5 (**-10**)

Total soil moisture
170 (**180**)

From groundwater
+45 (**+45**)

Transpiration
110 (**125**)

Evaporation
60 (**55**)

From streams
5 (**10**)

From irrigation
12 (**25**)

From irrigated areas
+5 (**+15**)

From unirrigated crops
42 (**35**)

From irrigated crops
13 (**35**)

Total groundwater
67 (**85**)

Total surface flows
180 (**185**)

From forests and other vegetation
55 (**55**)

Evaporation and raising of water table
9 (**5**)

Regeneration in streams
45 (**45**)

Storage in reservoirs and tanks
15 (**35**)

Flow in streams and rivers
165 (**150**)

Extraction for use
13 (**35**)

Evaporation
5 (**10**)

Utilisation
25 (**70**)

To sea and out of India
150 (**105**)

Other uses
2 (**9**)

Irrigation
11 (**26**)

Irrigation
24 (**51**)

Other use
1 (**19**)

13 (**35**)

Total irrigation
35 (**77**)

25 (**70**)

Total utilisation
38 (**105**)

To surface water
5 (**15**)

To soil moisture
5 (**15**)

To groundwater
12 (**25**)

To evaporation, transpiration, etc
16 (**50**)

35 , 1974 figures, in million hectare metres
(**77**), 2025 predictions, in million hectare metres

Figure 1.6 Water sources and use in India. *Source:* CSE (1985).

enough to caution that to display surface water discharges only is to display but a part of a complex overall equation. Yet surface flow in major river channels attracts most attention, particularly political attention, for a number of reasons. The main rivers are sometimes arteries of trade, and major cities lie on their banks, and rely on them for urban water demands, they have provided some of the largest and oldest (and energetically cheapest to run) irrigation schemes, they are sometimes the source of

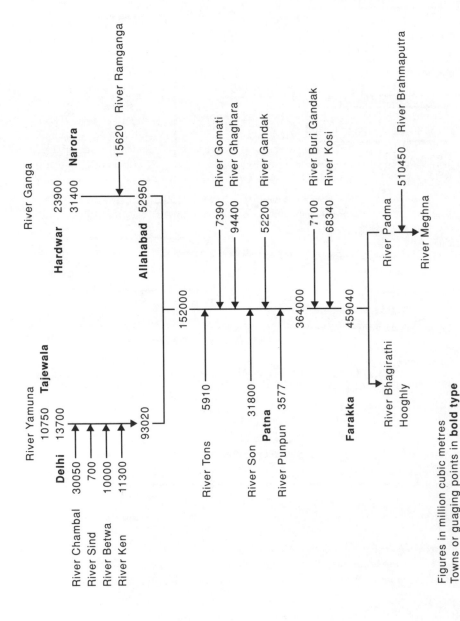

Figure 1.7 Discharges of the Ganga and tributaries. *Source*: Rao (1979).

major floods (but floods can also occur directly from impounded rainfall), they demarcate borders, and they can be sources of power and prized food.

Figure 1.7 shows the gross flow characteristics of the rivers of the basin. There are several features which immediately attract attention. The south bank tributaries (left side of figure) contribute less than the northern tributaries; the discharge at Delhi, far upstream on the Yamuna, is relatively quite small; the total flow of the Brahmaputra is greater than that of the Ganges; and, significantly, no figure is given for discharge down the River Bhagirathi. This is a major issue for Chapter 10. What the simple figure does not show is: the huge fluctuation between monsoon flows and the low season, when many of the south bank rivers simply dry up, and the north bank rivers have a vastly reduced flow; the fluctuation from year to year; and current and projected storage dams and their capacities, which could smooth out the irregularities on an annual or inter-annual basis. These are issues which to some extent are taken up in later chapters. The more general point that we are making here is that for many seemingly important issues, either there are no data, or there are data but they are not centrally collected and no-one is sure who has them, or there are data but they are withheld from the public domain for political reasons. In other words, as we intimated at the beginning, a book such as this is floating in a sea of uncertainty and ignorance.

Structure of the Book

We adopt a simple approach by moving from upstream, through midstream, to downstream. The issues, the scales and the approaches taken vary greatly. Some of the chapters are about hard field science and the mechanics of soil erosion – others touch on the sociology of public participation, or the public understanding of science, or international political intrigue. Yet every chapter could be extensively cross-referenced to every other: the locations are interconnected, the analyses are complementary, and the interpretations widened by this variety. Some are also contradictory. To put such a plethora of approaches into context we start with a methodological chapter by Thompson – who explains how and why there will be these different perspectives. Far from throwing our hands up in horror at the confusion, we should welcome the variety of insights and contradictions as a necessary part of our understanding. We have also, as editors, in places introduced a chapter with a brief comment, alerting the reader to other sources on some issues raised, or perhaps to issues ignored.

A Note on Place Names

The names used for many rivers and places in India have a variety of forms in English. Sometimes this reflects changing policies, heavily Anglicized names reverting to more 'original' forms, and sometimes it simply reflects a variety of transliterations. The name 'Ganges' is an Anglicized form. The usual word in India is 'Ganga'. We use the former, for consistency. At other times we have tried to alert the reader to varying forms, but something may have escaped our net. The reader is asked to use his or her imagination if stumped. The Yamuna (a tributary of the Ganges) is also the Jumna. But unfortunately both names are also used to apply to the Brahmaputra when it flows inside Bangladesh. Benares is the anglicized name for Varanasi, whose inhabitants are still usually known as Baranasis, and whose university is known still as Benares Hindu University. There should not be too much confusion or time wasted staring at an atlas if the possibility of variant spellings is kept in mind.

References

Chatterjee, S.B. (1953) *Indian Climatology: Climatic Classification of India with Special Reference to the Monsoons*. Calcutta: N.p.

CSE (1985) *Second Citizens' Report on the State of India's Environment*. New Delhi: Centre for Science and Environment.

Encyclopaedia Britannica (1990) *Book of the Year: Events of 1989*.

Encyclopaedia Britannica (1992) *Book of the Year: Events of 1991*.

Ives, J.D. and Messerli, B. (1989) *The Himalayan Dilemma: Reconciling Development and Conservation*, London and New York: The United Nations University and Routledge.

King, L.C. (1983) *Wandering Continents and Spreading Sea Floors on an Expanding Earth*. Chichester: John Wiley.

Michel, A.A. (1967) *The Indus Rivers: a Study in the Effects of Partition*. New Haven and London: Yale University Press.

Muthiah, S. (1987) *A Socio-Economic Atlas of India*. New Delhi: Oxford University Press.

Rao, K.L. (1979) *India's Water Wealth*. New Delhi: Orient Longman.

Sundaram, K.V. (1993) The emerging new development paradigm. In A. Mukherjee and V.K. Agnihotir (eds), *Environment and Development*. New Delhi: Concept Publishing, Chapter 3.

Saxena, D.P. (1968) Indian agriculture during the Vedic period. In *Proceedings of Symposium on Land Use in Developing Countries*, 21st International Geographical Congress, Aligarh: International Geographical Union (IGU) Committee.

Singh, M.R. (1972) *A Critical Study of the Geographical Data in the Early Puranas*. Calcutta: Punthi Pustak.

Tapponnier, P., Peltser G. and Armijo, R. (1986) On the mechanics of the collision between India and Asia. In M.P. Coward and A.C. Ries (eds), *Collision Tectonics* (Geological Society Special Publication No.19), Oxford: Blackwell Scientific, pp. 115–57.

Tata Services (1989) *Statistical Outline of India 1989–90*. Bombay: Tata Services Ltd.

2

Policy-making in the Face of Uncertainty: the Himalayas as Unknowns

Michael Thompson

Introduction

'Description then prescription' is the mantra of normal policy science. First get the facts straight, then deduce from those facts what the problem really is, and then move on to the examination of possible solutions and their evaluation. Objective, scientific, fact-determining procedures get us through the first two stages; only at the last stage, so the conventional wisdom insists, do values enter into the calculus. An explicit example is to be found in National Academy of Science (1983). If only it were that simple! Facts, alas, are often reluctant to reveal themselves fully and, even when they do, they still have to be interpreted (that is they have to be placed within an explanatory framework – a theory). Facts, therefore, are seldom clear-cut and self-evident truths. More often than not they are 'smeared out' a bit, and it is up to us to pull them together. That people (1) do succeed in pulling them together, and (2) do not all pull them together in the same way, suggests that they are guided in their *choice* of facts by the values they hold. In other words, 'Description then prescription' is a non-starter.

The Himalayas, it so happens, provide one of the finest examples of this insurmountable obstacle to the practice of normal policy science. What is more, this obstacle is now clearly recognized by many of those who work on the region and its problems. These policy scientists, faced with the clear impossibility of doing what they are supposed to do, have redirected their efforts towards finding a way out of this impasse. The result has been an impressively rapid learning process, which I will call the 'Mohonk process' (after the venue of the international conference that set it on its way – see special issue of *Mountain Research and Development* (1987) and Ives and

Messerli (1989). It is with this learning process, and its implications for policy practice, that this chapter is concerned.

Uncertainty, Ancient and Modern

The treatment of uncertainty has remained unchanged in its essentials since Knight's (1921) celebrated pronouncements:

1 If you know for sure what is going to happen, that is *certainty*.
2 If you do not know for sure what will happen, but you know the odds, that is *risk*.
3 If you do not even know the odds, that is *uncertainty*.

This scheme is all right so far as it goes; the trouble is it hardly goes anywhere. Many (perhaps all) important areas of human endeavour are characterized not just by Knightian uncertainty – defined as merely the absence of certainty – but by *contradictory certitudes:* seriously divergent and mutually irreconcilable sets of convictions as to how the world is and people are.

Contradictory certitudes, of course, are the different choices of fact that people are guided to by the different values they hold. The great advantage of starting with these contradictory certitudes, rather than insisting that facts and values be kept separate, is that you can do it. Contradictory certitudes, therefore, are the way out of the impasse that normal policy science has landed us in.

The Himalayan Environment and the Pale of Uncertainty

The extensive deforestation that is seen as the root cause of the environmental degradation of the entire Himalayan region is conceptualized as a vicious circle: the forest is being used faster than it grows. There have been many attempts to measure these two rates, and it is an easy matter to tabulate and compare them. This exercise reveals that estimates of the per capita fuelwood consumption rate vary by a factor of 67 and that estimates of the sustainable yield from forest production vary by a factor of at least 150. Far from giving us a precise, quantitative description of the vicious cycle of degradation, these results tell us that (if the most pessimistic estimates are correct) the Himalayas will be as bald as a coot overnight and that (if the most optimistic estimates are correct) they will shortly sink beneath the greatest accumulation of biomass the world has ever seen (Thompson, 1988).

Good science, faced with this sort of situation, would start by recognizing the full scale of the uncertainty. It would then probe the sources of that uncertainty. 'Are there any ways we might reduce it?' would be one question it would ask. Another tack would be to look hard at the whole 'vicious circle' argument to see if there is anything wrong with that way of conceptualizing the various forces that are at work in the Himalayas. And this is exactly what one part of the 'Mohonk process' has done. Most scientists and policy makers, however, have not done this. Instead, they have zeroed in on just one plausible certainty, embraced it, and rejected all the others. In doing this they have, between them, set up a number of contradictory certitudes, each of which generates its own distinctive definition of what the problem is.

It is this plurality of problem (and solution) definition that distinguishes the contradictory certitudes approach from conventional policy science. This plurality, in the context of the Himalayas, is the main theme in Thompson *et al.* (1987) and also the main theme, in the wider setting of technology assessment, in Schwarz and Thompson (1990).

So the other part of the 'Mohonk process' has been concerned with explaining, in a practical and policy-relevant way, how this has happened. All this takes us right into what is called 'the social construction of reality', and the theory that accounts for all the strange things that are happening here is called *cultural theory.* Cultural theory (Thompson *et al.*, 1990) is the joint creation of anthropologists and natural resource ecologists, and it will be the main focus of this chapter. But first, let us look at another example of contradictory certitudes; one which, though it has nothing to do with the Himalayas, will help explain what is involved in the 'Mohonk process'.

What are the health effects of low levels of radiation? Or, more technically, what is the shape of the dose–response curve at low levels of ionizing radiation? At high levels, of course, the answer is well known: the relationship is *linear* (we know this from animal experiments, from human accidents and from follow-up studies to the Hiroshima and Nagasaki atom bombs). Higher doses cause proportionately more tissue damage. But does this simple linear relationship also hold for low levels? 'Yes', say the scientists from the UK Department of the Environment, and the safe doses and other standards are set accordingly. But other experts (the US organization, Scientists and Engineers for Secure Energy, for instance) argue that the curve is *quadratic*, defining a threshold below which no harm is inflicted. Still other experts (Alice Stewart at Birmingham University, for instance) argue in the opposite direction. The curve, they insist, is *parabolic*, causing proportionally greater harm at low levels of exposure than at higher ones.

If the quadraticists are right, then (provided nuclear technology is engineered below the threshold) there will be nothing to worry about. If the parabolists are right, then the more nuclear technology we have the more harm will befall us. If the linearists are right, then the technology will be 'neutral': since the risks it brings are not inherently one way or the other, they can (and should) be planned, managed and regulated. The acceptability of the entire technology, therefore, hinges on which of these contradictory certitudes is the right one. Unfortunately, to find that out you would have to try to give tumours to more mice than there are atoms in the universe! And then there would still be the vexed question of the extrapolation from rodents to humans!

It is important to note that the scientists could not make these rival claims at high doses. At least, if they did they would lose all credibility as scientists, because they would be denying the irrefutable evidence of the historical and experimental record. In other words, there is a *pale of uncertainty* (within which scientists can legitimately cling to different certitudes) and that 'pale' is then contained within the wider *realm of certainty* (within which different certitudes are not legitimate).[1] It is this 'pale of uncertainty' that is the key to the 'Mohonk process'.

The Mohonk Process

The vicious cycle, in which the Himalayan forests are being consumed faster than they grow, is the central component of what is now called the theory of Himalayan environmental degradation. It is this theory, endlessly repeated yet never questioned, that has provided the definition of *the problem*.

> Television viewers, with striking regularity, are assailed with dramatic visions of deforestation, landsliding, and large-scale downstream flooding, coupled with statements about uncontrolled population growth, increasing poverty, and malnutrition. These processes – physical, human, socio-economic and political – are frequently linked together into a gigantic cause-and-effect drama which is claimed to be pushing both the Himalaya and northern plains of the Indian subcontinent to the brink of environmental and socio-economic collapse. (Ives and Messerli, 1989, p. 1)

The key feedback loop in this theory, so far as policy is concerned, is the increased flooding in the plains as a result of the removal of forest cover in the hills. The forest is removed, so the theory has it, under the pressure of an increasing population, so as to create more agricultural land, which then becomes more prone to landslip, thereby increasing the pressure to clear more forest, which then leads to still more erosion and landslipping and, at the same time, eliminates the precious 'sponge' effect of the forest, and so on.

This upstream–downstream connection was such a foregone conclusion, once one bought the vicious cycle definition of the problem, that no-one had really bothered to establish its existence. However, just as the scientists on the ground were beginning to wonder about accumulating anomalies (the things that, according to the theory, ought not to be there), a piece of desk research (commissioned by the United Nations Environment Programme) tabulated the estimates of the two key rates – fuelwood consumption and forest production – and revealed the full and truly

Himalayan scale of the uncertainty that enveloped them (Thompson and Warburton, 1985, pp. 115–35). With the cat out of the bag (and despite some strenuous efforts by certain policy actors to put it back in again) those geomorphologists, soil scientists, hydrologists and foresters who were already wondering about all the anomalies were stimulated to re-examine their data in the light of this disturbing possibility: that the generally accepted definition of what was wrong with the Himalayas might be profoundly wrong.

There was, it turned out, very little evidence for this human input to the waterborne transport of solid material from the hills to the plains, and a great deal of evidence for its absence (see Chapters 3 and 4). Indeed, it is quite probable that the human contribution, though very small relative to the natural processes that are at work, is the other way. The well-maintained and superbly engineered terraced fields impound an enormous volume of water, which then deposits its suspended material instead of thundering on with it to the plains below. What is more, the farmers carry vast quantities of manure out to, and often up to, their fields (and this is increasing now that they are intensifying their farming systems and switching to the stall-feeding of their animals) and they routinely stabilize and re-terrace landslip scars that, left to themselves, would continue to erode.

With this key linkage in the theory of Himalayan environmental degradation smashed beyond repair, attention then turned to all the other feedback loops of that problem-defining framework. None has survived intact; at best, some of them have been shown to hold true in certain places and under certain conditions (see Hamilton, 1987). This means, quite simply and without qualification, that decades-worth of policy has been directed at providing the solution to what is not, in fact, the problem. Where, then, do we go from here?

This demolition of the theory of Himalayan environmental degradation does not mean that there is nothing wrong with the Himalayan environment, and nor does it mean that we know nothing about that environment. What this demolition has done, in the simplest and most general terms, is reveal the position and extent of the pale of uncertainty. For instance, the upstream–downstream linkage, which was long thought to be a certainty, can now be seen to have been a contradictory certitude: a contradictory certitude, moreover, that now lies beyond the pale of uncertainty. This means that, unlike, say, the various definitions of what development is (which all lie well within the pale and which I will come to in a moment), the definitions of problem and solution that have been derived from this purported linkage are no longer legitimate. What, then, happens to all the policy commitments that have been built upon that invalid linkage?

In one sense, it makes very little difference, because many of the sensible policy actions that are needed in the mountains if the mountain environment itself is to be improved (the afforestation of impoverished and almost bare hillsides, for instance, and the reform of land tenure systems so that tenants can better enjoy the benefits of their capital and labour inputs) are also the sensible actions that would be needed in the hills if there *was* a causal link between the behaviour of the hill farmers and the flooding in the plains. But, in another sense, it makes all the difference in the world, because it removes the trans-boundary quality of the cause-and-effect relationship. Since mountain farmers in Nepal and Bhutan now harm only themselves, it is no longer possible for those in the plains – the Indians and the Bangladeshis – to point the finger of blame at them. Or, to be more precise, it is no longer possible for their governments to claim scientific support for that line of argument. Nor, conversely, is it possible for Nepal and Bhutan to argue with any conviction for a disproportionately high disbursement of international aid, on the grounds that the root cause of a huge regional problem is located within their boundaries.

That, in a fairly small nutshell, is what the notion of contradictory certitudes, and its associated idea of the pale of uncertainty, has done for policy, and for science-for-policy, in the Himalaya/Ganges region.

There is, of course, a great deal more that I could say about this part of the Mohonk process and what it has done to all the long-cherished linkages in the theory of Himalayan environmental degradation. But, since most of this is already published, I will now move on to the second part of that process and explain something about where the various contradictory certitudes *come from*, and how policy can be redesigned so as to make the most of the wisdom that each of them contains.

Cultural Theory

It is, cultural theory points out, not too surprising if those who are in the business of controlling tend, wherever possible, to see things in a way that renders those things susceptible to control: inherently *fixable* by those with the requisite knowledge and organization. The Food and Agriculture Organization (FAO), for instance, has surveyed the various estimates of fuelwood consumption and forest growth in the Himalayas and has then drawn a line between those it considers credible and those it considers incredible (Figure 2.1). The credible range of values then defines a problem that is nicely matched to the solution FAO is eager to provide. Outside of that range in one direction, there would be no need for FAO to do anything; outside of it in the other direction, nothing that FAO *could* do would make a blind bit of difference.

By contrast, those (like the radical conservative economist Lord Bauer) who advance under the banner 'Without international aid there would *be* no Third World' tend to see as credible that excluded section of the range

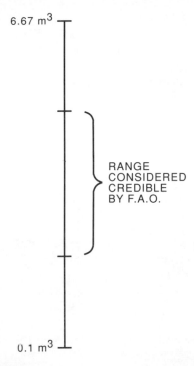

6.67 m^3

RANGE
CONSIDERED
CREDIBLE
BY F.A.O.

0.1 m^3

Figure 2.1 The range of estimates of fuelwood consumption in Nepal (per capita per annum).

that, if true, would remove the justification for FAO's involvement in the region. Conversely, those such as the 'deep ecologists' who join together in rejection of both unfettered individualism and bureaucratic, top-down intervention will tend to see as credible the other excluded section which, if true, would demand a solution so drastic that there would no longer be a place for either markets or hierarchies, Bauers or FAOs. And finally, there are those – the hill-farmers – who, though they actually *know* what is happening to the forests in their localities, are unable to make themselves heard above this cacophony of voices, each claiming to speak on their behalf (Figure 2.2).

This thumbnail sketch of cultural theory makes it clear that, though interests are certainly involved, there are more profound forces at work here. This is not a fourfold clash between similar actors who happen to have dissimilar interests. The actors themselves are fundamentally different in that they are committed to rival and incommensurate ways of life: *hierarchy, individualism, egalitarianism* and *fatalism*. Two of these ways of life – individualism and hierarchy – correspond to the classic social science distinction between markets and hierarchies. Cultural theory, however, shows us that there is more to life than *just* markets and hierarchies.

Hierarchies, cultural theory points out, institute inequality and limit

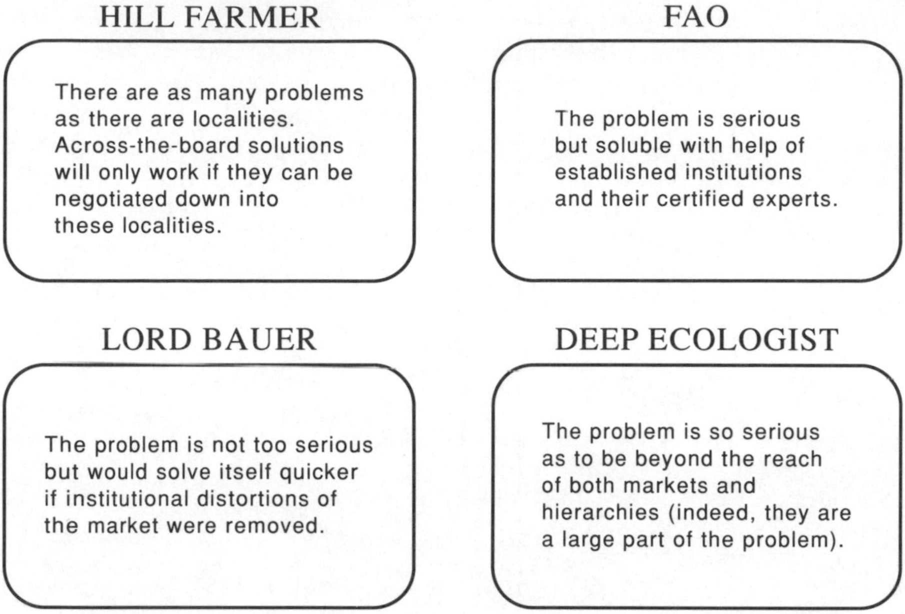

HILL FARMER

There are as many problems
as there are localities.
Across-the-board solutions
will only work if they can be
negotiated down into
these localities.

FAO

The problem is serious
but soluble with help of
established institutions
and their certified experts.

LORD BAUER

The problem is not too serious
but would solve itself quicker
if institutional distortions of
the market were removed.

DEEP ECOLOGIST

The problem is so serious
as to be beyond the reach
of both markets and
hierarchies (indeed, they are
a large part of the problem).

Figure 2.2 Four definers of the problem, each supported by his own choice of facts.

competition; markets institute equality and promote competition. There are, in other words, two dimensions at work here, and the full typology of social arrangements must include the other two permutations: equality without competition (egalitarianism) and inequality with competition (fatalism).

Without going too deeply into the details of cultural theory, we can see that each of the four ways of life has its distinctive pattern of social relationships: ego-focused networks for the individualists, hierarchically nested groups for the hierarchists, egalitarian bounded groups for the egalitarians, and a life on the outside of these structured arrangements for the fatalists. What is more, these ways of life are in competition for adherents (to put together ego-focused networks you have to dismantle the group-based patterns, and so on) and this means that it is never enough to just *have* a way of life; you have to support it against the others. This is where the contradictory certitudes come in.

In all those situations where the true state of the world is not entirely certain (global warming, for instance, or the risks from 'mad cow disease', or the future of fusion energy, and, of course, Himalayan deforestation and low-level radiation), the followers of each way of life tend to choose those possible states that best support their way of organizing and most discomfort those of the rival ways of life. These 'social constructions of reality' are so predictable and so enduring that natural resource ecologists have been able to deduce them from recurrent regularities within the managed ecosystems they study. Indeed it was ecologists, not anthropologists, who first developed this part of cultural theory and who classified the social constructions in terms of four distinct and mutually irreconcilable *myths of nature* (Holling, 1979, Timmerman, 1986). Each of these myths, they showed, can be represented by a little picture of a ball in a landscape, and each of them, by a few simple steps of socio-logic, can be shown to be necessary to the viability of its associated way of life (Figure 2.3).

Egalitarians, for instance, speak of 'natural resources' whilst individualists speak of 'raw materials', those raw materials becoming resources only when human skill, ingenuity and daring have been successfully brought to bear upon them. For egalitarians, therefore, resources are finite – they are what nature has given us (hence the precariousness of our position as we draw upon them). For individualists, however, resources are something we ourselves create out of the 'clay' that nature has provided (and there is plenty of that!). Resources, therefore, are limited only by our lack of

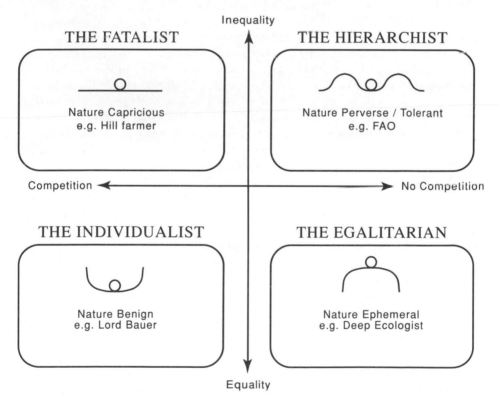

Figure 2.3 The two dimensions of sociality, the four ways of life, and their supporting myths of nature.

imagination and by our unwillingness to engage in trial and error. Of course, if our first experiment was likely to be our last (as it would be if nature was ephemeral, and might be if nature was perverse/tolerant) or if we could never learn anything from our experiments (as would be the case if nature was capricious) we would be in serious trouble. Nature, therefore, has to be benign. Where egalitarians construct for themselves a world of *resource depletion* (a Malthusian world in which we must all be frugal and no one should have more of anything than anyone else) and individualists construct a world of *resource abundance* (an Adam Smithian world in which the skilful, the forceful and the lucky benefit everyone by the exuberant pursuit of their self-interest), the hierarchist prefers a world of *resource scarcity.*

Hierarchists do want the resource cake to grow bigger, but only when it is controlled by their certified experts. If the resource cake could not grow (worse still, if it kept getting smaller) hierarchists would find it increasingly difficult to share it out unequally, and they would find it ever more difficult to attract followers to their way of life. On the other hand, if the cake could grow just by unleashing the free-for-all of individualistic trial and error there would be no need for all the carefully planned procedures, expertises, proper channels, statutory regulations and so on that are the means by which the hierarchical way of life institutes and reproduces itself. The social construction that sustains the hierarchist, therefore, has a positive-sum pocket beyond which lies trouble: a world in which everything hinges on finding out where the dividing line lies and then making sure that people stay on the right side of it.

And so it goes – each way of life, as it were, supplying its followers with the convictions, the preferences and the moral justifications that will support that way of life and, at the same time, discomfort the rival ways. Yet, for all their rivalry, each way of life ultimately needs the others. For instance, we have already seen how each one's Himalayan problem is largely constituted by the other three's solutions, and the mutualities cut even deeper than that. Ways of life *define* themselves in contradistinction to one another and they simply could not do that if the others were not there.

If there were no unruly elements the hierarchist's task would be so easy that anyone could do it, in which case there would be no need for all the expertise and specialization on which hierarchies are built and by which the inequalities they institute are justified. Similarly, if individualists finally got rid of all traces of hierarchy there would no longer be any extra-market authority to enforce the law of contract, and you cannot have markets without that. And egalitarians simply would not be able to muster the moral fervour that holds them together if there were no markets or hierarchies there to perpetuate their inegalitarian excesses on their fellow humans and their unsustainable abuses of Mother Nature. Nor, of course, could the fatalists be fatalistic if there were no hierarchists, individualists and egalitarians to exclude them from the decisions that shape their lives.

These mutualities can be conceptualized as a *hypercycle* (as those game theorists who work on the problem of pre-biotic evolution call it – see Eigen and Schuster (1977) and Sigmund and Hofbauer (1984)) in which each component does something vital for one or more of the others that it or they could never do for themselves. It is these mutualities that, by making it more difficult for the hypercycle to fall apart than to come together, confer viability on these four ways of life and their appropriate certitudes. This, of course, is pretty fancy social theory and there is certainly not time to go into all its supporting arguments here, but, fancy or not, the gist of it – that people cannot be relied upon to bring their risk perceptions into line with those of the experts, once their 'misperceptions' have been pointed out to them – has now been confirmed, time and time again, by both risk research and policy practice (Thompson *et al.*, 1990; Schwarz and Thompson, 1990).

But the hypercycle also shows us that this recalcitrance on the part of the 'misperceivers', far from being a troublesome obstacle in the path of well-designed policy, is a template for that policy's redesign. In a hypercycle, for one component to be there, they must all be there. Conversely, if one disappears they will all disappear. A policy that is neatly designed around just a single definition of the problem (that is, around just one of the contradictory certitudes) will inevitably strengthen the way of life that happens to be supported by that definition and weaken all the others. Pushed hard enough, the policy would end up forcing everyone into just one way of life, at which point that way of life too would become unviable. By contrast, *clumsy institutions* (some laws, 'broad church' professions, companies with the motto 'the customer is always right'), which fudge and bodge things enough for each definition to receive *some* recognition, are able to build upon and harness these mutualities that are the hypercycle's strength (Schapiro, 1988).

On the other hand, *gainly institutions* (which is what we mostly have at present) are neatly optimized around just one definition of 'the problem': just one of the myths of nature. They are therefore denied access to all the wisdom and experience that is captured by the other three myths. Such policies are highly *surprise-prone*, since they assume that nature is just one of at least four possible ways. They are also *unlikely to enjoy widespread consent*, since they deny the validity of the problem and solution definitions held by all those who happen not to subscribe to the chosen myth. A clumsy institution, however, could have this or that component strengthened or downgraded as Mother Nature revealed more of her hand, all the while enjoying a much higher level of consent than would any of the gainly policies that are generated by those policy experts who first insist on reducing the debate to a uni-rational frame.

Clumsy Institutions in the Himalayas

We in the West are so accustomed to offloading our obsolete technologies (car assembly lines, for instance) and our unfashionable ideologies (planning, for instance) on to Third World countries that we find it difficult to entertain the possibility of anything valuable ever coming the other way: 'from them, to us'. That, however, is what is now happening with the contradictory certitudes approach. While US Congressmen continue to demand 'one-armed scientists' (so that they cannot say 'on the other hand'), and British MPs still rant on about 'bogus professors' (by which they mean those recognized experts who happen not to share their particular certainty), social foresters in Nepal are actually getting the trees to grow by systematically modifying their 'Western science' idea of what a healthy forest looks like until it can mesh constructively with the villagers' 'home-made' idea of what a healthy forest looks like. Out go the eucalyptus seedlings, the straight line and the boundary fences; in come wind-seeded indigenous species, higgeldy-piggeldy layouts, and locally funded forest guardians (*naua*). The plurality of problem definitions, in other words, is seen as a valuable resource, not something to be got rid of before work can begin.

This is not to say that all the Himalayan policy actors have abandoned their 'single definition' approaches, but only that the plural rationalities framework *is* now in place: both in practice and in theory. Those who define the problem as 'too many people' are now able to debate constructively with those who see it as 'not enough food', and they are able to agree that, given the scale of the uncertainty that surrounds the facts at issue, both definitions are legitimate. The situation is similar with contradictory definitions of what development is. Those (the members of the Chipko Movement, for instance) who advocate land-based self-sufficiency are able to countenance those (the 'Trade Not Aid' campaigners, for instance) who favour a resurgence of the intensive trading that lay behind the original emergence of the Nepalese kingdoms, and both are then able to connect their arguments with the views of those (the Hunzas of the Pakistan Himalaya, for instance) who see development aid as a way of expanding their agricultural production, not in order to become self-sufficient, but in order to break *out* of their mountain fastnesses and *into* the global market-place.

Nor are the pluralized people of the Himalayan region just sitting there waiting for the debate over what development *is* to be resolved before they can start to do it. The self-sustainers (the 'tree-huggers' of the Indian Himalayas, for instance) are getting on with sustaining themselves (and, where necessary, chasing the corrupt forestry officials and the logging contractors who corrupt them out of the forest); the traders (the Manang-bhotis who live in the remote valley behind Annapurna, for instance) are merrily flying Apple computers into Kathmandu from Thailand and Tibetan carpets out to New York; and the exuberant agriculturalists of Pakistan have been so successful in breaking out that Hunza apricots can now be found on the shelves of any London wholefood store.

That all this is happening in the Himalayas is not in dispute. The dispute is over whether or not it is *sustainable* and, if it is not, what needs to be done about it. However, since the facts that would decide that are well inside the pale of uncertainty, each actor is free to construct his or her own answer.

Lord Bauer, were he to wander through the region, would see all this anarchic activity as a wonderfully encouraging sign, especially since no planning agency has planned for it, and especially since it flies in the face of all those direct predictions from the deep ecologists.

The planner, however, is alarmed. Sustainable growth, for him or her, is something that can only occur within 'an integrated approach to environmental management and development': one in which policies can be considered within 'a global framework of the interrelated phenomena of a planned process of development'.[2]

The deep ecologist, for his or her part, sees it all as an unmitigated disaster: a fatally unsustainable direction of change, given the inherent fragility of the resource base it so unthinkingly abuses and the gross inequalities of the social system that generates those gross demands.

These three characters, together with the much put-upon and little consulted 'villager on his remote hillside',[3] are the *myth-holders* and, in one guise or another, they provide the dramatis personae for the Himalayan drama. They also, when they are united with cultural theory, enable us to unravel the uncertainty in terms of the various socially constructed and mutually contradictory certitudes that it gives rise to. Lord Bauer's view is valid only if the myth of nature benign holds true, the planner's view requires nature to be tolerant within perverse (but discoverable) limits, and the deep ecologist's view is persuasive only to those who are convinced that nature is everywhere ephemeral (see Figure 2.3).

The practical argument from all of this is that, since each actor's myth captures *some* essence of experience and wisdom (otherwise it would have died out long ago), all of them must have *something* to contribute. That, of course, is why we need clumsy institutions.

Notes

1   This is not to say that those facts that lie within the realm of certainty are true; only that they are not 'viably challengeable'. Nor is the line that separates the two realms fixed for all time. That which is viably challengeable may become unchallengeable and vice versa. Indeed, shifting that line is what science is all about.

Whether or not it is really true that water flows downhill, we do tend to get quite good results when we act on the assumption that it is. Conversely, we tend to get rather poor results if we assume that water flows uphill. Whilst this 'practical performance' criterion does not apply to everything that is in the realm of certainty (sometimes there may be no way of testing the facts we are all agreed on, sometimes other choices of fact, if chosen and acted on by someone, would work just as well or even better) it does play an important part in the process by which the line is endlessly drawn and redrawn. The idea is to harness policy to that process, rather than to just one of the contradictory certitudes that are involved in it (which is what normal policy science does). A corollary of this is that policy design should pay heed not just to scientists but to all practical testers: farmers, for instance, and engineers, and all those holders of 'tacit knowledge' who so often find themselves excluded by top-down prescription.

2   These quotes are from a United Nations Environment Programme document.

3   This quote is from a Food and Agriculture Organization document.

References

Eigen, M. and Schuster, P. (1977) Emergence of the hypercycle. *Naturwissenschaften*, **64**, 541–65.

Hamilton, L.S. (1987) What are the impacts of Himalayan deforestation on the Ganges–Brahmaputra lowlands and delta? Assumptions and facts. *Mountain Research and Development*, **7.3**, 256–63.

Holling, C. (1979) Myths of ecological stability. In G. Smart and W. Stansbury (eds), *Studies in Crisis Management*. Montreal: Butterworth.

Ives, J.D. and Messerli, B. (1989) The Himalayan Dilemma: Reconciling Development and Conservation. London: Routledge.

Knight, F.H. (1921) *Risk, Uncertainty and Profit* (republished in 1965). New York: Harper and Row.

Mountain Research and Development (1987) **7**, (3).

National Academy of Science (1983) *Risk Assessment in the Federal Government: Managing the Process*. Washington DC: National Academy Press.

Schapiro, H.M. (1988) Judicial selection and the design of clumsy institutions. *Southern California Law Review*, **61.6**, 1555–69.

Schwarz, M. and Thompson, M. (1990) *Divided We Stand: Redefining Politics, Technology and Social Choice*. London: Harvester-Wheatsheaf.

Sigmund, K. and Hofbauer, J. (1984) *Evolution of Hypercycles*. Cambridge: Cambridge University Press.

Thompson, M. (1988) Uncertainty and its uses. In P. Blaikie and Tim Unwin (eds), *Environmental Crises in Developing Countries*. Monograph No. 5. Developing Areas Resource Group. London: Institute of British Geographers.

Thompson, M. and Warburton, M. (1985) Uncertainty on a Himalayan scale. *Mountain Research and Development*, **5.2**, 115–35.

Thompson, M., Warburton, M. and Hatley, T. (1987) *Uncertainty on a Himalayan scale*. London: Ethnographica.

Thompson, M., Ellis, R. and Wildavsky, A. (1990) *Cultural Theory*. Boulder, Colorado and Oxford: Westview.

Timmerman, P. (1986) Mythology and surprise in the sustainable development of the biosphere. In W. Clark and R. Munn (eds), *Sustainable Development of the Biosphere*. Cambridge: Cambridge University Press.

PART II

Upstream and Highland–Lowland Interaction

3

Terrace Irrigation of Mountainous Hill Slopes in the Middle Hills of Nepal: Stability or Instability

Kegang Wu and John B. Thornes

Editors' Note

It is easy to make a simple off-the-cuff correlation between deforestation for agriculture, and subsequent increased soil erosion. This chapter is an example of the very detailed and careful work that has to be done to establish for some sites in some conditions whether the claim can be substantiated or not – but even then it would be difficult to extrapolate to all sites under all conditions. However, it does tend to suggest that farmers have known for a long time what they were doing – even if they could not explain why in scientific detail. The chapter has an element of 'hard science' about it, but terms are explained in the glossary at the front of the book.

Introduction

Terrace agriculture is one of the most common agricultural land use types in the world, especially in Southeast and East Asia. Ninety-three per cent of the population of Nepal are dependent upon subsistence agriculture (Kienholz *et al.*, 1983, p. 208), of which the most common type is terrace agriculture on steep mountainous slopes. Of the total cultivated area, hill-slope cultivation accounts for 43.3 per cent (Figure 3.1) (Land Resources Mapping Project, 1986a).

The Middle Hills region, which comprises one-third of Nepal's total area of 14.7 million hectares (Land Resources Mapping Project, 1986a, p. 5), is the most dense in terms of both population and agriculture. The continuous increase in food demand caused by increased population has led to a tendency to cultivate any marginal land possible and to convert sloping, dry bari terrace to level, irrigated khet terraces. Consequently, hill-slope terrace agriculture has been blamed for various environmental problems in the Himalayas such as deforestation, soil erosion, land sliding, gullying and flooding, and increasing sedimentation in the downstream Gangetic plains. In recent years it has been at the centre of the controversy about the validation of the theory of Himalayan environmental degradation.

In a comprehensive review, Ives and Messerli (1989) summarized the theory as a series of linked vicious circles. These suggest that an unprecedented wave of population growth (2.6 per cent per year for the 1971–1981 census decade) led to rapidly increasing demands for food, fodder, fuelwood and constructional timber. This led to massive deforestation, the decrease of forest cover amounting to a loss of half the reserves of Nepal during the period 1950–1980, a loss of crisis proportions in terms of the population it must support. The deforestation, especially for agricultural terraces on steeper and more marginal mountain slopes, in turn led to a sharp increase in soil erosion and the loss of productive agricultural land due to accelerated surface erosion, gullying and landsliding. The increase of erosion in turn increased overland flow on hill slopes and produced catastrophic amounts of sediment during intense rains, causing numerous problems in downstream areas, including disastrous flooding in the Ganges plains and in the Brahmaputra delta, siltation of reservoirs, siltation of lowland agricultural land and accumulation in river beds. The continued loss of terraces on steep hill slopes then led to another worse round of deforestation to enable the cultivation of more new terraces.

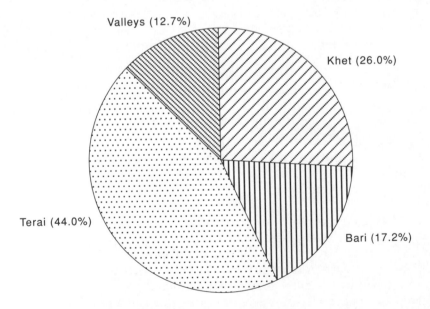

Figure 3.1 Types of cultivation in Nepal.

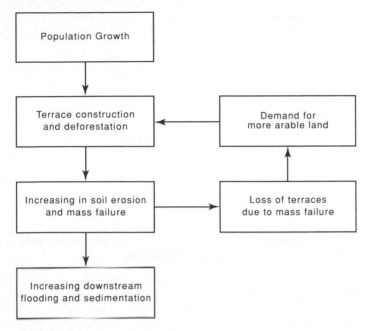

Figure 3.2 Vicious circles in the theory of Himalayan environmental degradation.

One of the major arguments against the theory is that many investigators trained in geology and physical geography view the geological structure, lithology and climatic conditions as far more important determinants of landsliding than human activity, because of the natural dynamic, tectonic and climatic conditions (Brunsden *et al.*, 1981; Ramsay, 1985, 1986; Caine and Mool, 1982; Wagner, 1981, 1983). From their experiences of the Nepal Mountain Hazards Mapping Project, Ives and Messerli (1989) reversed their earlier view of human accelerated erosion to argue that the construction and maintenance of agricultural terraces and irrigation systems actually helps to stabilize the vulnerable steep hill slopes. Regarding the environmental problems in the downstream area, they believe that fluctuations in annual stream flow and the high sediment loads of the huge rivers are the consequences of natural (especially climatic) processes. Local flooding and excessive sedimentation on the plains may be due to human intervention on the plains themselves rather than to the activities of subsistence farmers in the mountains.

The soil erosion, gullying and landslides of the Middle Hills have attracted a lot of attention, and current research mainly covers the following aspects:

1   The classification, mapping and statistical evaluation of the distribution, causes and triggering mechanisms of large-scale slope failures which are mainly linked

with road construction or mapping projects (Laban, 1979; Wagner, 1981, 1983; Brunsden *et al.*, 1981; Caine and Mool, 1982; Kienholz *et al.*, 1983, 1984; Ramsay, 1985, 1986).

2   The monitoring and estimation of soil erosion, slope failure processes and annual denudation rate (Caine and Mool, 1982; Ramsay, 1985, 1986; Shah *et al.*, 1991; Gardner *et al.*, 1992).

3   The stability of mountain ecosystems (Ives and Messerli, 1988; Kienholz *et al.*, 1984).

4   The soil fertility, productivity and conservation of agricultural terraces. A few preliminary reports on soil hydraulic properties and water balance (Aubriot, 1991; Fontenelle, 1991) have been produced.

This chapter emphasizes another issue – the movement of soil moisture in terraced land and its relation to slope failure and erosion.

1   What is the subsurface water movement on the two types of terraced slopes found in Nepal?

2   Given the combination of soil physical situation, soil water, slope condition, rainfall, and irrigation management, under what condition will slope failure occur?

3   Will the change of land use on terraces cause slope failure under certain conditions? In other words, what is the relationship between the hill-slope stability and the terrace hydrological behaviour which relates to agricultural water management?

Agriculture and Agricultural Terracing

There are two types of agricultural terraces that are very different in either their natural or agricultural characteristics: khet (wet, flat, bunded irrigated terrace) and bari (sloping, dry, or rain-fed terrace). In the Kakani area these two terraces together make up 44.5 per cent of the total area (Kienholz *et al.*, 1984, p. 249).

Generally, khet is a levelled, bunded, periodically inundated terrace found at the lower elevation of hill slopes. In the Kakani area (Kienholz *et al.*, 1983, p. 202) khet is rarely situated above 1750m, which is also the average maximum altitude for rice cultivation in central Nepal (Donner, 1972, p. 288). And most of the khet lands are located on slopes of 15–40° (Figure 3.3).

Bari is a sloping, unbunded, rain-fed terrace on the higher and steeper hill slopes. The most common hill-slope angle for the location of bari is 20–40°. The lower levels of bari cultivation coincide approximately with the average of the higher levels of khet, where the two types interdigitate (Johnson *et al.*, 1982, p. 180).

There is a large difference in water management between khet and bari because the crops cultivated are different (Table 3.1). Khet fields are mainly built in the lower parts of slopes where the land is irrigated by canals which take water from upstream and run along the contours to feed the lower slope. Bari is mainly found on upper slopes where land is not irrigated.

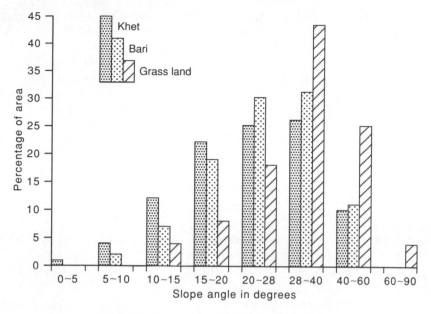

Figure 3.3 Slope angles of terraced hillsides in Nepal.

Table 3.1 Major annual crop rotation system in khet and bari in the Middle Hills, Nepal

	March–June	*July–Sept.*	*Oct.–Feb.*
Khet			
Water excess	Paddy rice	Paddy rice	Fallow
Full irrigated	Paddy rice	Paddy rice	Wheat
Partial irrigated	Corn	Paddy rice	W/F
Bari	Corn	Millet	W/F/Veg

W = wheat; F = fallow; Veg = vegetable

Paddy rice is the most valuable crop and only grows on khet land where it may be intercropped with wheat. Certainly khet is the most valuable land. Its cultivation is so intensive that in land suitable for khet there are hardly any settlements, roads, trees or shrubs. Wherever water is available khet is built, even though it requires heavy energy inputs for maintenance, careful levelling, tilling, fertilizing and irrigation control. In the Lumle area of Nepal, 1974 data show that one hectare of transplanted rice requires about 5000 hours of work compared with 800–1200 hours in other Asian countries (Ruthenburg, 1980, p. 206).

Landslides and the other slope failures have long been a severe natural hazard in this dynamic mountainous region. Caine and Mool (1982) estimate that in the Kakani area landslides occupy about 1 per cent of the total with a mean age of 6.5 years. These landslides comprise an estimated

2.2 × 10⁶ m³ of sediments which could be converted into an annual denudation rate of 12 mm/year. The quantitative relationships between the distribution of agricultural terraces and slope failures remain to be determined even though landslides and other slope failure can be seen everywhere on terraced hill slopes, especially small, shallow failures. Ramsay estimated that small shallow failures in the Phewa Valley account for 95 per cent of the total slope failures (Ives and Messerli, 1989). In the Kakani region, of the 15 landslides surveyed by Caine and Mool (1982, p. 161), the average depth of shallow planar slides was 1.63 m, and that of rotating failures 2.25 m, compared with a mean depth of debris flows of 7.1 m.

There are three different scales of slope failure occurring on terraced hill slopes: individual terrace riser collapses, shallow slides (including planar and rotational slides) and debris flows. Detailed information about the effect of the terrace cultivation, especially water management, on these slope failures is still not available.

Table 3.1 shows that in most of the khet, two rice crops are cultivated annually between March and September. During the growth of paddy rice, standing water is required on the terrace for most of the time, so the terrace soils are saturated with water in that period. The simultaneous occurrence of rice cultivation and monsoon rain adds further to the water in the soil and load on the slope, both directly from surface infiltration and, as shown below, laterally from slope throughflow.

Terrace Hydrological Monitoring

In this section we report both on general models and knowledge of water movement in these fields, and also on first-hand results from our own detailed field surveys conducted in the monsoon of 1992 at adjacent sites in Nepal. The Likhu Khola Watershed (GR:27°50′N, 85°20′E), where the field site is located, is representative of the Middle Hills area of the Himalayas. The catchment is about 25 km from Kathmandu and immediately north of the Kakani area. It is one of the main branches of the Trisuli River, which eventually joins the Ganges River. The main rock types in the watershed are gneiss and mica schist, which are among the main rock types of the Middle Hills area. Its typical monsoonal mountain climate and vegetation species (sal, *Pinus roxburgi*, evergreen oak, schima, and *Quercus*), and its agricultural pattern of terraces are also representative of the region.

The relief of the area ranges from 700 m to 2500 m with very steep hill slopes ranging from 20° to 40° and deeply incised stream channels and ravines. The main valley is characterized by gentle lower slopes with river terraces and benches, and steeper upper slopes. The network of tributary valleys and ravines is characterized by steep V-shape cross-sections and stepped profiles, entrenched much more deeply in their lower reaches.

Slope failures along the stream banks are not uncommon and gullies are found in the lower end of ridges where deep red soils occur.

Four field sites, called Khetland A and Khetland B and Bariland A and Bariland B, have been selected. All sites are located in the lower part of the valley slope at elevations between 600 and 800 m.

To assess stability of a hill slope, the conventional method is the Mohr–Columb failure criterion:

$$S = C + (T - U_w) \tan A \qquad (3.1)$$

where S is the shear strength of the material of interest, C is the effective cohesion, A is the effective angle of internal friction, T is the total normal stress and the U_w is the pore water pressure. The equation applies to the situation of saturated soil. When the soils are unsaturated the equation becomes (Fredlund, 1987):

$$S = C + (T - U_a) \tan A + (U_a - U_w) \tan X \qquad 3.2$$

where U_a is the pore air pressure, and X is the increase in shear strength due to matric suction in unsaturated soil.

In the above formulae, C and A are constants for the particular soil type; U_a is usually very small and hence negligible. Therefore the dynamic variables are pore water pressure U_w, normal stress T and internal friction increase due to suction X, which can be deduced from A and C and the soil suction–moisture relation curve. It is clear that these variables are either hydrological variables proper such as U_w or are effected by soil water movement as in the case of X and T.

Slope stability is defined by relating the shear strength available, S, to the shear strength required, S_r. If S is less than S_r then failure will occur. A slope may be stable while it is dry, but since S is controlled by hydrological variable U_w or soil-moisture-related variables X and T, when the monsoon comes S may be reduced and a failure occur. Therefore, subsurface hydrology, or soil water movement, is the key to assessing the stability problem, for any given geological setting. Of course the sensitivity – rates of change of S in comparison with S_r – will vary with background geology and soil type.

Geological Controls

The study sites are all on north-facing valley slopes, near the intersection of three different tectonic zones: the Sheopuri injection gneiss zone, the Nawakot meta-sediment zone and the Gsarnkund gneiss zone. The intensively faulted and folded tectonic block structure is the main factor which controls large-scale landslides, rockfalls and debris flows. Discussion at this scale of the impact of structure on patterns of mass failures is beyond the scope of this chapter. But it is clear that such controls operate:

particular dip and strike orientations account for the fact that most of the large-scale landslides occur in the south-facing slopes of our selected valley.

Another geological factor which affects mass failure is the common presence of mica in metamorphic rocks in the Middle Hills area. It has been noted (Vaughan, 1990, p. 470) that mica acts as a platy clay mineral, and this will be discussed later.

Most hill-slope mass failures involve only the weathered mantle above the bedrock. The thickness of weathered material may be up to 10 m in the subtropical Middle Hills area (Peter and Mool, 1983). In the Likhu Khola, mica schist has been seen weathered commonly to depths of 4–5 m. This is relatively thin compared with the other subtropical area due to the steepness of the hill slopes. The profile varies greatly in terms of different horizons but the general characteristics are similar. The Middle Hills rocks are subject to intense chemical weathering processes under the subtropical geographical conditions, and the weathered material (or *in situ* residual soils, saprolite) has undergone varying degrees of change in response to the varied amount of weathering. The generation of clay minerals and the alteration of fabrics are most important.

The presence of clay minerals created by chemical weathering is common. The platy clay minerals with a low coefficient of friction can reorientate when shearing occurs (Lupini *et al.*, 1981). This gives rise to a low residual frictional strength and to polished shear surfaces. The effect of platy clay combined with decomposition of the cement increases porosity, which in turn increases the permeability, and makes the weathered *in situ* soil lose most of its cohesion and reduces its angle of internal friction.

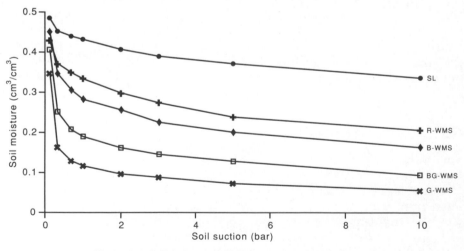

Figure 3.4 Soil moisture characteristics at field sites in Nepal.

The presence of soil clay minerals also changes the soil moisture characteristics. The capacity for holding water is well related to soil constituents. Soil retention curves observed in the laboratory (Figure 3.4) reveal that the soil moisture content at a given suction decreases with depth in the soil in the following sequence; cut and fill material (SL), red soil (R-WMS), brown soil (B-WMS), browny grey soil (BG-WMS) and grey weathered mica schist (G-WMS). Therefore the upper part of the weathered profile has greater water-holding capacity. This matches with the change of permeability which increases with the depth of soil profile. This means that during the wet season the upper part of the slope would be saturated first, hence increasing the effective stress on the potential shearing surface.

Figure 3.3 shows that about one-quarter of khet and one-third of bari land are in the slope range of 28–40°, and 10 per cent of each in that of 40–60°. The average angles of the khet and bari terracing are respectively 24° and 28° compared with 36° for grassland.

Table 3.2 Critical slope angles of debris.

Lithology	Critical slope angles (degrees)	
	drained	saturated
Phyllite	32.8	18.5
Biotite gneiss	41.5	20.8
Augen gneiss	44.2	24.4
Granite	42.8	21.8

Based on Caine and Mool (1982).

Caine and Mool (1982) worked out the critical slope angles on the failed debris of weathered materials (Table 3.2). It seems from this that during the wet season, if the soil profile is saturated, most cultivated land is near or in a critical condition. Terraces on steeper slopes are susceptible to failures of the entire hill slope such as debris flows and landslides, while the risers of terraces are prone to individual riser collapse because they are much steeper, ranging mainly from 40° to 70°. This may be true of the bari. On the other hand, failure on khet slopes may relate more to the water management of the agricultural terraces as discussed later.

Agricultural hill slopes are particularly prone to failure if located immediately above incised river cliffs or near deeply cut ravines. The situation is not uncommon because of the active neotectonic uplifting and active downcutting of river channels in ravines.

Weather conditions

The annual rainfall in the area ranges from 1500 mm to over 3000 mm. Precipitation records over the long term are rare in Nepal. The available long-term record from the stations at Kakani and Kathmandu have helped to reveal the characteristics of the rainfall pattern. The Kakani station, at the top of the southern dividing range (2703 m) of the catchment, has an average of 2800 mm annual rainfall. With reference to slope stability, there are two notable characteristics of the rainfall. Firstly, most of the annual precipitation falls in the monsoon season from June to September, with peak monthly rainfalls in July and August. The average rainfalls in July and August are 681 mm and 703 mm respectively. The highest monthly rainfall of the fieldwork period was in July 1992 at 1194 mm. The four-month rainy season supplies a more or less continuous recharge to the soil and leads to soil moisture saturation. Secondly, individual rainfall events are of a high intensity, frequently greater than the infiltration capacity of the soil.

Vegetation is always considered as a stabilizing factor for soil conservation. However, it is a more complicated problem in relation to soil stability. Greenway (1987) indicated that vegetation effects on hill slopes can be both beneficial and adverse to stability. Tree roots reinforce soil and hence increase soil shear strength, and roots may anchor into firm strata, providing support to the upslope soil mantle. On the other hand, the weight of trees surcharges the slope, increasing normal and downhill force components which can be either beneficial or adverse. Greenway concluded that they will be beneficial only in case of high soil friction and relatively gentle slopes. These are obviously not the conditions of the hill slope in the Middle Hills area.

In summary, the natural conditions on the hill slopes are sensitive and prone to mass failure. The intensely faulted and folded geological structure, well-developed bedding, the lamination of bedrocks, the lower strength of weathered saprolites with platy clay and mica minerals, the critical slope angle and the dynamic monsoonal rainfall when taken together make the hill slopes liable to failure.

The Impact of Cultivation on Subsurface Water

The natural soil starts to wet up in the pre-monsoon season and reaches saturation in the monsoon season. The continuous monitoring of soil moisture change in bari has shown that the soil moisture gradually increases in relation to the rainfall increase throughout the monsoon season (Figure 3.5) even though it does not behave exactly the same as the non-arable hill slopes.

But the controversy about terrace farming relates to khet irrigation which overlaps with monsoon rains. As shown in Table 3.1, the pre-monsoon

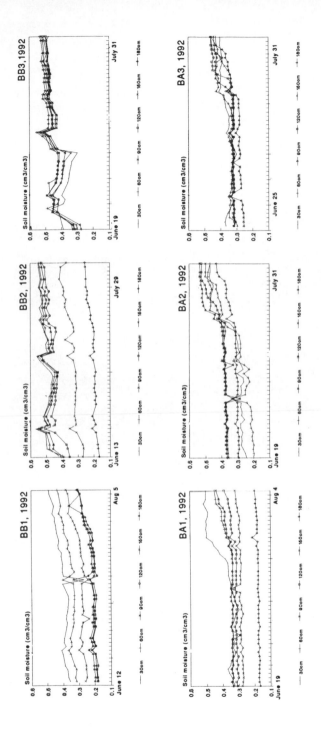

Figure 3.5 Soil moisture change in two bari sites.

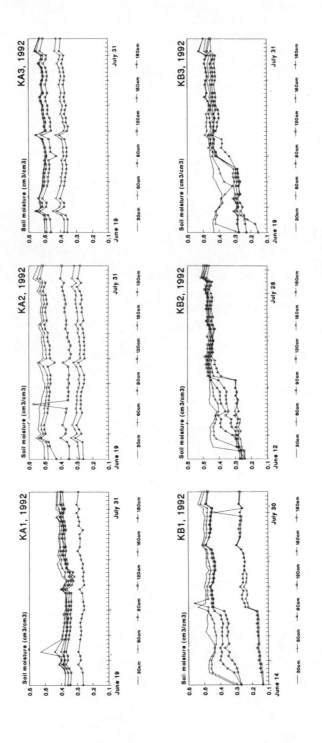

Figure 3.6 Soil moisture change in two khet sites.

and monsoon rice cultivation needs irrigation in the periods March to June and July to September, continually for more than half the year, during which there is intermittent standing water in the khet terraces except for a few days after transplanting and a few days before harvesting.

To understand the effect of terracing and irrigation on subsurface hydrology and slope stability, it is important to know how the terraces have been constructed and maintained. It was presumed by many investigators that the terraces were constructed in the way shown in Figure 3.7a. The maintenance of the terrace includes two practices: repair after terrace riser failure and annual routine trimming of the riser to get rid of weeds and thereby avoid their competition with crops for nutrients. The latter practice has led to the assumption that they are widened and progressively flattened through time (Blaikie *et al.*, 1980). Detailed study of the soil profiles at varied positions of terraces shows a cut-and-fill soil profile (Figure 3.7b). The fill material covers not only the outer part of the terrace surface and the upper part of a terrace riser but also the inner terrace surface and the lower part of a terrace riser. The cut-and-fill materials are quite different in terms of their soil physical properties and affect the hydrological behaviour of the terraces.

The terracing affects the infiltration processes in different ways on the bari and the khet. One of the special hydraulic soil characteristics of the

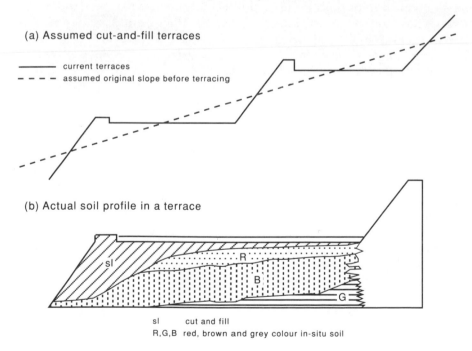

(a) Assumed cut-and-fill terraces

——— current terraces
– – – – assumed original slope before terracing

(b) Actual soil profile in a terrace

sl   cut and fill
R,G,B   red, brown and grey colour in-situ soil

Figure 3.7 Assumed and actual terrace profiles in Nepal.

weathered *in situ* soil is that the permeability of soil increases with depth within the weathered horizons, and therefore the topsoil has the lowest permeability in the profile of the weathered horizons. The creation of a terrace firstly enlarges the surface area of a hill slope; secondly, it lowers the slope angle of most or part of the slope to zero in the case of khet or into less than 15° in most cases of sloping bari terraces; thirdly, and most importantly, ploughing before planting greatly loosens the top layer of soil.

The combination of effects is clear in the case of bari: there is a significant increase in infiltration. Because the subsurface layers have greater permeability, the increased infiltration of the topsoil results in greater percolation into the soil. Field experiments in the sloping terrace show an infiltration rate of 1.11×10^{-3} cm/s to 5.073×10^{-3} cm/s in the topsoil of bari terrace compared with the one of 4.7×10^{-5} cm/s to 1.94×10^{-4} cm/s for natural *in situ* red soil or 2.15×10^{-4} cm/s to 1.782×10^{-3} cm/s for brown *in situ* soil.

In the case of khet, however, the infiltration effect due to cultivation is more complex. Infiltration is firstly increased by ploughing the field for transplanting rice, but subsequent puddling seals the bed and reduces the infiltration dramatically to a rate of 1.4×10^{-5} cm/s to 7.5×10^{-5} cm/s.

The increased infiltration has both positive and negative effects. In a sloping bari terrace the increased infiltration reduces the overland flow, thus reducing the surface erosion. On the other hand, increasing the percolation rate in the soil increases soil moisture, reduces soil suction and builds up pore water pressure, hence decreasing the factor of safety. This is particularly the case with khet because the terrace is full with standing water after ploughing and transplanting. However, infiltration in the khet is quickly reduced by puddling or sealing.

Khetland B site was left fallow during the pre-monsoon crop, so this allowed us to observe the soil moisture increase with the ploughing and transplanting of the monsoon rice in early June (Figure 3.6).

Irrigation occurred at the site on 2 July 1992 and it was ploughed the same day. Soil moisture at six different depths throughout three profiles at the front, middle and back of the terrace showed a sharp increase the following day, and most of the terrace reached near saturation except the two deepest positions (1.5 and 1.8 m) at the back of the terrace. This indicates that ploughing and irrigation at the beginning of crop cultivation does speed up the increase of moisture in the terrace soil sharply but within a certain limit, such as 1.8 m at the front and middle of the terrace and only 1.2–1.5 m at the back of the terrace. The infiltration rate decreases when puddling or sealing occurs.

The Impact of Cultivation on Surface Water

One of the other important effects of irrigation is the redistribution of surface water. This results from increasing soil water storage due to increased infiltration and the reservoir capacity of khets. The increase of infiltration leads to an increase in percolation, because in the upper part of the soil the water-holding capacity is much higher than deeper down the profile, especially in the cut-and-fill slope-forming materials which are at the top of the terrace. Retaining the water in the upper part of terrace soil helps to reduce the surcharge of ground water and reduces the overland flow/run-off ratio. It also increases the evapotranspiration after rainfall because of greater available soil moisture. The reservoir effect of terraces helps to detain and redistribute rainfall and overland flow, reducing surface erosion and making peak flow in stream channels less peaky. A khet is constructed with a bund at its front for keeping the irrigated water in the terrace. Usually the bund is 20–30 cm high but the standing water in the terrace is about 10 cm or less. This means that the terraces have the capacity to hold a 10–20-cm depth of water body – a storm size of 100–200 mm of rainfall before the water in the terraces overflows.

One might argue that the outlets which interconnect the terraces are draining water during the rainfall, hence invaliding the reservoir effect. However, the drainage is minor compared with the collection area of the whole terraced slope. Often the outlet is only 10–20 cm in width. In making the outlets for every terrace, farmers normally ensure that the inlet and the outlet of one terrace are as far apart as possible to allow for maximum time for the water to fill up the terrace before it drains into the next terrace. The farmer thus also makes the best use of the limited time quota he gets for irrigating his land under the self-organized community management. The farmer of Khetland B site reported that it normally takes him four days to fill his 2-ha terraced slope with full canal inflow. It can take up to 12–15 days if the canal supply is limited. Therefore the terrace can detain the rainfall and surface overflow for hours, if not days, hence effectively reducing the contribution of drainage to downstream flooding. This is very significant, for we are talking about catchments with as much as 26 per cent of the area of all agricultural land of the Middle Hills region. Furthermore, the surface erosion on the khet hill slope is reduced to an insignificant level because the water has to meander around at an extremely low speed from terrace to terrace.

Another effect on redistribution is that the canals take more water from streams when it is not raining on the terraces. Given the uneven distribution of mountain rainfall, this effectively helps to reduce stream peak discharge and to even out the water distribution, hence reducing the risks of local flooding downstream.

For the bari land the surface erosion problem does exist. But this is mainly a problem in the pre-monsoon season and some times in August when maize is harvested and a new crop is still to be planted. During the rest of monsoon season the bari lands are well protected by the dense maize crop. Brown (1985) summarized a comparative case study in eastern Nepal on surface erosion rate as: 13.35 t/ha/per year for bare denuded land; 8.146 t/ha/per year for an old forested landslide; 2.547 t/ha/per year for grassland; 2.885 t/ha/per year for bari land; and only 0.088 t/ha/per year for khet land.

Figures 3.5 and 3.6 also depict the seasonal soil moisture change from the beginning to the middle of the monsoon for bari and khet. The soil water movement in the bari only responds to rainfall because of its non-irrigated character. Most of the bari profiles show a tendency to increase steadily through the whole period, except when intensive continuous rainfall occurred on some days such as 7 to 10 July (an average of around 50 mm/day), during which time in the bari land BB there was a perturbation in the middle of the terrace and a sharp increase at the front of terrace. In the other bari site BA, the moisture remained quite stable until about 20 July, when it rained intensively and continuously for a week. It is interesting to compare the seasonal moisture change of the two khet sites. In Khetland B most of the soil profile was saturated when the farmer irrigated on 2 July, and then remained saturated. But in the Khetland A site, where both pre-monsoon and monsoon rice were planted, the moisture remained fairly stable with small perturbations throughout the season. Field results from tensiometers revealed that suction in most of the soil profiles was near zero, ranging from 10 kPa of suction to 10 kPa of positive pressure.

The spatial distribution of soil moisture may be more important in terms of slope stability because either positive or negative pore water pressure (suction) plays an important part in the slope stability analysis (Equations 3.1 and 3.2). The moisture and suction values obtained from monitoring at varied depths and different locations has enabled some other spatial variations to be examined. All the soil moisture profiles share some common characteristics. All profiles show that the soil moisture *decreases* with depth. That is, the deeper the soil, the less the moisture content. This is also reflected in the soil suction, which increases with depth. By the end of July, the peak of monsoon rainfall, however, in some profiles, such as the middle of Khetland A, the back of Khetland B, the back of Bariland A and the middle of Bariland B, the soil moisture contents at deeper positions remained as low as 0.2–0.3 proportional volume throughout the whole rainy season, even though suction was reduced to near zero by the end of July. The reduction in moisture is due to the increased permeability of the schistose structure in the weathered saprolite. This provides macropores, which drain water by gravity. The development of saturation by irrigation of the terrace is limited to the front and middle of an individual terrace, because the well-drained saprolite prevents the pore water pressure building up. This can be further demonstrated by the ground water level monitoring results.

Water Pressure in the Soil: the Piezometric Surface

If the ground water table is able to rise and fall freely in the soil or rock of a confined aquifer, the surface level of the water reflects simply the air pressure above. If, however, there is an impermeable membrane in the soil, the membrane forms the surface level of the ground water table, but at that surface the pressure may be above the simple local air pressure. The piezometric surface is the imaginary surface that the water would attain if the membrane were punctured.

The pore water pressure has been monitored by a network of piezometers at each site to find the fluctuation of ground water. Depths monitored range from 2.5 m up to 4 m. Three out of the four terrace hill slopes had no positive pore water pressure within the depths investigated. Khetland B was the only site which had ground water starting at the end of July at the foot of slope, and by early September it was at the upper middle of the slope. The build-up of pore water pressure is a major factor causing slope instability, acting as a lubricant, especially when the pore water pressure built up at the upper middle of the slope at a very fast speed because it was at the middle of a concave valley shape. That the build-up of pore water pressure is not due to the terracing or irrigation (except in so far as it

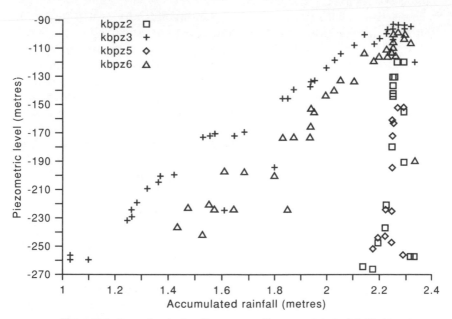

Figure 3.8 Ground water level increases with accumulated rainfall in Nepal.

generates excess throughflow) but rather is due to the topography can be deduced from the following two aspects.

Firstly, as mentioned before, the Khetland A site had two seasons of rice cultivation in the monitoring year, and hence had been irrigated from March to September, while Khetland B had only been transplanted with monsoon rice and hence had been irrigated from July to September. Interestingly, ground water in Khetland A did not increase to the depth of the piezometers, while in Khetland B it did. Khetland A lies on a divergent spur from which water would drain, in contrast to the valley hollow of Khetland B.

Secondly, the correlation between the ground water level change and accumulated rainfall in Khetland B shows a good linear relationship. The pore water pressure increased to a depth of 2.6 m below the ground surface in the lower part of slope when accumulated rainfall reached around 1000 mm, and then linearly increased along with the increase of the accumulated rainfall. When the accumulated rainfall increased to 2150 mm, the pore water pressure at the upper middle of the slope shifted quickly up from 2.65 m deep to 1.2 m deep in about 20 days (Figure 3.8).

The Impact of Cultivation on Soil Cohesion and Shear Stress

The detailed modelling of the subsurface hydrology and its coupling with slope stability analysis is still under investigation and is not included in this chapter. But a brief discussion is necessary to see the potential effect of agricultural terracing on the slope failure.

The construction of terraces changes the effective stress distribution on the hill slope locally in a terrace. The cut-and-fill process reduces stress at the back of the terrace and adds load at the front. It also creates a much steeper segment of slope at each terrace riser, with an average slope angle of 57°. Beneath the cut-and-fill materials the uppermost high clay content horizon of weathered material may remain to form an impermeable or semi-impermeable layer so that pore water pressure could build up above the layer. This was actually seen when a soil pit was dug for sampling in a terrace in early August. Water percolated from the water of the pit at a depth of about 1 m down the profiles.

To be stable, calculation suggests that the angle of slope should be less than 14° or so. However, most of the potential shearing surface between the cut-and-fill material and the underlying *in situ* soil is greater than 30–45°. Therefore it is clear that the construction of a terrace does increase substantially the risk of failure at the front of a single terrace. Field observations demonstrate that individual terrace front failure is the most common type of mass failure in the area investigated. However, the effect of the terracing farming and irrigation on the mass failure of this type is limited in scale to a single terrace, and any material from the failure accumulates in the next terrace down.

In terms of mass failure involving more than a single terrace, the effect of terracing farming and irrigation is more due to the change in soil moisture. As stated above, the natural hill slope is saturated by the peak or late monsoon, late July or August. What the irrigation does is to slightly advance the onset of saturation towards early July in the case of khet land. This reduces soil suction and adds the weight of water as loading at the potential shearing surface. Since the porosity of the soil is around 0.5, the saturated bulk density of the soil increases by about one-third above the dry bulk density, hence increasing the normal stress on the steep potential shearing surface. However, the effectiveness of the stress increase does not reduce the factor of safety to the critical value of 1 because, firstly, the saturation is limited to the first 2 m of the slope profile, and secondly, infiltration on khet land is reduced by the puddling or sealing effect. Also, pore water pressure is still below the potential failure surface in early July. Field research has shown that mass failure rarely occurs in early July at this scale. The information from field observation and farmers' interviews demonstrated that most shallow failures occur in August and September, during which period the monsoon enters its peak and late stage. By that time the saturated soil in the hill slope is affected by intensive continual rainfall events, rising ground water levels, increased lateral flow at the base of the weathered horizons and the effect of topographic convergency (valley hollows), and these together result in the failure of terraced hill slopes in appropriate topographic conditions.

Terrace Management

We have discussed above the effect of construction, farming and irrigation of agriculturally terraced hill slopes on mass failure. What has not been covered is the farmers' work to maintain the terraces. Two of the most important aspects are the re-terracing of failed slopes and the repair of collapsed irrigation canals.

It has been noted by many researchers that farmers reclaim their failed terraces as soon as they can within the constraints of available labour (Ives and Messerli, 1989; Johnson *et al.*, 1982; Ives, 1987). The failures involving an individual terrace are mostly repaired immediately by rebuilding the failed materials back and reinforcing the terrace riser, farmers being well aware of the risk of leaving the failure to expand. Immediate repair prevents the failed material from being carried downslope by the irrigation water. Larger scales of mass failures which involve a group of terraces may take years to reclaim. Ives used repeat photography to demonstrate how a large debris flow (failed in 1978) involving a series of terraces was completely reclaimed when it was revisited in 1986 (Ives, 1987). Farmers usually start to re-terrace failed hill slopes in the year after failure. Being aware of critical conditions, after failures many of them re-terrace the khet fields into bari terraces instead.

Farmers have a variety of effective community schemes for the management of their irrigation canals. Use of water is usually by rotation for all farmers whose land is within the coverage of the canal. Meetings are called before the farming season to make decisions on rotating use of water and major repairs to canals. Any minor break or damage of a canal is repaired by the farmer who happens to be irrigating his land that day. Larger failures are repaired by all the farmers in the community together. Because irrigation is required by rice for the whole growth period, the irrigation canals are therefore effectively maintained in this way throughout the whole pre-monsoon and monsoon seasons.

Conclusions

We are now able to review the questions posed in the previous section and to provide preliminary, if not unequivocal, answers. In the construction, farming and irrigation of the hill slopes, terracing does change the hydrological behaviour of the hill slope. The effects are not necessarily negative; rather they are positive. Irrigation takes in and redistributes stream water, and the reservoir effect of khet land retains the rainwater and overland flow, both significantly reducing the surcharge of the stream flow and the latter also preventing slope erosion. Increased infiltration also helps to reduce overland flow in both khet and bari lands.

Crop plant cover protects the surface soil of the terraces except in the pre-monsoon when only low intensity and less frequent rainfall events occur. In the case of subsurface hydrology, the increased infiltration does advance saturation although it is limited temporally to the early stage of the monsoon and vertically within the first 2 m of the soil profile. The timing of intensive failures does not match with this advancing saturation except for the individual terrace riser failures which are under the farmers' complete control if repaired immediately. Therefore individual terrace failures do not contribute any sediment to the downslope and stream flow although they are the results of terrace construction and irrigation.

The mechanisms of larger scale terraced slope failures which involve a few or dozens of terraces are much more complicated. While a complete analysis awaits the next stage of modelling, the above discussions have revealed that the natural factors in the hill slope environments are the most critical variables: (1) form – most hill slopes are steeper than critical slope angle with deep-cutting river channels and ravines below them; (2) material – the deeply weathered *in situ* soil proves to be prone to failures due to the decomposition of cementation, presence of platy clay mineral and abundance of mica mineral, well-developed schistose structures and the existing impermeable horizons; and (3) processes – intensive, continual and frequent events throughout the monsoon season, the saturation of soil profile, the building up of the pore water pressure from the peak of the monsoon season and active stream and ravine incision. Even at this scale of failure, farmers who manage terraces and irrigation canals on land naturally prone to erosion and failures can effectively repair most failures and induce lower sediment transport and overland flow.

Acknowledgements

The authors gratefully acknowledge the financial support given to the fieldwork of this research from University of London Central Research Fund, Department of Geography, King's College London and the Sargeaunt Travel Fund. Special thanks are owed to the ODA Nepal 'Water, Soil and Land Use Management' project and its directors, Dr Alan Jenkins of the Institute of Hydrology and Dr Rita Gardner of King's College London, for allowing use of the project facilities and weather station data. Mr John Harper's help in making field equipment is warmly appreciated and thanks are extended to Mr R.B. Maskey, Mr Y.G. Khodka, Mr K.B. Thapa and Mr Him Prasad Panday for their valuable assistance in Nepal. The first author is K.C. Wong Scholar.

References

Arita, K., Ohta, Y., Akiba, C., and Madue, Y. (1973) Kathmandu region. In Y. Ohta and C. Arita (eds), *Geology of Nepal Himalayas*. Sapporo, Japan: Hokkaido University.

Aubriot, O. (1991) Rice cultivation and water balance evaluation in a terraced rice field in Nepal. In P.B. Shah, S.J. Schreier, S.J. Brown, and K.W. Riley (eds), *Soil Fertility and Erosion issues in the Middle Mountains of Nepal* (Workshop Proceedings of International Development Research Centre of Canada), pp. 218–21.

Bajracharya, D. (1983a) Deforestation in the food/fuel context: historical and political perspectives from Nepal. *Mountain Research and Development*, 3(3), 227–40.

Bajracharya, D. (1983b) Fuel, food or forest? Dilemmas in a Nepali village. *World Development*, 11(12), 1057–74.

Bandyopadhyay, I., Jayal, N.O., Schoettli, U., and Singh, C. (1985) *India's Environment, Crises and Responses*. Dehra Dun, UP, India: Natraj Publishers.

Blaikie, P., Cameron, J. and Seddon, D. (1980) *Nepal in Crisis*. Delhi: Oxford University Press.

Boyce, J.R. (1985) Some observations on the residual strength of tropical soil. *Proceedings of the 1st International Conference on Geomechanics Tropical Soils. Brasilia*, 1, 229–37.

Brown, A. (1985) A study of soil erosion on the Kosi hills of Eastern Nepal. Unpublished BSc thesis, King's College, London.

Brunsden, D., Jones, D.K., Martin, R.P., and Doornkaup, J.C. (1981) The geomorphological character of part of the Low Himalaya of Eastern Nepal. *Z. Geomorph*. NF Suppl.- 37, 25–72.

Caine, N. and Mool, P.K. (1981) Channel geometry and flow estimates for two small mountain streams in the Middle Hills, Nepal. *Mountain Research and Development*, 1 (3–4), 231–43.

Caine, N. and Mool, P.K. (1982) Landslides in the Kolpu Khola drainage, Middle Mountains, Nepal. *Mountain Research and Development*, **2**(2), 157–73.

Donner, W. (1972) *Nepal: Raum, Mensch and Wirtschaft*. Wiesbaden: Otto Harrassowitz Verlag.

Eckholm, E. (1975) The deterioration of mountain environments. *Science*, **189**, 746–70.

Eckholm, E. (1976) *Losing Ground*. New York: Worldwatch Institute. W.W. Norton & Co. Inc.

Fontenelle, J. (1991) Water management analysis of a rice growing network. In P.B. Shah, S.J. Schreier, S.J. Brown, and K.W. Riley (eds), *Soil Fertility and Erosion issues in the Middle Mountains of Nepal* (Workshop Proceedings of International Development Research Centre of Canada), pp. 213–17.

Fredlund, D.G. (1987) Slope stability and analysis incorporating the effect of soil suction. In M.G. Anderson and K.S. Richards (eds), *Slope Stability*. John Wiley and Sons, pp. 113–44.

Gardner, R., Blaikie, P., Gerrard, J., Thornes, J., Collins, R., Curtis, A., and Wu, K. (1992) *Land Use, Soil Conservation and Water Resource Management in the Middle Hills of Nepal*. Working paper No. 1 of the Soil Erosion Group. London: Royal Geographical Society.

Gilmour, D.A. (1991) Trends in forest resources and management in the Middle Mountains of Nepal. In P.B. Shah, S.J. Schreier, S.J. Brown, and K.W. Riley (eds), *Soil Fertility and Erosion Issues in the Middle Mountains of Nepal* (Workshop Proceedings of International Development Research Centre of Canada), pp. 33–46.

Greenway, D.R. (1987) Vegetation and slope stability. In M.G. Anderson and K.S. Richards (eds), *Slope Stability*. John Wiley and Sons Ltd, pp. 187–230.

Griffin, D.M., Sheperd, K.R., and Mahat, T.B.S. (1988) Human impacts on some forests of the Middle Hills of Nepal. Part 5: Comparisons, concepts, and some policy implications. *Mountain Research and Development*, **8**(1), 43–52.

Ives, J.D. (1987) Repeat photography of debris flow and agricultural terraces in the Middle Mountains, Nepal. *Mountain Research and Development* **7**(1), 82–6.

Ives, J.D. and Messerli, B. (1988) *The Himalayan Dilemma*. London: Routledge.

Johnson, K., Olsen, E.A., and Manandhar, S. (1982) Environmental knowledge and response to natural hazards in mountainous Nepal. *Mountain Research and Development*, **2**(2), 175–88.

Joshi, S.C. (ed.) (1986) *Nepal Himalaya: Geo-ecological Perspectives*. Nainital, UP, India: Himalayan Research Group.

Kienholz, H., Schneider, G., Bichsel, M., and Mool, P. (1983) Mountain hazards mapping in Nepal's Middle Mountains: maps of land use and geomorphic damages (Kathmandu-Kakani area). *Mountain Research and Development*, **3**(3), 195–220.

Kienholz, H., Schneider, G., and Tamrakar, R. (1984) Mapping of mountain hazards and slope stability. *Mountain Research and Development*, **4**(3), 247–66.

Laban, P. (1979) Landslide occurrence in Nepal. *Phewa Thewa Tal Project Report No. SP/13*. Kathmandu: ICIMOD.

Lall, J.S. and Moddie, A.D. (eds) (1981) *The Himalaya: Aspects of Change*. New Delhi: Oxford University Press.

Land Resources Mapping Project (1986a) *Land Utilization Report*. Kathmandu: Kenting Earth Sciences Limited.

Land Resources Mapping Project (1986b) *Land System Report: The Soil Landscapes of Nepal*. Kathmandu: Kenting Earth Sciences Limited.

Lupini, J.F., Skinner, A.E., and Vaughan, P.R. (1981) The drained residual strength of cohesive soils. *Geotechnique*, **31**(2), 181–213.

Mahat, T.B.S., Griffin, P.M., and Sheperd, K.R. (1986a) Human impact on some forests of the Middle Hills of Nepal. I: Forestry in the context of the traditional resources of the state. *Mountain Research and Development*, **6**(3), 223–32.

Mahat, T.B.S., Griffin, P.M., and Sheperd, K.R. (1986b) Human impact on some forests of the Middle Hills of Nepal. II: Some major human impacts before 1950 on the forests. *Mountain Research and Development*, **6**(4), 325–34.

Mahat, T.B.S., Griffin, D.M., and Sheperd, K.R. (1987a) Human impact on some forests of the Middle Hills of Nepal. III: Forests in the subsistence economy of Sindhu Palchok and Kabhre Palanchok. *Mountain Research and Development*, **7**(1), 53–70.

Mahat, T.B.S., Griffin, D.M., and Sheperd, K.R. (1987b) Human impact on some forests of the Middle Hills of Nepal. IV: A detailed study in southeast Sindhu Palchok. *Mountain Research and Development*, 7(2), 111–34.

Myers, N. (1986) Environmental repercussions of deforestation in the Himalayas. *Journal of World Forest Resource Management*, **2**, 63–72.

Peter, T. and Mool, P.K. (1983) Geological and petrographical base studies for the mountain hazard mapping project in the Kathmandu–Kakani area, Nepal. *Mountain Research and Development*, **3**(3), 221–6.

Ramsay, W.J.H. (1985) Erosion in the Middle Himalaya, Nepal, with a case study of the Phewa Valley. Unpublished MSc thesis, University of British Columbia, Vancouver.

Ramsay, W.J.H. (1986) Erosion problems in the Nepal Himalaya – an overview. In Johsi, S.C. (ed.), *Nepal Himalaya: Geoecological Perspectives*. Nainital, UP, India: Himalayan Research Group.

Ruthenburg, H. (1980) *Farming Systems in The Tropics*. Oxford: Clarendon Press, pp. 1178–250.

Sandroni, S.S. (1985) Sampling and testing of residual soils in Brazil. In E.W. Brand and H.B. Phillipson (eds), *Sampling and Testing of Residual Soils*. Hong Kong: ISSMFE, Scorpion Press, pp. 31–50.

Shah, B.P., Schreier, S.J., Brown, S.J., and Riley, K.W. (eds) (1991) *Soil Fertility and Erosion Issues in the Middle Mountains of Nepal*. Kathmandu: ISS/UBC/IDRC.

Singh, J.S. (ed.) (1985) *Environmental Regeneration in Himalaya: Concepts and Strategies*. Nainital, UP, India: Central Himalayan Environment Association.

Singh, J.S. and Kaur, J. (1985) *Integrated Mountain Development*. New Delhi: Himalayan Books.

Sterling, C. (1976) Nepal. *Atlantic Monthly*, **238**(4), 14–25.

Thompson, M. and Warburton, M. (1986a) Uncertainty on a Himalayan scale. *Mountain Research and Development*, **7**(3), 332–44.

Thompson, M. and Warburton, M. (1986b) Knowing where to hit it: a conceptual framework for the sustainable development of the Himalaya. *Mountain Research and Development*, **5**(3), 203–30.

Vaughan, P.R. (1990) Characterising the mechanical properties of in-situ residual soil. In Publications Committee of 2 ICOTS (ed.), *Geomechanics in Tropical Soils*, Vol. 2. Netherlands: A.A. Balkema, pp. 469–87.

Wagner, A. (1981) Rock structure and slope stability study of Walling area, central west Nepal. *Journal of Nepal Geology Society*, **1**(2), 37–43.

Wagner, A. (1983) *The Principal Geological Factors Leading to Landslides in the Foothills of Nepal: a Statistical Study of 100 Landslides; Steps for Mapping the Risks of Landslides*. Kathmandu: Helvetas/Swiss Technical Cooperation/ITECO.

4
Assessing the Impact of Anthropogenic Land Use Change in the Himalayas

Bruno Messerli and Thomas Hofer

Editors' Note
Towards the end, this chapter touches on the question of highland–lowland interaction – in this case the problem of floods in the plains. This is a question about which there has been considerable public controversy in recent years. The authors here give only one set of flood data without space for detailed explanation, and qualification. A recent comprehensive review of floods by CSE (1991) in India points out that data on flooding are variable and unreliable. No-one has accurate data on inundated areas – most statistics refer to loss or damage, something which may change as human settlement patterns change, rather than because river behaviour has changed.

Introduction

The several hundred million people living in the Himalayas and their adjacent vast lowlands are forced to use their land with increasing intensity. Is this region consequently running into an ecological catastrophe in the next years or decades? More and more people are concerned with this question, among them scientists and politicians. The chain of mechanisms seems to be very clear: population growth in the mountains; increasing demand for fuelwood, fodder and timber; uncontrolled and increasing forest removal in more and more marginal areas; intensified erosion and higher peak flows in the rivers; severe flooding in the densely populated and cultivated plains of the Ganges and Brahmaputra. These convincing conclusions have been subscribed to carelessly by some scientists and adopted by many politicians in order to point at the culprit. In the article 'Bihar floods: looking northward', published in *India Today* in

October 1987, the Kingdom of Nepal and its population are found responsible for the flood catastrophies in the Gangetic plain (Farzend, 1987). One month later the authors of an article in *Newsweek* claimed that 75 per cent of the forests in the Everest region have disappeared since 1953 and that at the same rate of forest removal the Himalayas will be barren of trees in 25 years (Begley *et al.*, 1987).

What is the reason for such theories? To what kind of data do the authors have access? Where are the scientific fundamentals of such stirring statements? Who is responsible for them, laden as they are with sensation and conflict potential?

The aim of the Highland–Lowland Interactive Systems programme (renamed later as Mountain Ecology and Sustainable Development) of the United Nations University (UNU) is to promote a more serious scientific analysis of these crucial problems, which in the light of increasing population and expanding land use are of growing importance for the tropical mountains and their surrounding areas. This chapter focuses on Nepal and the plains of the Ganges and Brahmaputra, as we have our own field experiences in these regions; a first summarizing overview is available (Ives and Messerli, 1989), and it is intended to continue research in this area (Hofer, 1989).

Population Growth and History of Deforestation

The census of 1971 showed a population of 11.5 million for Nepal and a 2 per cent rate of growth, which would mean a doubling of the population every 35 years. Although it was thought that the introduction of family planning would reduce this rate, the census of 1981 showed a population of 15 million and a 2.6 per cent rate of growth, meaning a doubling of the population every 27 years (Goldstein *et al.*, 1983). The 1991 data give a total of 19.4 million and a growth rate of 2.6 per cent per annum. From these limited data we could conclude that the desire for land in the erosion-threatened mountains of Nepal should increase enormously. A closer examination of the situation reveals that from 1952/54 to 1971, the population in the subtropical Terai, which had once been infested with malaria, increased from 35 per cent to only 38 per cent of the total population. However, between 1971 and 1981 this proportion rose from 38 to 47 per cent. It was accompanied by a period of immense population growth in the cities at an annual rate of over 10 per cent. By 1981 over 6 per cent of the total population lived in cities. Thus the decade from 1971 to 1981 was one of fundamental demographic change; the population of the Terai and the cities grew to comprise almost 50 per cent of the total population, while in mountainous and hilly areas population increase was relatively small as a result of migration (Goldstein *et al.*, 1983).

Even without further consideration of the politically sensitive question of uncontrolled migration from India to the Terai, the accuracy of the census, the different birth rates among different castes, etc., this astoundingly rapid demographic change still shows clearly that relationships between population growth, settlement of new land and deforestation are not simple and one-dimensional. They must be perceived as much more differentiated in local and regional terms.

The history of deforestation must be examined in a new light in exactly the same way. Studies published in recent years clearly demonstrate that forest use and degradation are not confined to this decade or even this century. On the contrary, these processes have been going on for hundreds of years. It was on the Ganges plain that land use was first intensively expanded over wide areas at the expense of forests. The first period of massive deforestation in the Himalayas occurred during the 1850s and 1860s as a result of two forces: the establishment of British control in the upper Ganges and Indus plains, and the penetration of that region by railways (Tucker, 1987; see also Richards *et al.*, 1985; Griffin *et al.*, 1988). These few examples suffice to show how easy it is for inhabitants of the plains to accuse inhabitants of the mountains of doing what they themselves did much earlier and more intensively.

An examination of specific, detailed studies of the problem clearly reveals how varied the conditions of deforestation are. In a UNU study, a comparison of photographs taken in the period 1955–1963 and up to 1984 identified no significant changes in the forest cover over wide areas of the Everest region. At the most, forest stands were observed to be less dense in some places. Settlement and clearing of this high mountain region by Sherpa immigrants from Tibet date from the first half of the sixteenth century (Opitz, 1968; Limberg, 1982; Zimmerman *et al.*, 1986; Byers, 1987). This unique landscape thus has a much longer history of deforestation. Today it is a landscape of impressive cultural and ecological harmony, although we must not overlook the problems for future development in terms of tourist-related structural changes.

The Tinau Watershed Project in the hills between Pokhara and the plain constitutes a much more striking intervention. The amount of forest cover in this district is assumed to have dropped from 42.5 per cent in 1955 to 25.5 per cent in 1984; forest cutting along roads is substantially greater. For 12 years from 1972 to 1984, during which more precise aerial surveys were done, annual replacement of forest cover was determined to be 0.30 per cent, being replaced by 0.07 per cent bush, 0.09 per cent grass, 0.12 per cent cultivated fields, and 0.015 per cent degraded land (Strebel, 1985). With regard to erosion, these figures show the extent to which these surface areas have been transformed and are now either covered by completely acceptable forest substitutes or are areas of potential hazard. If forest is replaced with sympathetic agriculture or at least suitable vegetation cover, neither surface run-off nor erosion will increase. We shall return to this point.

Change in land use is undoubtedly most apparent in the plains of the Terai, where settlement has been extensive since the successful fight against malaria. In the period 1964–1977 alone, 2500 km^2 or 10.2 per cent of the forest cover was cleared (His Majesty's Government of Nepal, 1983). Even if we have no exact chronological data, it is doubtless accurate to say that deforestation here has proceeded exactly as it did decades or centuries ago in the Ganges plain of India.

In the Hengduan mountains in China we came across the same problem. The turmoils of the Cultural Revolution were blamed for the forest removal in numerous mountain areas. The verification in the field and the comparison with old maps, pictures and travel documents, however, clearly showed that this phase of deforestation took place much earlier (Ives and Messerli, 1989). These observations are confirmed by the following conclusions of Menzies (1988):

> Western visitors to China during the nineteenth century remarked on the scarcity of forests, and on the apparently relentless destruction of what little forested land remained. The disastrous floods and famines which occurred during the early twentieth century led some to conclude that deforestation, followed by severe erosion and siltation in sensitive watersheds, was one of the major factors accounting for rural poverty in China.

First investigations in the Indian Himalayas, based on maps of 1923 and 1969 as well as LANDSAT imagery of 1986, show an increase of forest cover in the upper Beas[1] Valley (Kuster, 1989). In the investigation area of roughly 5000 km^2, afforestation exceeds deforestation by 46 km^2. Only in the vicinity of the tourist resort of Manali is there a significant decrease of forest cover. The afforestation programmes concentrate on the steep, erosion-prone portions of the slopes.

Although the statements with regard to forest history are limited they may show that these processes are much older and temporally more differentiated than is generally accepted. It is harmful to provide political authorities and decision makers in any position with non-reviewed or even wrong reports as did the World Bank (1979); 'Nepal has lost half its forest cover within a thirty-year period (1950–1980) and by AD 2000 no accessible forests will remain.'

Forest and Mountain Agriculture and Their Effects on Run-off and Erosion

So far, we have been using the term 'deforestation' without careful definition. But we should be clear that the term 'deforestation' is too general and therefore causes a lot of misunderstanding and misinterpretation (Hamilton, 1987). Different kinds of forest use and forest conversion have different impacts on soil erosion and run-off. 'The emotive term "deforestation" compounds the problem and should be eliminated from both technical and popular thinking unless used with qualifying adjectives or phrases to indicate the real nature of the forest land-use change' (Hamilton, 1987). Hamilton suggests the following specifications to be used in context with problems of 'deforestation'.

Uses or alterations:
1   Harvesting minor forest products.
2   Shifting agriculture.
3   Harvesting fuelwood and lopping fodder.
4   Harvesting commercial wood.
5   Grazing on forest land.
6   Burning forestland.

Conversion of forest:
7   Conversion to forest tree plantations.
8   Conversion to grassland or savanna for grazing.
9   Conversion to food or extractive tree crops.
10 Conversion to annual cropping.
11 Conversion to agroforestry.

Restoration of forest:
12 Reforestation or afforestation.

To discuss the effects of different land use types on run-off and erosion we quote three specific field research projects with their very instructive findings.

Phewa Watershed Project, Nepal

Table 4.1 contains some decisive figures from a project in the Phewa Watershed in Nepal (Impat, 1979). Erosion rates were calculated on test plots under different land use types.

Table 4.1 Land cover and erosion rates.

Land use	Area (ha)	Erosion rate (t/ha/year)	Annual soil loss (t/y)
Forest	4 128	5.2	21 465.6
Scrub	509	17.5	8 907.5
Grazing land	858	30.2	2 585.1
Irrigated rice terrace	4 020	4.5	18 090.0
Non-irrigated rice terrace	2 173	17.4	37 810.2
Total	11 686		88 858.4

Source: Impat (1979).

Although the data are a result of only one year's measurements, we may conclude the following:

1   An overused grassland certainly has a higher erosion rate than forest.
2   If we turn forest area into non-irrigated terraces, erosion will increase.
3   If we convert the land into irrigated rice terraces, there will be no change of the
    erosion rates; the situation will even slightly improve compared to forest area.

The figures show very clearly that if we change forest area into well-managed agriculture units, the erosion rate will not increase.

Nepal–Australian Project

The main topic of the Nepal–Australian project was the difference of water infiltration under forest and non-forest with compacted soil (Gilmour *et al.*, 1987). In one of the research areas there had been forest cutting for probably a century and heavy grazing. The surface was very much compacted down to a depth of 10 cm. Although only one rainy season has been measured, the results are most interesting: only on 6.7 rain-days (17 per cent of all rain-days) of the monsoon season did the five-minute intensity exceed the surface infiltration rate, which resulted in surface run-off. Only for a limited time on these 6.7 days was there more precipitation than the compacted soil was able to absorb. In a second test area trees were planted and the infiltration rate continuously measured. Not until 12 years after the plantation of trees did infiltration begin to change slowly towards higher rates.

The effect of soil compaction and of forest removal or afforestation on surface run-off seems not very important. Against this background the Australian team suggests we think over the contention that 'deforestation' necessarily results in an increase in large-scale flooding, and conversely that afforestation would decrease the frequency or magnitude of such flooding.

India

As a third example we present the results of a research project of the Central Soil and Water Conservation Research and Training Centre in Dehra Dun, India (CSWCRTI, 1976). Up to 1963 the investigated watershed of 80 ha was highly degraded through forest removal and land use. From 1964 to 1975 fast-growing grass, shrubs and trees were planted and soil conservation measures began. In order to observe the effect of these measures, data on precipitation, discharge and erosion were recorded regularly (Figure 4.1).

With a range from 800 mm to about 1700 mm the variability of annual precipitation is very high, as is typical for monsoon climates. The variation in run-off is less. But most interesting is the graph of actual erosion: within three years of the commencement of conservation measures, the amount of erosion decreased from about 80 t/ha/per year to almost 10 t/ha/per year, a

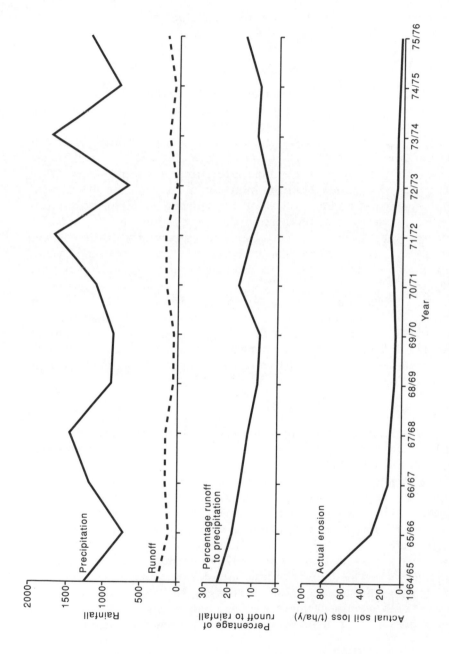

Figure 4.1 Annual rainfall, run-off, erosion and actual soil loss from small treated watershed near Chandigarh. *Source:* CSWCRTI, (1976).

reduction of nearly 90 per cent. In the last year of measurements, the erosion rate was 5 t/ha/per year, close to the rate of soil replenishment. The percentage of run-off to rainfall also decreases, but much less than the erosion rate.

Land use practices and soil conservation measures have much more effect on soil loss than on run-off. Again we have to emphasize that forest removal as such is not so important with regard to run-off and soil erosion as the other use to which the land is converted.

In addition to these three instructive examples, Hamilton (1987) emphasizes another aspect of trees and forests with respect to soil erosion: it is a well-known, generally accepted fact that trees protect the soil against erosion. But in reality this again seems to be a subject of misinterpretation. Important experiments by different scientists (Lembaga Ekologi, 1980; Mosley, 1982) have shown that raindrop impact on bare soil under tree canopies greater than 10 m in height is higher than on bare soil in the open. This is mainly due to larger raindrops which are formed on the tree leaves and which have a higher terminal velocity than normal raindrops. With the increase of the drop size, the erosivity increases. Therefore it is not the high trees of a forest that protect the soil from splash and sheet erosion, but the organic matter, the surface litter and the low canopy vegetation. 'If surface erosion is to be minimized, the upper tree canopy myth must be abandoned, and attention focused on the management of the soil/litter/vegetation interface' (Hamilton, 1987).

As a whole we may conclude, based on the data available today: 'Forest cutting followed by abusive agriculture and grazing may aggravate flooding, forest cutting followed by conservation farming should not aggravate flooding.' This is certainly true also for soil erosion.

> Deforestation of the Himalayas is not likely to have a significant effect on the extent of the floods in the plains and the delta below. The high monsoon rains in the mountains, combined with steep slopes and seismically unstable terrain, ensure that this zone will have rapid run-off and high sedimentation whatever the land cover may be, as was true before human settlement in the region. (Rogers *et al.*, 1989)

River Discharge: Human-induced Trends or Natural Fluctuations?

The basic information comprises data of discharge and sediment load, which for political reasons are too often not available. Hydrological data are classified and very difficult to get. Therefore our information is still limited and we have to concentrate on some selected river systems. Always we have to keep in mind the very high precipitation especially in the eastern part of the Himalayas, not only in the mountains, but also in the plains.

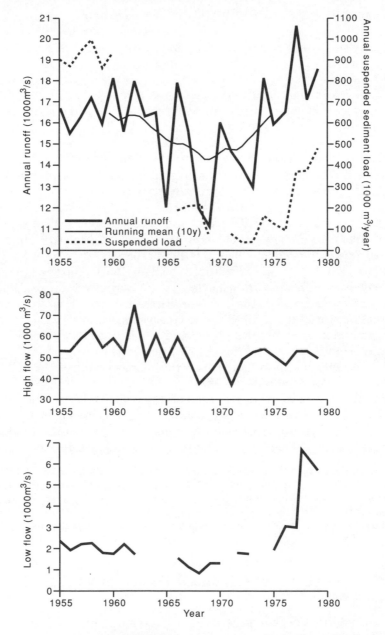

Figure 4.2 Brahmaputra: run-off, sediment loads, high and low flows, at Pandu. *Source:* Goswami (1983).

Brahmaputra

The data used in Figure 4.2 have been published by Goswami (1983). For the 25 years of available data the variability of the annual discharge is extremely high. But a striking feature is the obviously clear increase of annual discharge since 1969. The same trend can be observed in the graph of annually suspended sediment load. Is this change the result of lower water retention and of higher soil erosion in the upper parts of the catchment area? The three following facts contradict this deduction:

1 The high-flow hydrograph follows a decreasing trend and the low-flow hydrograph an increasing trend during the late 1970s. If human influence played an important role, for instance through accelerated forest cutting and poorly maintained agricultural terraces, then it should have an increasing effect on high-flow river discharge, i.e. we should have observed the high-flow discharge increasing and the low-flow discharge decreasing.
2 In the 1960s the annual discharge reached similar levels as in the 1970s. We have to be very careful in analysing trends of short time series as they might represent part of a natural cyclicity.
3 From 1955 to 1960 the suspended sediment load was much higher than from 1970 to 1980. This has nothing to do with forest clearing or land use patterns. Goswami (1983) associates the high sediment load of the Brahmaputra from 1955 to 1963 with tectonic events. The great earthquake of 1950 increased soil creep and slippage over wide areas, enhanced erosion and therefore provided a large debris load for the rivers.

On the basis of the available data, changes in land use or forest cover do not provide a satisfactory explanation of discharge and sediment load variations. After his very intense research in the Assam region, Goswami (personal communication) puts the anthropogenic influence on erosion and discharge in the last position. Natural factors such as relief, tectonic activities, erosion-prone geology and high precipitation with extreme intensities are dominating the discharge processes and are overlapping the anthropogenic influence up to now.

Ganges

Farakka is a gauging site very close to the India–Bangladesh border. At Farakka the river has a stable cross-section with a long history of monitoring. In Figure 4.3 information on the annual volume of water flow of the Ganges is shown.

The hydrography does not show any trend in the hydrological characteristics of the Ganges from 1950 to 1985. The annual fluctuation is extremely high, but there is no obvious change over the recorded time period. However, we have to emphasize that the Ganges at Farakka does not represent the total natural flow as enormous amounts of water are diverted upstream for irrigation and other purposes.

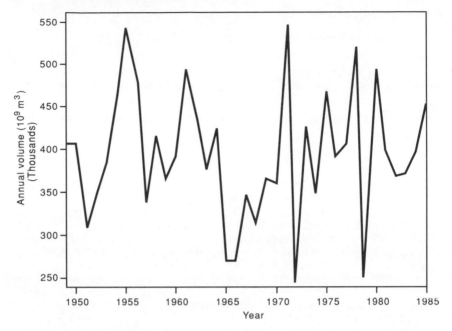

Figure 4.3 Annual discharge in the Ganges at Farakka. *Source:* Rogers *et al.* (1989).

Beas[1] (Himachal Pradesh)

After the discussion of the large-scale processes we shall comment on two examples of meso-scale rivers. The gauging site of Thalot is located about 40 km upstream of Mandi, just above the reservoir of Pandoh. The data are recorded by the Electricity Board of Himachal Pradesh. At Thalot the catchment area of the Beas is approximately 5000 km^2. The monthly data in Figure 4.4 are calculated from average 10-daily discharge records.

The annual fluctuation of water flow is very high. The variability of high flow in the summer months is remarkable. The river flow in summer mainly consists of monsoonal run-off combined with snow-melt discharge. The low flow in winter is more or less constant. The graph describes typical hydrological phenomena of Himalayan rivers (Hofer, 1989). There is absolutely no evidence of change over the recorded 40 years which could be a result of ecological degradation in the catchment area. Neither high flow nor low flow nor annual average of discharge follow any significant trends whatsoever. But we have to emphasize that unfortunately only average 10-daily data were available for the investigation and not daily records.

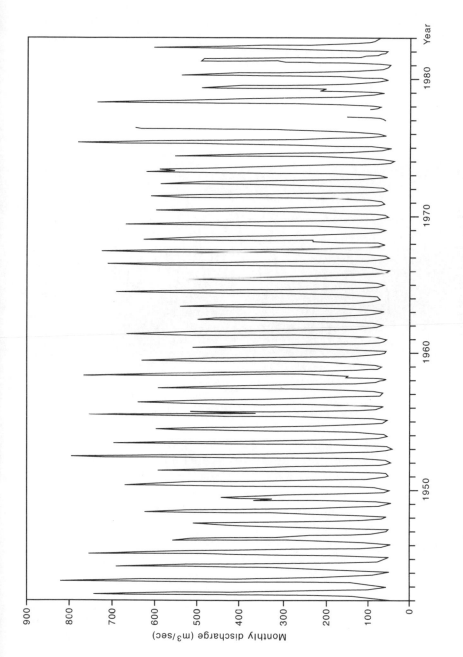

Figure 4.4 Monthly discharge of the River Beas at Thalot. *Source:* Hofer (1989).

Sutlej (Himachal Pradesh)

For the Sutlej river, discharge data for almost 60 years could be made available. Again the original information is given in average 10-daily discharge. The graph in Figure 4.5 represents the annual average of river flow. The gauging site of Wangtu Bridge is located on the inner line border between India and China. Again the Electricity Board of Himachal Pradesh is responsible for the measurements.

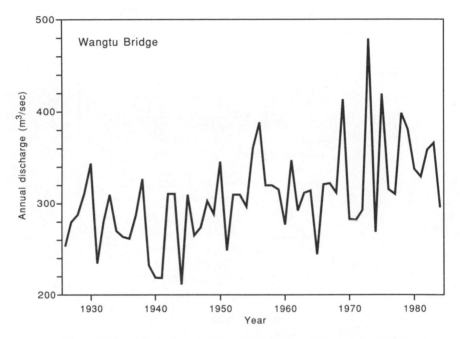

Figure 4.5 Annual discharge of River Sutlej at Kilba. *Source:* Hofer (1989).

The hydrograph in Figure 4.5 is clearly indicating an increasing discharge trend. Not only are the values as such increasing, but also the frequency of years with high average annual flow. Through regression analysis it is possible to show that the trend is statistically significant. Is this hydrological change the result of forest removal or land use intensification in the watershed?

The precipitation records, computed in Figure 4.6 provide us with the answer. Kilba is a climatological station located some kilometres upstream of Wangtu Bridge. The graph of annual precipitation shows exactly the same trend as discussed with the average annual discharge: over the last 60 years precipitation has been generally increasing. This trend, too, is statistically significant (Hofer, 1989). Interestingly, specific years with high precipitation do not necessarily correlate with years of high river flow. This

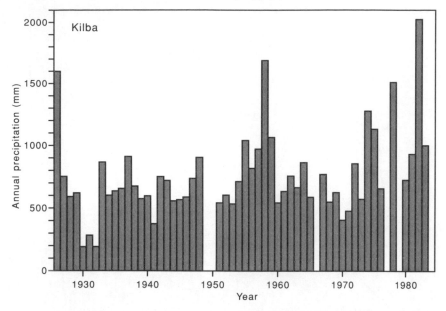

Figure 4.6 Annual precipitation at Kilba. Source: Hofer (1989).

is due to the fact that an important part of annual precipitation is stored as snow or ice. Thus the annual discharge is more related to the intensity of solar radiation during the summer months than directly to precipitation. Over longer periods, however, precipitation and discharge are highly correlated.

To summarize the Sutlej example, there is no evidence that artificial watershed degradation has influenced natural processes.

Floods and Sedimentation: Natural or Artificial

Flooding and high sedimentation are natural processes in the foothills and the plains due to high-intensity rainfall, geologically loose material in the lowest ranges and active tectonic movement in the Himalayan ranges. Carson (1985) points out that according to ancient chronicles the Ganges appears to have been behaving long ago in exactly the same manner as it behaves today. Drilling has intersected more than 5000 m of alluvial sediments adjacent to the Himalayan foothills. The sketch map of Sapt Kosi alluvial fan in Figure 4.7 shows the dynamic nature of the river's distributaries over the past 250 years. During this period the Sapt Kosi River has moved over 100 km to the west as a result of ongoing erratic sedimentation, and 12 distinct mainstream channels can be identified.

This indicates very clearly that the Sapt Kosi has been depositing vast amounts of sediment on its fan for a much longer period than that of recent

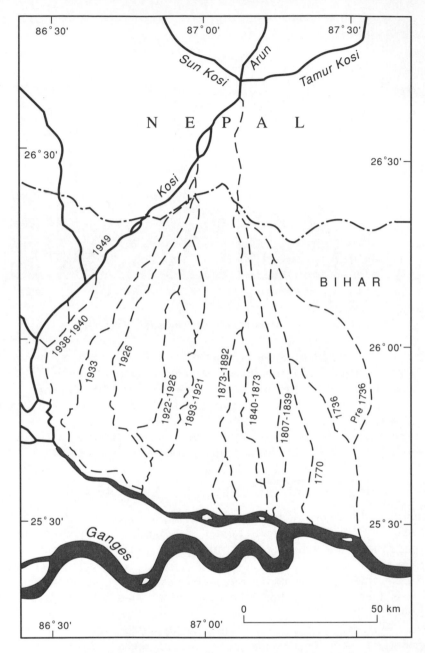

Figure 4.7 The changing course of the River Kosi on its alluvial fan. *Source:* Carson (1985).

human watershed intervention through forest removal or land use intensification. Flooding must have been a common process on the Sapt Kosi alluvial fan.

Floods in the Gangetic Plain: A General Investigation

It is a generally accepted fact that the dimension of floods in the Gangetic plain has been increasing over the last few decades. Is it possible to prove this assumption? Or is it only the flood damage that is increasing and not the water involved? The collection of reliable flood information is a very difficult task. With the available information it is not possible to give a final answer to this important and politically most sensitive question, but we would like to stimulate a broader aspect of thinking with regard to this problem.

The information on flood events used in this and the next section is quoted from Chaphekar and Mhatre (1985). Only the data on annually flooded areas were analysed, as other figures given in the statistics (population affected, damage to houses, loss of cattle and number of deaths) are variable in time, being much more the results of population growth, intensification of land use and extension of settlements into flood-prone areas rather than of the actual amount of water involved. The climatological information is quoted from Parthasarathy *et al.* (1987). Figure 4.8 shows the annually flooded area computed for the states of Uttar Pradesh, Bihar and West Bengal from 1953 to 1981.

The dimension of the flood catastrophies is extremely variable from year to year. In Bihar and West Bengal there was no increasing trend of the flooded area over the analysed period. In Uttar Pradesh the frequency of severe flooding has been higher for the last few years. However, with regard to the variability of the flood events as well as of the monsoon rains, it is too early to attribute this to a significant long-term increasing trend of flood catastrophies in Uttar Pradesh. But more important are the following observations:

1 Except for the years 1971 and 1979 the three graphs do not show any obvious correspondence of the flood events.
2 At the beginning of the recorded period, from 1953 to 1959, there was one heavy flood event in all three states, but not in the same year: Uttar Pradesh 1955, Bihar 1954 and West Bengal 1956.
3 Whereas in Uttar Pradesh and Bihar there were several remarkable floods in 1960–1967, West Bengal was almost exempt from flooding.
4 All the three states faced some flood problems in 1968–1980, but on a totally different scale. In Uttar Pradesh, the flood dimension was catastrophic. In Bihar, the flooded area was average. The inundation in West Bengal can be overlooked.

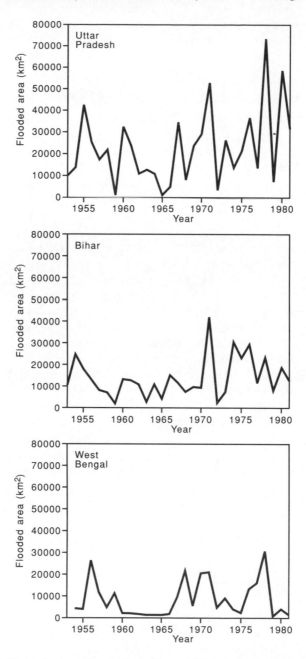

Figure 4.8 Flooded areas, Uttar Pradesh, Bihar and West Bengal. *Source:* Hofer (1989).

As only annual data could be analysed the question of whether the effect of short-term rainfall peaks (daily data) on flooding has increased or not cannot be answered.

With the few available data it is not possible to prove a significant increase of flooding in the Gangetic plain. Obviously the floods are regionally and temporally considerably differentiated. They are a function of the variable precipitation, especially of the regional distribution of heavy rainfall events. If the flood damage has increased, then it is much more an effect of the growing number of people living in flood-prone areas. (We thank Dr. G. Goswami for this very interesting personal information.)

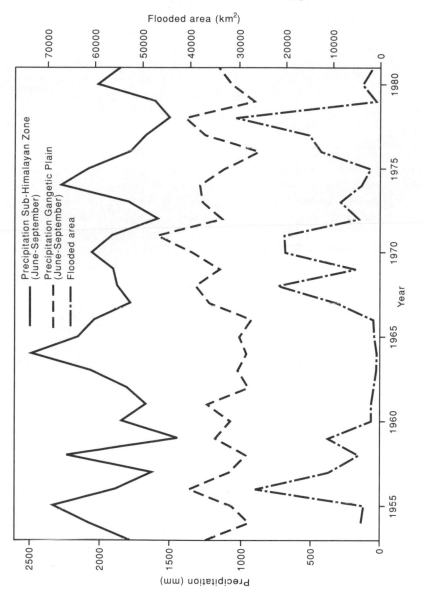

Figure 4.9 Precipitation in hills and plains, and flooded area. *Source:* Hofer (1989).

Floods in West Bengal in Comparison with Monsoonal Rainfall

Due to orographic effects, the rainfall in the Sub-Himalayan zone is higher than in the plains (Figure 4.9). It is a striking feature that the two graphs of precipitation are far from being parallel. In the years 1954, 1958, 1959–1967 and 1978 they even follow an opposite trend. Obviously the precipitation processes in the mountains and in the plain are very much differentiated and perhaps not even caused by the same climatological events. The annually flooded area in West Bengal is very well correlated with the precipitation of the plain itself. Extraordinary floods always coincide with high monsoonal rainfall within the plain (1956, 1959, 1968, 1971, 1978).

As the Sub-Himalayan zone of West Bengal belongs hydrologically to the catchment area of the Brahmaputra, this graph cannot be compared with the flood statistics of West Bengal (see Figure 4.8). Some of the floods in West Bengal are 'home-made'; they are mainly caused by the precipitation on the plain itself and not by the rains in the hills and mountains. Thus, regionally limited phenomena are influencing the flood situation to a large extent.

Sedimentation

Erosion in its different forms – sheet or gulley – occurs over the whole land surface of a catchment at some specific rate. At any point on a river it is therefore in theory possible to measure total erosion in the catchment upstream of that point, and also to observe how much sediment passes the point. Dividing the latter by the former gives the 'sediment delivery ratio' for the catchment. While this ratio may be 90 per cent for a drainage area of 1 ha, it probably averages only 50 per cent for an 80-ha area, and is less than 30 per cent for any drainage area larger than 500 ha. The material that does not pass the gauging point has therefore been eroded from one place in the catchment and deposited somewhere else – i.e. it has in some sense restabilized locally. Use of a theoretical sediment delivery ratio curve for a river basin of the size of the Ganges gives a ratio of well below 10 per cent (Hamilton, 1987). Thus major rivers carry only a modest amount of the material eroded in the mountains. This shows that anthropogenic influences in the mountains have only a limited impact on the plain. Even if we could eliminate all potential hazards and conserve every slope, the effects on sediment load on the plain would barely be detectable even decades later (Hamilton, 1987). In addition, precipitation is so intense in the central and eastern southern escarpment of the Himalayas that catastrophies are inevitable regardless of the type and density of forest cover and land use; see, for example, Darjeeling 1950 and 1968, which cites amounts up to 500 mm/day (Starkel, 1972; Zollinger, 1979). It should be remembered that the monsoon of 1993 also led to extreme rainfall and the severest flooding for decades along almost the entire Himalayan front.

Particularly in cases where heavy precipitation falls on saturated soil, it no longer matters whether the catchment area is forested or not. Furthermore we saw that catastrophic events in the mountains such as a glacial outburst in the Khumbu area had no effect on the plain. The Dudh Kosi hydrological station located where the river debouches onto the plains, at an altitude of 460 m, registered only a small peak compared with the high-run-off events caused by normal monsoonal precipitation (Figure 4.10; Zimmerman *et al.*, 1986).

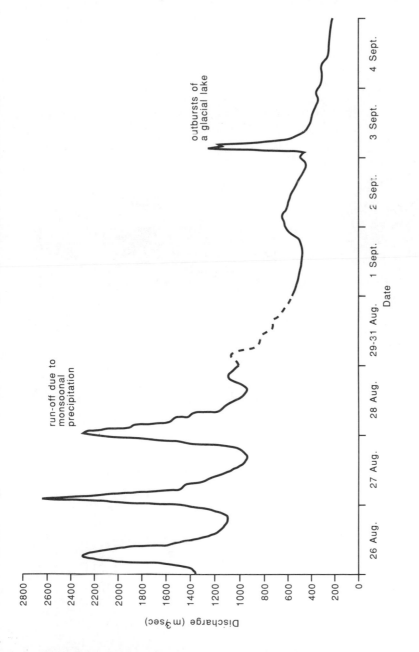

Figure 4.10 Catastrophic outburst of a glacial lake. *Source: Zimmerman et al.* (1986).

Conceptual Summary Model and Future Research

Three scales were defined with regard to Himalayan catchments: micro-level (small catchments up to approximately 50 km²); meso-level (medium-sized catchments up to approximately 20 000 km²); and macro-level (large catchments over 100 000 km²).

Damage resulting from flooding and sedimentation occurs virtually every year at all three levels. Distinctions must be made, however. Human activities have the greatest influence in small catchment areas, while natural hazards are much more significant in medium-sized catchments and human influences are concealed by the overwhelming dimensions of natural processes in large catchment areas (Figure 4.11).

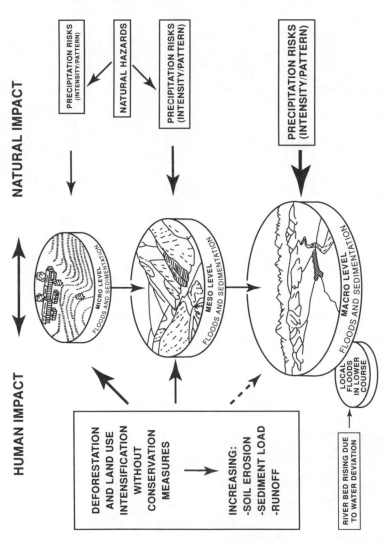

Figure 4.11 Human and natural impacts of floods and sediments in small, medium and big catchments. *Source:* Lauterburg (1985).

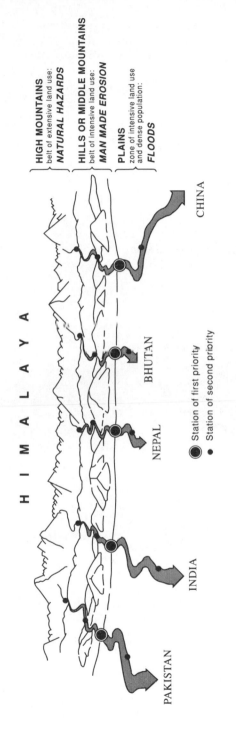

Figure 4.12 Highland–lowland interaction. *Source: Ives et al.* (1987).

HIGH MOUNTAINS
belt of extensive land use:
NATURAL HAZARDS

HILLS OR MIDDLE MOUNTAINS
belt of intensive land use:
MAN MADE EROSION

PLAINS
zone of intensive land use
and dense population:
FLOODS

H I M A L A Y A

CHINA

BHUTAN

NEPAL

INDIA

PAKISTAN

⊙ Station of first priority
● Station of second priority

Because our knowledge is based on qualitatively and quantitatively insufficient data, we propose a research strategy for the future which could serve inhabitants of the mountains and the plains as a foundation for ecologically sound land use and better mutual co-operation. All countries that share the large Himalayan water reservoir in the broadest sense should understand the processes in one of their catchment areas at different levels between the mountains and the plains, using a station network they have devised themselves (Figure 4.12).

The different scales of research should no longer be an obstacle to combining and connecting various orders of magnitude. The principle of the zoom lens may help us to see the key factors and the key processes from the local to the meso- and macro-level (Figure 4.13). We need more integrated and interdisciplinary research projects and strategies to understand the interaction of natural and artificial processes. This must be a long-term programme so that the effects of extremely dynamic land use

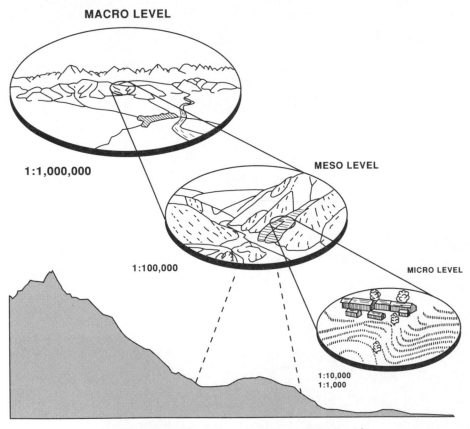

Figure 4.13 Scales of research, an integrated approach.

change can be constantly monitored, even if great time intervals between action and effort influence the processes being measured. A research approach such as this, with uniform methods and comparable data, would certainly be the most emphatic realization of the highland–lowland research programmes. If new trust between the countries and the inhabitants of the mountains and the plains is finally created by disclosure of data and findings, and if the inclination to act in the interests of ecologically sound land use can be realized, then there is a prospect of contributing something meaningful to the maintenance and development of this unique mountain environment and to its forelands.

Conclusions

Taking into account the very low sediment delivery ratio of the Ganges and Brahmaputra in the lower reaches, we must assume that most of the sediment loads result from material removed from storage places and from channel erosion. If we also consider that precipitation of 400–500 mm can occur within 24 hours, especially in the monsoon season when soils are clearly saturated, then nothing can prevent floods. Disastrous floods will occur even if the entire basin is forested (Hamilton, 1987). Knowing that every year about 2.7 billion tons of topsoil are deposited in the Bay of Bengal, creating new land, Safiullah of the Disaster Management Institute in Bangladesh stated: 'It is an unproven hunch that soil erosion and deforestation in the Himalayan region has anything to do with this' (Khanal, 1990).

Although currently available data are insufficient, we can assume that most of the catastrophic floods in the plains are the result of heavy monsoonal precipitation in the plains or in the Sub-Himalayan zone. Catastrophies are inevitable, particularly when the pressure of growing population subjects previously avoided hazardous zones to intensive use. Forest removal in the mountains plays a relatively modest role in major monsoonal floods in the lower Ganges plain. This, however, does not absolve mountain inhabitants from their responsibility to develop new, ecologically sound systems of land use, something which will enhance forests, pastures and farmlands to their benefit.

Notes

1   The Beas and Sutlej are Punjabi tributaries of the Indus system.

References

Begley, S., Moreau, R. and Mazumdar, S. (1987) Trashing the Himalayas, a once fertile region could become a new desert. *Newsweek*, Nov. 9.

Byers, A. (1987) Landscape change and man-accelerated soil loss: the case of Sagarmatha (Mt Everest) National Park, Khumba, Nepal. *Mountain Research and Development*, 7(3), 203–16.

Carson, B. (1985) Erosion and sedimentation processes in the Nepalese Himalaya. *ICIMOD Occasional Paper* No. 1. Kathmandu.

Chaphekar, S.B., and Mhatre, G.N. (1985) *Human Impact on Ganga River Ecosystem*. New Delhi: Concept Building Company.

CSE (1991) *State of India's Environment: A Citizen's report: 3: Floods, Flood Plains and Environmental Myths*. New Delhi: Centre for Science and Environment.

CSWCRTI (1976) Dehra Dun (UP, India); Central Soil and Water Research and Training Centre, *Annual Report*.

Farzend, A. (1987) Bihar floods: looking northward. *India Today*, Oct. 15.

Gilmour, D.A., Bonell, M. and Cassells, D.S. (1987) The effects of forestation on soil hydraulic properties in the Middle Hills of Nepal: a preliminary assessment. *Mountain Research and Development*, 7(3), 239–49.

Goldstein, M.C., Ross, J.L., and Schuler, S. (1983) From a mountain-rural to a plains-urban society. Implications of the 1981 Nepalese census. *Mountain Research and Development*, 3(1), 61–4.

Goswami, D.C. (1983) Brahmaputra River, Assam (India): suspended sediment transport, valley aggradation and basin denudation. PhD. University Microfilms International, Michigan.

Griffin, D.M., Shephard, K.R. and Mahat, T.B.S. (1988) Human impacts on some forests of the Middle Hills of Nepal. Part 5: Comparisons, concepts and some policy implications. *Mountain Research and Development*, 8(1), 43–52.

Hamilton, L.S. (1987) What are the impacts of Himalayan deforestation on the Ganges–Brahmaputra lowlands and delta? Assumptions and facts. *Mountain Research and Development*, 7(3), 256–63.

His Majesty's Government of Nepal (1983) *The Forests of Nepal*. Ministry of Water Resources, Water and Energy Commission, Report No. 4/2/200783/1/1, Kathmandu.

Hofer, T. (1989) Abholzung-veränderte Abflüsse-Ueberschwemmungen: Mythos oder Wirklichkeit? Eine hydrologische Untersuchung am Beispiel des·Sutlej, Beas, Chenab und Jhelum in nordwestindischen Himalaya. Unpublished Master's thesis. Department of Geography, University of Berne.

Impat, P. (1979) *Hydrometeorology and Sediment Data for Phewa Watershed*. Working Paper 15, UNDP/FAO/DSCWM-IWM Project, Kathmandu.

Ives, J.D. and Messerli, B. (1989) *The Himalayan Dilemma. Reconciling Development and Conservation*. London: Routledge.

Ives, J.D., Messerli, B. and Thompson, M. (1987) Research strategy for the Himalayan region. *Mountain Research and Development*, 7(3), 332–44.

Khanal, P. (1990) Disaster management Institute, Bangladesh. *Himal*, 3 (1), 21.

Kuster, H. (1989) Waldveränderung im indischen Himalaya. Eine Kartierung im oberen Einzugsgebiet des Beas-River. Unpublished. Institute of Geography, University of Berne.

Lauterburg, A. (1985) Erosion und Sedimentation im zentralen Himalaya (Nepal). Unpublished Master's thesis. Institute of Geography, University of Berne.

Lembaga Ekology (1980) *Report on a Study of Vegetation and Erosion in the Jatiluhur Catchment*. Bandung: Institute of Ecology.

Limberg, W. (1982) Untersuchungen über Siedlung, Landbesitz und Feldbau in Solu-Khumbu (Mount Everest-Gebiet). *Khumbu-Himal 12*. Universitätsverlag Wagner, Innsbruck.

Menzies, N.K. (1988) Trees, fields and people. The forests of China from the seventeenth to the nineteenth centuries. PhD Berkley, USA (unpublished).

Messerli, B., Ives, J.D., Hofer, T., Lauterburg, A. and Wyss, M. (1988) Himalaya: Erosion und Abfluss als Zeugen ländlicher Entwicklung und natürlicher Ressourcen. In R. Mackel and W.-D. Sick (eds), *Natürliche Ressourcen und ländliche Entwicklungsprobleme der Tropen. Festschrift für W. Manshard*. Stuttgart: Franz Steiner Verlag, pp. 218–36.

Mosley, M.P. (1982) The effect of a New Zealand beech forest canopy on the kinetic energy of water drops and on surface erosion. *Earth Surface Processes and Landforms*, **7** (2), 103–7.

Opitz, M. (1968) Geschichte und Sozialforschung der Sherpa. *Khumbu Himal 8*. Universitätsverlag Wagner, Innsbruck.

Parthasarathy, B., Sontakke, N.A., Monot, A.A. and Kothwale, D.R. (1987) Droughts/floods in the summer monsoon season over different meteorological subdivisions of India for the period of 1871–1984. *Journal of Climatology*, **7**, 57–70.

Richards, J.F., Haynes, E.S. and Hagen, H.R. (1985) Changes in the land and human productivity in Northern India 1870–1970. *Agricultural History*, **59**, 523–48.

Rogers, P., Lydon, P. and Seckler, D. (1989) *Eastern Waters Study: Strategies to Manage Flood and Drought in the Ganges–Brahmaputra Basin*. Washington D.C. US Agency for International Development.

Starkel, L. (1972) The role of catastrophic rainfall in the shaping of the relief of the lower Himalaya (Darjeeling Hills). *Geographica Polonica*, **21**, 103–47.

Strebel, B. (1985) Recent land changes in Palpa (Nepal). Report submitted to Helvetas (Zürich) and GTZ (Eschborn). Unpublished.

Tucker, R.P. (1987) Dimensions of deforestation in the Himalaya: the historical setting. *Mountain Research and Development*, **7** (3), 328–31.

Vuichard, D. and Zimmerman, M. (1986) The Langmoche flash flood, Khumbu Himal, Nepal. *Mountain Research and Development*, **6**(1), 90–4.

World Bank (1979) *Nepal: Development Performance and Prospects*. A World Bank country study, South Asia regional office. Washington DC: World Bank.

Wyss, M. (1988) Naturraum Himalaya. Unpublished Master's thesis. Institute of Geography, University of Berne.

Zimmerman, M., Bichsel, M. and Kienholz, H. (1986) Mountain hazards mapping in the Khumbu Himal, Nepal, with prototype map, scale 1 : 50,000. *Mountain Research and Development*, **6** (1), 29–40.

Zollinger, F. (1979) *Analysis of river problems and strategies for flood control in the Nepalese Terai*. UNDP Integrated Watershed Management Project. Working Paper 12, Kathmandu.

5

Nepal's Water Resources: the Potential for Exploitation in the Upper Ganges Catchment

K.B. Sajjadur Rasheed

Editors' Note
This chapter treats the topic of large dams and power generation from what Thompson in Chapter 2 has termed a 'hierarchist' position. An alternative view follows in Chapter 6.

Introduction

The Himalayan kingdom of Nepal possesses a rich resource endowment in terms of water – which, in fact, holds the key to the country's progress. Located between the Tibetan plateau and the Gangetic plain, Nepal's unique physical setting along the southern Himalayan slopes has contributed to this natural wealth. Almost the entire area of Nepal (147 181 km^2) lies within the Ganges basin, which is about 13 per cent of the total area of the basin. Four major left bank tributaries of the upper and middle Ganges flow southward from Nepal, and along with the other lesser tributaries, Nepal's contribution to the Ganges flow at Farakka (West Bengal, India) amounts to about 45 per cent. The country has over 6000 rivers and streams with the total length of the water courses exceeding 45 000 km. But development of this resource is far from straightforward, mostly because of the highly seasonal nature of precipitation and discharge. In addition, inter-annual variation is also high. This hydrological uncertainty is made more complex by the problems of funding water development projects, inadequate local infrastructure and lack of a clear picture of the market for water power. Hydropower is, by far, the most important resource to be harnessed in Nepal; the other sectors of water resource utilization are irrigation and navigation. This paper focuses on

Nepal's potential for utilizing the Ganges waters for hydroelectricity generation.

An Environmental Profile of Nepal

Nepal is a landlocked and mountainous country with altitudes ranging between 200 m and 7500 m. It can be divided into five distinct ecological zones from north to south. These zones are the High Himal (literally 'snows'), the High Mountains, the Middle Mountains, the Siwaliks and the Terai. The High Himal (over 4000 m high) is largely unpopulated, and, together with its southern zone, the High Mountains, accounts for over one-third of the total land area. The Middle Mountains zone forms the central belt of the country. It is heavily populated, covers nearly 30 per cent of the country, and is a region of rugged terrain and deep valleys. The Siwaliks comprise of a series of low ridges and settled valleys, covering 13 per cent of the country's land area. The southernmost zone is the Terai; it is a low plain of fertile land and dense forests accounting for about 14 per cent of the land area.

The physical environment of Nepal offers a vast potential of water resources. Yet, the geological history of the Himalayas demonstrates the region's proneness to earthquakes. Consequently, any major structural intervention for harnessing water wealth requires caution and comprehensive assessment. One other hazard to be taken note of in Nepal's water resource utilization is glacier lake outbursts and flooding. The northern zones have a large number of these lakes, and an occasional breaching of the pondage has often caused severe flooding and destruction downstream.

The climate of Nepal varies widely and dramatically because of the extreme altitudinal range. It varies from a tundra climate in the northern High Himal zone to a hot subtropical climate in the Terai. Precipitation is in the form of both rainfall and snowfall. The mean annual precipitation is about 1500 mm – ranging from 200 mm in the northwest to about 4000 mm in the eastern sections of the country. The southwest monsoon, which lasts from June to September, brings most of the rainfall to Nepal – especially in the southern slopes of the mountains and hills. Snowfall accounts for nearly 10 per cent of the total precipitation. Snow and glaciers make significant contributions to the run-off in the major rivers of Nepal.

Surface Water Systems

Nepal's abundant wealth of water resource is largely in the form of surface water, although there are some ground water resources in the Terai. The general alignment of the surface water drainage is toward the Ganges in the south. The drainage system is comprised of three categories of rivers (Zollinger, 1979). The most important category includes the four snow- and

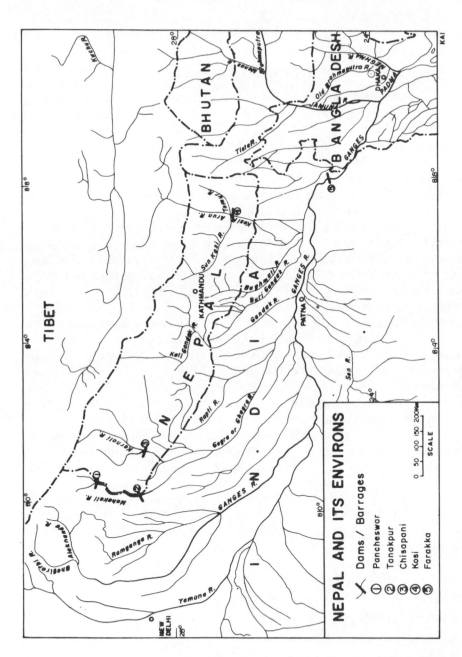

Figure 5.1 The rivers of Nepal.

glacier-fed Himalayan tributaries of the Ganges, i.e. the Mahakali (also known as Sarda in India), the Karnali, the Gandak and the Kosi, and their tributaries (Figure 5.1). The flow in these four sub-basins accounts for about 75 per cent of the annual flow during the monsoon, and the dry season flows are also substantial. The next category of rivers, like the Bagmati, Rapti, Mechi, Kankai and Babai, have their sources in the Middle Mountains. They are mostly rain-fed and have low dry season flows. The rivers originating in the Siwaliks or further south belong to the third category. They have smaller catchments, dry season flows are minimal, and wet season flows often come in the form of violent spate floods with high sediment loads. The westernmost of Nepal's four major rivers – the Mahakali – forms part of the Indo-Nepalese border. After flowing into India, it meets with the Karnali. Nearly 35 per cent of the Mahakali drainage area lies within Nepal. The Karnali river dominates the drainage area of western Nepal. The river originates in Tibet (China), forms a deep gorge at Chisapani in the Siwaliks, and, after receiving several tributaries within Nepal, meets the Mahakali in India. It is then known as the Ghagra and joins the Ganges upstream of Patna (India). The Gandak river drains central Nepal and its volume is enhanced with flows from seven major tributaries. After emerging out into the plains, the river flows in an easterly direction to meet the Ganges near Patna. The biggest river of Nepal is the Kosi, which drains the eastern third of the country. The Kosi's headwaters come from Tibet and its major tributaries are Arun, Sunkosi and Tamur. Following the three tributaries' confluence at Tribeni, the Kosi (now known as Sapt Kosi) cuts through the Siwaliks, emerges into the plain near Chatra and continues its flow toward the Ganges.

Table 5.1 Energy consumption in Nepal, 1990 (by fuel type).

Fuel type	Percentage of total energy
Biomass	94.6
Fuelwood	74.5
Crop residues	11.8
Animal dung	8.3
Petroleum products	3.9
Coal	0.5
Electricity	0.8
Others	0.2
Total	100.0

Source: WECS, Power Absorption Study, 1990.

The Energy Scenario

The abundant supply of water and the favourable terrain offer excellent opportunities for hydropower development in Nepal. However, due to technical and financial constraints, this advantage has been little developed so far. At present, only 11 per cent of the population have access to electricity. In order to evaluate Nepal's potential for exploitation of the upper Ganges waters for electricity generation, it is necessary to first look into the current energy consumption pattern (Table 5.1). Nepal heavily depends on traditional non-commercial energy sources – mainly biomass. Commercial energy consumption (coal, oil and electricity) is only around 5 per cent. In fact, per capita consumption of commercial energy in Nepal is one of the lowest in South Asia; it is 25 KOE as compared to 57 KOE in Bangladesh and 231 KOE in India (World Bank, 1992). Biomass energy sources include fuelwood, crop residues and animal dung, and these are the dominant fuel sources in the domestic sector. Even in the industrial sector, nearly 66 per cent of the energy consumed comes from fuelwood and crop residues (IIDS, 1993). Fuelwood has traditionally been a non-commercial fuel, but it is now increasingly commercialized, especially in the urban areas.

Fuelwood primarily comes from public forest lands and some private woodlots. Overexploitation of these forest resources for fuelwood has led to adverse environmental problems in the recent decades. Rice straw is the major type of crop residue used for domestic cooking, especially in the Terai, where fuelwood is relatively scarce. Animal dung for cooking competes with manure demand in the crop fields. Nepal has, nonetheless, achieved modest success in developing small biogas plants using dung and crop residues. The value of these plants is that after the methane has been extracted and used as fuel, there still remains a valuable fertilizer residue – in contrast to the burning of dung, which leaves effectively nothing. Over 5000 family-sized biogas plants have been established so far.

The current installed capacity for electricity generation in Nepal is 249 MW, of which 227 MW is generated from water and the rest from diesel. The relief of Nepal provides sufficient scope for run-of-river hydro-power generation. Within the past decade, small and micro hydropower plant development has received considerable attention among the energy planners. Both coal and oil are imported into Nepal. India is the main supplier of coal, while petroleum products are bought from the international market elsewhere.

Hydropower

The absence of fossil fuels in Nepal and the progressive depletion of forest wealth from fuelwood exploitation make it imperative that indigenous water resources be developed for the production of electricity. The water wealth in the Nepalese rivers of the Ganges basin is indeed phenomenal. The estimated volume of the annual run-off of the rivers within the country is around 175×10^9 m^3 (Pradhan and Shrestha, 1986). These rivers include

Table 5.2 Nepal: water volume and hydropower potentials of river basins.

River basins	Percentage of mean annual run-off	Percentage of hydropower potential (theoretical)	Potential of hydropower potential (identified)
Mahakali	4.1	—	2.7
Karnali	23.8	43.5 (including Mahakali)	56.9
Gandak	28.9	24.8	12.5
Kosi	18.8	26.8	25.8
Other rivers	24.4	4.9	2.1
Total	100.0	100.0	100.0

Sources: IIDS (1993) and GOB/HMGON (1989).

the four perennial rivers of Mahakali, Karnali, Gandak and Kosi as well as the rain-fed rivers of the south. The volume of water in Nepal's rivers has a theoretical hydro potential of about 83 000 MW, of which the economically feasible potential is around 42 000 MW (WECS, 1989). However, as noted earlier, the current installed capacity of electricity production is only 227 MW, which is a mere 0.27 per cent of the theoretical potential. This figure underscores the enormous water power potential of Nepal, which it is anxious to exploit. Table 5.2 shows the vast hydropower resources of the four major mountain rivers. These rivers account for almost 98 per cent of the economically feasible potential for hydropower generation.

Nepal's development of water power utilization had been slow due to financial constraints and the limited nature of the domestic market, both of which reflect the dual attributes of a small population and a low per capita income. Nevertheless, the peak load demand within the country has steadily increased in recent years; power demand between 1984 and 1989 increased at an annual average rate of 14 per cent (NEA, 1990) and the Nepal Electricity Authority estimates that the country is likely to experience an energy deficit by 1995. To think in terms of the domestic market alone is of course wrong. There is already a large potential market to the south for the export of hydropower to the northern Indian states where demand is high, and this will increase rapidly in future decades.

Nepal has few proven natural resources, other than its agriculture and its scenery which draws so many tourists, and its water. Hydropower development potentially holds the key to the country's best chances of economic progress.

Development Options

The first hydroelectric plant in Nepal was constructed in 1911 (Sharma, 1983) with an installed capacity of 500 kw, about 15 km south of the capital, Kathmandu. However, because of certain technical and economic realities, Nepal was faced with a choice between developing storage-type large projects on the one hand, and micro hydro plants and run-of-river projects on the other. The scattered nature of the rural population in the hills and mountains and the availability of a large volume of surface run-off in the rivers make micro hydro plants very attractive. In 1990, the Nepal Electricity Authority was running 29 micro plants with a capacity of 4.2 MW; also, there are smaller sites owned by the private sector (IIDS, 1993). Agro-processing and rural electrification are the main sectors of electricity consumption from these plants. But the electricity produced from micro plants can be transmitted only over a moderate distance, and there might be problems, in some cases, in linking up with the national transmission network. The economies of scale enjoyed by the medium and large plants may also make micro plants cost-ineffective in the longer run.

Nepal also faces a development option of going after run-of-river projects as against large storage-type power projects. Run-of-river projects are considered attractive from the points of view of terrain, the rainfall distribution pattern and the social disbenefits such as population relocation. Yet, these projects do not utilize the water resource optimally, and as demand for energy increases in the export sector, run-of-river projects are likely to yield to the storage-type projects for greater economic gains. The storage projects are multipurpose in nature, i.e. besides generating electricity, they also provide irrigation, navigation and flood moderation benefits. However, storing water behind dams also entails displacement of people and the need for rehabilitation.

Market Potential

Nepal's water power is its principal export commodity. The logical market is northern India, although it is often argued by some energy planners in Nepal that the country will also be able to transmit electricity across India to Bangladesh and Pakistan in the long run – assuming more stable political relations between these states. However, the immediate market for Nepal's hydropower exists in the northern region of India, especially the states of Bihar and Uttar Pradesh. The load forecast for the next 10 years in this region shows an annual growth rate of about 10 per cent. Of the current installed capacity in northern India, 43 per cent is of hydel origin and over 52 per cent is from fossil fuels. By 2005, an additional generation of about 35 000 MW will be required to meet peak load demand in northern India (HMGON, 1989). Hence, instead of constructing more thermal plants, India can import clean hydropower from Nepal to meet its growing consumption needs. The exploitation of the northern Indian market is, therefore, an essential component of Nepal's planning strategy for water resource utilization. In the long run, the interconnection of the grids of Nepal and northern India could enjoy the benefits of an integrated system. The income earned by Nepal from its sale of power to India could be used

Table 5.3 Mega project features.

Project	Capacity (MW)	Dam (height) (m)	Reservoir storage (million m³)	Submerged area (ha)
Karnali (Chisapani)	10 800	268	16 210	33 900
Mahakali				
(Pancheswar)	1 335	262	4 800	4 750
(Poornagiri)	1 065	156	1 240	6 500
Kosi High Dam	3 000	269	9 370	19 500

Sources: Sharma (1983), GOB/HMGON (1989) and Verghese and Iyer (1993).

to service its debts incurred for the construction of hydropower projects. The additional benefit would be savings on fuel oil imports and diminished fuelwood consumption.

Nepal's Hydropower Programme and the South Asian Dimensions

Co-operation in water power development between Nepal and India had actually started in 1920 with an agreement to construct a barrage on the Mahakali (Sarda) river along with a hydropower plant within Indian territory (Verghese and Iyer, 1993). The agreement provided for mutual exchange of land between the two countries in order to have the project located completely within India. Nepal, under the agreement, was to receive about 28.3 cumecs (1000 cusecs) of water annually, but, since the barrage was under Indian control, Nepal never received more than 12 cumecs (400 cusecs). It serves as an example of the dangers of failure in regional efforts at water resource development when mutual trust and transparency of action are lacking. The Kosi river basin, which has nearly one-fourth of the country's total power potential, received early attention from both Nepal and India. In 1950, India had proposed to build a high dam at Barakshetra (near the confluence of the Sun Kosi, Arun and Tamur rivers) to produce 1800 MW of power along with providing substantial irrigation and flood attenuation benefits. However, instead of this mega project, the policy makers opted for the less ambitious Kosi barrage project in 1954, which was designed to yield power, irrigation and flood moderation benefits. The two countries amended the agreement in 1966 in order to acknowledge and ensure Nepal's right to all kinds of upstream water uses in the Kosi basin. This was necessary as a confidence-building step and also to dispel Nepal's fear of losing its water wealth due to earlier appropriations from trans-boundary rivers by the lower riparian, i.e. India. (Although it might seem that the upper riparian state can physically appropriate water without consideration of lower riparian states, legally it is normal that all subsequent developments have to take account of prior developments, regardless of location on the river. In other words, historical precedence is a legal principle). However, irrigation benefits to Nepal from the Kosi project, in terms of areal coverage, were only one-sixth of the projected total on account of certain locational and structural problems.

The next project of co-operative endeavour was on the Gandak river basin. Under the agreement between Nepal and India in 1959 (subsequently revised in 1964), a barrage was to be constructed on the international boundary. This was primarily an irrigation project to supply water to about 57 000 ha of land in the Terai and even larger tracts in the northern Indian states of Uttar Pradesh and Bihar. An important part of this agreement on the Gandak river was the recognition of Nepal's rights of upstream water withdrawals and negotiated trans-valley use of waters in the Gandak basin. Nonetheless, the Gandak project too, like the earlier Kosi project, did not bring Nepal its legitimate amount of benefits from a collaborative water resource utilization scheme. The proportion of irrigation benefits obtained by Nepal from the Kosi and Gandak projects amounted to only 2.4 per cent of the total area served by the two projects.

Nepal is expected to experience an electrical energy deficit by 1995, and power conservation through load shedding has already become a regular nightly phenomena. An NEA study on planning the expansion of power has considered this energy deficit situation against the projected load demand as well as the export market potential in future, and arrived at a sequential power development programme through utilizing the upper reaches of the Karnali, Gandak and Kosi basins. It involves the construction of five projects in varying sequences depending upon the production cost and the export potential. These projects are Upper Arun 3, Upper Karnali, Kali Gandaki and Burhi Gandaki. All of these are run-of-river projects except for the last one, which has a gross storage capacity of over 3.2×10^9 m^3 and energy capacity of 600 MW. All five projects, if completed, will increase Nepal's capacity of electricity generation by over 1300 MW. This will also enable Nepal to link its national distribution network with the northern Indian grid, and thus assure itself of regular power export.

In the light of the prospects of an energy market in northern India (and possibly even in Bangladesh), Nepal feels encouraged to utilize its water potential through large and mega projects. Nepal is unable to embark on the construction of such projects alone and must, therefore, seek funds from multilateral donors. The latter, in turn, will finance the projects only if they are assured of a market for the surplus power as well as of the water-sharing rights between Nepal and India. The role of India is very crucial in this context – it needs to make genuine efforts to remove past wrongs and to help to create a climate of trust, and collaborate in the establishment of projects through technical and financial support. In the past three decades, India has demonstrated its interest in developing large water resource projects in Nepal. The principal potential sites for mega projects are in the river basins of Karnali (at Chisapani), Mahakali (at Pancheswar) and Kosi (at Barakshetra) (Table 5.3). All of these projects involve large storage dams and are multipurpose in nature, i.e. besides power generation they are expected to yield irrigation benefits and to moderate flood effects downstream. The power potential of these three basins was investigated in the mid-1950s, and both Nepal and India showed eagerness to develop it.

Nepal undertook feasibility surveys in the Karnali basin in the 1960s and Chisapani was identified as the most suitable site for a major hydropower plant. Subsequently, several other studies were conducted in the Karnali basin and, finally, a comprehensive feasibility study of the basin recommended in 1989 a hydro plant at Chisapani with an installed capacity of 10 800 MW. The project will consist of a 270-m-high dam with active storage volume in the reservoir exceeding 16 km^3. The capacity of this project to produce electricity far exceeds Nepal's need in the foreseeable future, but by the year 2007 – when the Karnali is expected to be commissioned – it would be able to meet the increased demands for power in northern India as well as displacing some of the coal- and gas-fired generators there. The Karnali project, therefore, plans to link up with the northern Indian electricity grid through over 300 km of cables. Besides power generation, the Karnali project would also bring vast irrigation benefits to both countries. For Nepal, irrigation potential would extend over 190 000 ha of undeveloped land, while India would receive irrigation facilities in about 3×10^6 ha of land. The cost of the project would be around $5 billion at 1989 prices. The handsome benefits that India would derive from this project make it an eager partner in developing the Karnali potential.

The Kosi basin is the next important basin with potential for mega projects. The earlier plan for a high dam at Barakshetra is now being revived. The storage reservoir would not only produce power, but could also moderate floods in Nepal and northern India. The current scheme of the Kosi high dam project at Barakshetra includes a 269-m-high dam with an installed capacity of over 3000 MW. As the previous Kosi barrage project and flood control embankments did not yield projected benefits, the Kosi high dam seemed more promising as a multipurpose venture. The project would also irrigate lands in eastern Nepal and Bihar state (India).

The Mahakali (Sarda) river, which marks the boundary between western Nepal and India, offers yet another site for a large high dam project. The feasibility studies recommended a cascade development of the potential with two dams – one at Pancheswar and another at Poornagiri – having a combined installed capacity of 2400 MW. This project would be another exercise in the often difficult and sensitive field of Indo-Nepalese joint ventures in water power development.

Role of Seismicity

The building of high dams for mega projects in Nepalese rivers is, however, not without problems. One such area of concern is related to the vulnerability of the dams to seismic hazards in the Himalayan region. Moreover, dams themselves have been known to trigger earthquakes – a famous case being the filling of the Koyna reservoir in Maharashtra, which triggered an earthquake in 1967. Although the weight of water on or near a fault is sometimes cited as the causal factor, the increase in overburden is negligible in most cases: it seems mostly that the reservoirs cause changes in ground hydrology, and that they increase the chances of lubricating a fault, thus activating it. Changes in hydrology can also destabilize hill slopes – and there have been several dam disasters in which a massive landslip has occurred into a reservoir, causing tidal waves which have overtopped the dams, and also of course reducing reservoir capacity, and in some cases damaging the dam structure itself. The Himalayan belt and its foothills as well as northeastern India are active seismic zones. In fact, this area has experienced four great earthquakes (with magnitude of over 8 on the Richter scale) during the past 100 years in Assam (1897), Uttar Pradesh (1905), Bihar/Nepal (1934) and Arunachal Pradesh/Assam (1950). Earthquakes with a lesser intensity, but devastating in terms of loss of lives and property, also hit this belt in 1988 (Bihar/Nepal) and 1991 (north-western India/western Nepal). Thus seismic proneness of the Nepalese Himalayas has often been cited as a limiting factor in the construction of large dams. The Chisapani (Karnali) dam is projected in a highly seismic zone, although it is designed to withstand an earthquake of magnitude greater than 8 on the Richter scale. However, concern about seismicity should not be the principal factor limiting the development of such dams. Better and comparative studies and data are required for a fuller assessment of earthquake hazards in the Himalayas. It would improve the identification of the seismic source zones and the designs of earthquake-resistant dams. The International Commission on Large Dams (ICOLD) has formulated certain principles or guidelines for the design, construction, maintenance and operation of high dams (Verghese and Iyer, 1993). Technologically it is now possible to design and build stable and earthquake-resistant high dams.

Land Submergence and Population Displacement Associated with Large Dams

Another area of concern for Nepal in water resource development is the spectre of population displacement due to storage reservoirs and this displacement caused by the submergence of houses and agricultural land has, of late, become a major human rights issue of dramatic proportions.

Even though the proposed reservoirs in Nepal are located in low-density remote areas, they would, nonetheless, inflict traumatic hardships on many people. The reservoir behind the Chisapani (Karnali) dam would displace more than 60 000 people over a period of 10 years. It would also submerge about 8000 ha of cultivated land in the valley and over 20 000 ha of forests. The displacement of people and their relocation on other lands are inseparable parts of water development, although the costs of rehabilitation along with provision for land and alternative employment are high in both social and economic terms. For Nepal, it is an extremely challenging task that needs careful assessment of costs and benefits before the implementation of any large project. One brighter aspect of the problem is that most large water resource projects have a gestation period of 8–12 years or even more. This gives the planners a breathing time to prepare and implement relocation measures in phases so that the ordeal of displacement among the affected people can be minimized.

Conclusions ✳

Nepal possesses water wealth of immense proportions, which, if developed for power, can usher in an economic miracle. Besides power generation, the tributaries of the Ganges within Nepal offer opportunities for irrigation in the dry season. However, three-quarters of the irrigable lands are concentrated in the southern Terai region of the country. Small irrigation systems, managed by farmers, have operated in Nepal for centuries. In the present century, irrigation from surface water has increased through barrage construction, and the building of large multipurpose projects in the future would provide perennial irrigation in the country (CIWEC, 1989). Inland navigation in the Nepalese rivers had always been minimal due to the terrain and draft problems. As a landlocked country, Nepal needs transit through India and Bangladesh for outlet to the sea. The Ganges tributaries – as they emerge from the hills – may be developed for inland water transport in order to gain maritime access through the Ganges, through the use of navigation locks at appropriate places. Although hydropower is Nepal's major natural resource, its development faces several problems, including the international character of the market, seismic hazards, population displacement and rehabilitation, and the loss of agricultural lands and forests. The debate on whether Nepal should go for some or all of its hydropower potential through mega projects could be a never-ending exercise. Yet the ideal combination of an energy generation potential at home and a market for energy export in the neighbouring region seems a sufficient justification for the exploitation of Nepal's water asset without delay. The mega projects would no doubt be expensive, yet the income earned from the sale of energy would help to invigorate Nepal's sluggish economy. Moreover, the price of delaying hydropower generation efforts would be even greater because of increasing infrastructural, environmental and social costs. It may, therefore, be prudent for Nepal to plan for a mix of medium and large projects with the aim of obtaining an optimal scale of utilization.

Another dimension of Nepal's hydropower development relates to genuine and equitable regional co-operation, which, in fact, is germane to the utilization of a trans-boundary resource like water. It was noted earlier that Indo-Nepal co-operation in water resource development had not always been at the most satisfactory level. It started with a bilateral agreement for the Mahakali (Sarda) project. But Nepal was unable to obtain her allocated share of irrigation facilities for decades, and the co-operative spirit was, thus, stillborn. Next followed the Kosi and Gandak projects of the 1950s which, too, did not bring dividends to Nepal in proportion to the projects' potentials. In recent years, India has demonstrated active interest in participating in Nepal's water resource development for mutual benefits. However, this new dimension has also been clouded by a controversy regarding the Tanakpur project (120 MW) on the Mahakali river. This project involves some cession of Nepalese territory, and Nepal also feels aggrieved by the promise of getting only one-sixth of the generated power. These misgivings could have been avoided if Nepal had been adequately consulted at the pre-planning stage and a consensual atmosphere created through trust and transparency. Nonetheless, these hurdles are not insurmountable. And, despite the thorny nature of the co-operative path, the future of the Nepalese economy lies in the upper Ganges waters.

References

CIWEC (1989) *Master Plan for Irrigation Development in Nepal.* Main Report. Kathmandu: Canadian International Water and Energy Consultants and East Consult (P) Ltd.

GOB/HMGON (1989) *Report on Flood Mitigation Measures and Multipurpose Use of Water Resources.* Dhaka and Kathmandu: Bangladesh–Nepal Joint Study Team, Government of Bangladesh and His Majesty's Government of Nepal.

HMGON (1989) *Karnali (Chisapani) Multipurpose Project Feasibility Study.* Main Report. Kathmandu: Ministry of Water Resources, His Majesty's Government of Nepal.

IIDS (1993) *Water Resources and National Development: Nepalese Perspectives and Nepal Country Report.* Kathmandu: Institute for Integrated Development Studies.

NEA (1990) *Reconfirmation of Arun Hydroelectric Project.* Kathmandu: Nepal Electricity Authority.

Pradhan, B.K. and Shrestha, H.M. (1986) *Opportunity Costs of Delay in the Development of Himalayan Water Resources – A Nepalese Perspective.* Kathmandu: N.p.

Sharma, C.K. (1983) *Water and Energy Resources of the Himalayan Block.* Kathmandu: N.p.

Verghese, B.G. and Iyer, R.R. (1993) *Harnessing the Eastern Himalayan Rivers: Regional Cooperation in South Asia*. New Delhi: Centre for Policy Research.

WECS (1989) *Energy Issues and Options and the Eighth Five Year Plan*. Kathmandu: Water and Energy Commission Secretariat.

World Bank (1992) *World Development Report 1992*. Washington DC: World Bank/ IBRD.

Zollinger, F. (1979) *Analysis of Water Problem and Strategy for Flood Control in the Nepalese Terai*. Kathmandu: HMGON/FAO/UNDP.

6

Disputed Facts:
A Countervailing View from
the Hills

Michael Thompson

Editors' Note
This chapter began as an Editors' Note to the preceding chapter which, we feel, sets out just one of the 'visions of the future' that are at present competing for the attention of both policy makers and voters. However, as it grew in length and scope, we decided that it would be more sensible to make it a chapter. Even so, it is really little more than an extended critique of the preceding chapter, which it uses as a robust base from which to explore the more diffuse scenario that is discerned by some of those who look towards the plains and the delta from their vantage points high in the Himalayas.

Counter-arguments Against the Case for Large Projects

The preceding chapter makes a strong pitch for the large-scale, centralized and capital-intensive development of Nepal's water resources. However, many of the facts on which that scenario is justified are not unanimously agreed on. In particular, they are seriously disputed by those who favour a countervailing scenario of small-scale, decentralized and labour-intensive development. This, I hasten to add, does not mean that the facts as stated in the preceding chapter are wrong; only that they are somewhat 'elastic'. Far from being the sort of 'glistening nuggets' that we learnt about in school science, these facts are smeared out a bit, and it is up to us to gather them together, this way or that, to our own satisfaction.

1 The parlous state of Nepal's forests is attributed, as it so often is, to their being overexploited for fuelwood. However, many now argue (Thompson *et al.*, 1986; Ives and Messerli, 1989) that the forests have suffered, not because of population and development pressures, but as a result of the inappropriate

institutional arrangements that were introduced following the overthrow, in the 1950s, of the Rana regime. The nationalization of the forests, they point out, destroyed the village-level commons-managing institutions, replacing them with a large-scale and cumbersome system of district forests that did not work and did not enjoy the consent of the villagers.

There is now considerable evidence in support of this argument, and the government of Nepal is currently committed to a policy of returning much of this land to local control and to helping the villagers to design the modern equivalents of their traditional commons-managing arrangements. Many small village forests are already in much better health than they were a few years ago.

2 Whilst it may well be true that water is Nepal's most valuable resource, it does not automatically follow that it is the key to Nepal's economic progress. The key may well lie, not in Nepal's physical endowments, but in the resourcefulness of the Nepalis. And many of those who are opposed to the large-scale, centralized and capital-intensive scenario argue that its pursuit will seriously deplete this most precious of all resources. Experience suggests that many of those who are displaced will lapse from vigorous self-sufficiency into fatalistic dependency, and that this may also be the path taken by the totality – the nation itself – if lead-times, capital costs and forecasts of future energy demand turn out (as they so often *have* turned out, elsewhere in the world) to be wildly overoptimistic.

3 That small-scale hydro projects will be ineffective in the long run, because of the economies of scale that are built into their meso and macro competitors, is also challengeable. Economies of scale feed through only when they are not outweighed by countervailing diseconomies of scale – a slow learning curve, poor matching of built capacity to the demand curve (unless the latter is rising steadily), increased industrial unrest, unspread risk (all your eggs in one basket) and so on. And even the most celebrated economy of scale – the 'two-thirds power law', as it is called – is valid only if, in the scaling-up process, none of the other vital relationships change (which, of course, they do).[2] The fact is that bigger is not always better and small is not always beautiful. The best size is often somewhere in between and, to complicate things still further, there may be more than one best size within this middle range (in which case the most sensible strategy may be to develop some flexible mix of these differently scaled technologies). What all this means is that economies of scale are never trump cards that, once slammed down on the table, rule out all the alternatives. After all, if those who operated under the rule 'Go for the biggest' were never surprised, then white elephants would never have acquired the meaning they now have!

4 One of the arguments for large-scale storage systems (rather than run-of-the-river) is that, as well as providing a steady year-round supply of electricity, they enable the provision of three other benefits: irrigation, navigation and flood mitigation. Whilst this is true, it is by no means certain that you can enjoy all of these benefits all of the time. If, at certain times, navigation needs require that the water be released whilst some other need requires that the gates be closed then you cannot have both benefits. And, as you go from two benefits to four, so the chances of your enjoying them all, all of the time, decrease dramatically.

Add to this the appalling problems entailed in managing these conflicting demands when each of them is being made from a base that is the exclusive preserve of a powerful government department, and the stage is all set for an outcome in which none of the promised benefits are delivered!

5 That water power is (or will be) Nepal's principle export commodity is also debatable. Since Nepal is landlocked, and India is not a signatory to the

international convention on landlocked countries, Nepali entrepreneurs have shrewdly directed their energies to developing those industries – tourism and hand-made carpets – in which the 'added value' is so high as to justify the products flying out *over* India (in the case of tourism, of course, the tourists fly *in* but the effect is the same). Electricity, we should note, cannot fly out over India.

Yet those who favour the large-scale scenario argue that the sale of electricity to India will quickly repay the vast debts Nepal will incur in building the dams and power plants. The scale of the financial risk, it should be pointed out, is unprecedented: the optimistically estimated cost of just one of the proposed high dams is more than 10 times the annual budget of Nepal. Hydropower, under these sort of conditions, may well be a recipe, not for getting rich quick, but for losing sovereignty quick!

6   To say that mutual trust is lacking when it comes to the co-operative development of Himalayan water resources, and that this needs to be rectified if the sorts of solution advocated by those who favour the large-scale scenario are to be put in place, is true enough. However, that said, there is another question that needs to be asked: are these requirements achievable within the available time-scale? History, especially the recent history (some of which is outlined in the preceding chapter), suggests that we would be less than wise to assume that the answer is an unequivocal 'yes'.

Some very recent developments (in particular a series of non-governmental international conferences on Himalayan water) indicate that Nepal may well be able to build the requisite levels of trust with those Indian states – Bihar and Uttar Pradesh – that, like Nepal itself, are landlocked, but that increase in mutual trust may well put a strain upon those Indian states' relationships both with their bordering states and with Delhi. A vast, centralized and highly managed electricity-generating and distributing system would not fit comfortably with a balkanized South Asia. Nor is it at all likely that the installation of such a system would do anything to weaken these balkanizing forces.

7   Statements such as that Nepal is anxious to exploit its water power potential skate lightly over serious divergences *within* Nepal over the nature of that potential and how best it might be exploited. These divergences have always existed, but they have blossomed now that democracy has broken out in Nepal. The result is that previously unchallenged pronouncements by 'HMG' (the unrepresentative 'Panchayat' system that has now been overthrown) are being questioned.

Whilst few if any voices are demanding that there be no further development of Nepal's water resources, there is a healthy controversy over which development path – large-scale with bought-in expertise or small-scale with home-grown competence – should be followed. The advocates of the latter path point out that if the large-scale path is chosen then Nepal's indigenous technological capabilities will not enjoy any increase, despite the vast sums of money the country will have borrowed and spent. On top of these institutional and 'human resource' objections to the large-scale scenario, there are, these critics point out, some daunting engineering and governance problems.

8   The assertion that 'technologically it is now possible to design and build stable and earthquake-resistant high dams' is bitterly resisted in some quarters. The influential International Rivers Network, for instance, insists that all high dams (not just those in earthquake-prone locations) are 'incomplete experiments'. To this blanket rejection of claims to safety can be added the recent discovery that ground acceleration during fairly severe earthquakes can exceed -1 g. What this means is that when the ground is moving downwards during an earthquake

anything that is lying loose on the surface – a boulder, for instance, or a high dam and its contents – will be left hanging in the air!

Dams in the Himalayan region are also at risk from sudden catastrophic events upstream of them. The preceding chapter mentions the quite frequent break-outs from ice-dammed lakes (one of which, in Khumbu, has recently destroyed an almost completed small dam). Most of these break-outs, though awesome in their effect immediately downstream, are scarcely noticeable by the time they reach the plains. Also, since the local people are careful not to build their houses in the path of these break-outs, the loss of life is usually remarkably small in relation to the violence of the event. If engineers were to work on the hubris-free assumption that, sooner or later, their dams are going to fail, then the size and location of these natural and naturally failing dams would provide them with some useful guidance for how best to site and build their artificial ones.

However, in addition to these modest break-outs, there are some recurrent events that do not dissipate themselves before they reach the plains. About 700 years ago there was an outburst from a moraine-dammed lake behind the mountain Machapuchare which, in addition to its water content, shifted 5.5 km^3 of solid material (Heuberger *et al.*, 1984). And about 25 000 years ago a landslide in the Langtang Himal shifted 10 km^3 of solid material (though some of it became molten in the process) (Fort and Freytet, 1982). Since the Himalayas are still rising faster than they are being worn down, these cataclysms are not things of the past, like dinosaurs. They *have* happened and they *will* happen. It is difficult to see how even the International Commission on Large Dams could formulate guidelines that would enable dams to stand up to that sort of insult.

9   The advocates of the large-scale scenario concede that, as well as the benefits, there will be some costs. There will be the loss of highly valued landscapes and habitats, and there will be displacement of people. Whilst some (the displacees among them) may argue that displacement is simply unacceptable, the advocates of the large-scale scenario see it as a price that is well worth paying. Egg-breaking, they note, is a necessary condition for omelette-making and, since we all like omelettes, the whole disruption is perfectly acceptable as long as those who are displaced are adequately compensated.

A recent study[3] has shown that, in none of the displacements that have happened to date, has there been adequate (in many cases, any) compensation; not even when, in one case in western Nepal, only seven people were displaced. Who, the critics ask, would trust an institution to compensate hundreds of thousands of displaced persons when it has already proved itself incapable of compensating seven? Trust, whether it be between national governments over the sharing of waters or between individual governments and their poorest citizens, is not something that miraculously appears because its presence is a necessary condition for a development path that those who are calling for the trust have set their hearts on.

These nine sets of objections (which, of course, could easily be extended) have done two things. They have put a spoke in the large-scale wheel, and they have prepared the ground for a small-scale alternative to that development path.

The Alternative Scenario

The large-scale, centralized and capital-intensive development scenario is the view from the plains: not the view of everyone in the plains, but of the hierarchists and large-scale individualists in the plains (Bandyopadhyay, 1991). It therefore needs to be contrasted with the view from the hills: not the view of the hierarchists and large-scale individualists in the hills (for that is pretty much the same as that of their counterparts in the plains) but of the egalitarians and small-scale individualists in the hills. Nor, since we should not assume that all the hilly hierarchists sit in ministerial offices in Kathmandu, should we ignore the small-scale hierarchists – the villagers who operate the commons-managing institutions that regulate water and forest resources on their tiny but vital patches.

If we zero in on these characters we will find that they have an impressive track record in the harnessing and managing of water power.[4] Water-wheels grind the corn and press the mustard seed in village after village across the Himalayas. It is estimated that there are around 40 000 water mills in operation in Nepal. Some of these mills (around 450 to date) have been converted so that they are driven by water pressure (rather than simply by its flow). A convenient stream or rivulet or ambitious trickle (often from a spring, which means that the flow is fairly constant over the year) is introduced into a metal tube with a turbine at its bottom end. The turbine then drives the cornmill and the oil-press (achieving a 50 per cent increase in yield) and, at night-time or during slack periods, the electricity generator (which, at the very least, lights the village).

The entire technology (except, at present, for the generator) is produced and maintained in Nepal, which has a long tradition of skilled metal-working. This technology is in the control of the local institutions and there is no reason why (in principle, at any rate), once it has satisfied its immediate customers (or 'passengers', as they are called in Nepali), its excess capacity should not be sold further afield. Both the total installed capacity and the size of the individual installations (which is limited by indigenous competence) are increasing year by year and, on present trends, will comfortably exceed the combined capacity of the proposed large-scale hydro plants by the time these projects are optimistically estimated to come on stream. Since there are plenty of villages, plenty of streams and plenty of resourceful Nepalis, there is no reason why this projection of the present trend should not be realized (or even exceeded).

Of course, such a system is unplanned, uncentralized and incremental in its pattern of growth, but these are precisely the qualities that are being extolled in the most highly developed reaches of northern technology – information systems, for instance, and all those 'sunrise' enterprises that see themselves as 'knowledge intensive'. So here, under the very noses of those development experts who advocate it, is an instance of 'leapfrogging' that is actually under way. Very soon, and as long as those who advocate the large-scale scenario can be beaten off, the Kathmandu-based consultancies will be selling their remarkable skills all around the globe, and that includes the northern part of the globe!

Conclusions

I have simplified and perhaps overstated the case in the above critique of the plains-based orthodoxy, but I feel that these short-cuts are justified. My aim is not to set out the alternative scenario in all its detail – that is something that the expert practitioners in Nepal are busy doing – but simply to show that an alternative scenario, along these sorts of lines, *does* exist. In our concluding chapter we will return to this scenario, and to the one it sets itself up in opposition to, and suggest how, if institutional arrangements that grant legitimacy to both visions of the future are put in place, the interactions between these two scenarios will result in a flexible line of development that really is sustainable.

Notes

1 For instance, the amount of metal in a beer vat increases with the square of its radius whilst its capacity increases with the cube of its radius. Since the vat itself is a cost whilst the beer in it is a profit, the sensible thing, this law tells you, is to make the vat as large as you possibly can.
2 An example: if a chemical reaction is mildly exothermic, then if it is taking place in a small vessel the ratio of volume to surface area may well result in so much heat loss that heat will actually have to be applied if you want the reaction to go at a spanking pace. Scale the vessel up a bit and the ratio will be such that the reaction will look after itself. But scale it up still further and it will proceed so violently that you will have to add a refrigeration system to your plant. Much the same applies to animals, which is why mice tend to be hairy whilst elephants are almost bald and are equipped with large heat-dissipating ears.
3 Much of the information and argument in this chapter has been gleaned from a special issue of the journal *Water Nepal* (Dixit, forthcoming), in which are published the key papers from the 1993 Kathmandu conference on 'The Cooperative Development of Himalayan Water Resources' jointly sponsored by the Nepal Water Conservation Foundation and the International Academy of the Environment. The study of displacement and compensation is by Ajaya Dixit.
4 The section that follows draws heavily on Bikas Pandey's contribution to the special issue of *Water Nepal* (Dixit, forthcoming).

References

Bandyopadhyay, J. (1991) Mountain development, plains bias. *Himal*, March/April.
Fort, M.B. and Freytet, P. (1982) The quaternary sedimentary evolution of the intra-mountane basin of Pokhara in relation to the Himalaya Midlands and their hinterland (West Central Nepal). In A.K. Sinha (ed.), *Contemporary Geoscientific Researches in Himalaya*, Vol. 2. Dehra Dun: N.p., pp. 91–6.

Heuberger, H., Masch, L., Preuss, E. and Schroecker, A. (1984) Quaternary landslides and rock fusion in Central Nepal and in the Tyrolean Alps. *Mountain Research and Development*, 4(4), 345–62.

Ives, J.D. and Messerli, B. (1989) *The Himalayan Dilemma: Reconciling Development and Conservation*. London and New York: Routledge.

Thompson, M., Warburton, M. and Hatley, T. (1988) *Uncertainty on a Himalayan Scale*. London: Ethnographica.

Numerous Authors (notably Dixit, A. and Pandey, B.). Special issue of *Water Nepal* (1994, forthcoming).

PART III

Midstream

7

The Ganges Plains

Graham P. Chapman

Introduction

For statistical purposes the central Ganges plains have been defined as comprising the state of Haryana, the two Union Territories of Chandigarh and Delhi, the plains districts of Uttar Pradesh and the state of Bihar. In broad terms this is an area 1400 km long (NW to SE) by 300 km across; the total area of the territories just named is 514 000 km², slightly less than the area of France. In 1991, the total population of this area was 246 million people, or about 5 per cent of the human race, and nearly five times the population of France. This figure is of course the beginning, not the end, of the story about population pressure. The growth rate of the population from 1981 to 1991 was 2.3 per cent annually, meaning that the first constraint on the development process will be the basic necessities of this ever-burgeoning total.

In Table 1.1 an attempt has been made to project the population to the year 2031, and also to calculate the urban percentage of the population. The assumptions are that population growth rates will have declined to 1.5 per cent annually by 2031, so the starting rates, which for each part of the basin vary around 2.3 per cent, are reduced slightly in each year. The assumption about urbanization is that there are two components to growth – the internal natural increase, and migration. The natural increase of both urban and rural areas is projected using the same growth rate as for the state, but then the urban growth is augmented by a migration component subtracted from the rural area, which is calculated as a specific multiple of the natural urban increase. The specific multiple changes according to a curve related to levels of urbanization. At 10 per cent the migration component is two times the natural increase. At 30 per cent the migration component is equal to natural increase (what has happened in broad terms in the last 10 years in India); at 90 per cent migration it is only 1 per cent of natural increase.

The results, wholly credible, suggest that in 35 years' time the population of the middle Ganges plain will be about 600 million or 100 million more than for the whole of the Ganges–Brahmaputra in 1991. The population will also be about 40 per cent urban rather than 20 per cent urban as now. The implication is that rural populations will increase by about 80 per cent, nearly doubling the pressure on land. The surest way to increase agricultural production and levels of employment – livelihood creation – has been shown above all to be through increasing irrigation, both from gravitational canals and by powered tubewells, and then secondarily by other means such as the use of fertilizers and new seeds.

The urban population will increase from the current 50 million to 250 million, of whom 140 million will be in the one state of Uttar Pradesh. In passing, we may note that Delhi's size is predicted to be 25 million by 2031. These urban populations will make demands on water for direct use, and indirectly through the demands for more power, much of it from hydro-electricity. But they will be in competition with the rural population, increasing from 385 million to 685 million. In sum, from the point of view of the plains, we have to consider what are the likely patterns of direct water demand by the following consumers: agriculture, urban non-industrial, urban industrial, and waste disposal.

Urban water Demand and Urban Sanitation

A case study of Delhi written by environmental journalists Shankar *et al.* (1994) provides an introduction to this topic. Delhi is split between the Delhi Municipal Corporation, serving old Delhi and many squatter areas, and the New Delhi Municipal Corporation, serving spacious and affluent suburbs, major hotels and embassies, and only a few squatter areas. In New Delhi, per capita water consumption is the highest in the country. It is provided both by purchases from Delhi Municipal Corporation, and by 84 tubewells – which are already pumping at or perhaps even above ground water replenishment rates. The rising middle class wants flush lavatories, but invariably buys those which flush at 10 litres per pull, rather than the 5 litre types which are also on offer, but which are paradoxically twice as expensive. Washing machine ownership is rising, and so is the ownership of cars and scooters, which are also washed frequently. The 17 five-star hotels consume 800 000 litres daily, enough for the requirements of the 1.3 million slum dwellers. Very few of the hotels have any recycling facility, but most have private boreholes to provide for much of their usage. There are an unknown and unregulated number of other private boreholes. A further unregulated activity – illegal but common – is for domestic users to add booster pumps to their domestic supply, in effect forcibly draining water from other areas.

External surface water is supplied to the capital area (both Delhis) by a link from the Bhakra canal and from the Upper Ganges canal – the former at one point recharging the Yamuna upstream of treatment works. The transmission losses in the canal and river are considerable. In addition there are high transmission losses in the delivery system itself. Shankar *et al.* claim that more than 200 million litres leak through the system each day – at average consumption rates elsewhere in north India this is enough for a city of 2 million people.

Local water wars have in effect started. Haryana, through which the Bhakra connection runs, reduced water supply to Delhi by 227 million litres a day from 10 January 1994. The stated reason was that Haryana needed the water for its rabi irrigation. Such problems will be averted, say the water planners, when three new dams are built in the Himalayas – the Renuka (on a Yamuna tributary), Kissau (on the Yamuna), and Tehri (on the Ganges) – which will also have some role in power generation and perhaps in flood control, but which are environmentally and socially contentious. They will be expensive, and provide costly water from a great distance. Rather than simply enhancing supply, demand should be limited by price, the critics say. Currently it is claimed all water is provided way below cost, and that regularized slum settlements with water connections subsidize the others – since they have to pay a flat rate of Rs 10 per month, which is collected, and which would pay for twice the amount that these households actually consume. The actual consumption figure per slum household is quoted at about 40 litres per day – something under 10 litres per capita. Consumption in parts of New Delhi is over 250 litres per capita per day.

In general I have found it very difficult to get any estimates or data on the general likely pattern of urban water demand. Supposedly supplies of water are provided by public authorities, though it is clear that many households and enterprises are not connected directly to the supply, and there are private water traders meeting some of the excess demand. Where water tables are high enough, handpumps can also be found in urban areas

Table 7.1 Suggested urban water requirements.

Purpose	Absolute minimum litres per capita per day (lpcd)	Desirable lpcd
Cooking and drinking	10	15
Bathing, flushing etc.	30	40
Washing utensils and clothes	30	35
Total	70	90

Source: GOI (1988, p. 294).

– but within urban areas there is a very high chance that water is contaminated. The National Commission on Urbanization (GOI, 1988) has provided a sketchy overview of some of the issues and requirements. It notes that currently per capita water supply in large cities may be over 100 litres per day – but that the distribution as in Delhi is highly unequal, with a majority of households not directly supplied. The connection for sewage is similarly unequal: only one-third of households in urban areas nationally are connected to a closed water sewer.

The same source quotes some figures which are slightly confusing – it is difficult to work out what have been stated as target figures by the Planning Commission (note: not the National Commission on Urbaniz- ation) and what are current achievements. It appears that to provide for a complete coverage of the urban population by the year 2001 with 150 litres per day, the state would have to make an investment of Rs 15 000 crores (£3 billion or $4.5 billion) annually (from 1988 to 2001). Noting that this is an impossible financial target, the National Commission on Urbanization suggests a more modest approach, with lower targets to aim for, and a more multifaceted distribution system. The norms are shown in Table 7.1 – they are much more modest than the Planning Commission's target of 323 lpcd for Delhi (225 lpcd for domestic purposes, the remainder for industrial and civic purposes). Even to achieve this and equitable distribution, simple means of distribution – such as neighbourhood holding tanks with tapped outlets, and standpipes – are postulated, plus private provision from ground water, although clearly with the proviso that either private or public regulators have the ability and mandate to monitor quality.

In the past the public water utilities have been owned and directed by urban local government. However, over the last 20 years, the status and power of local urban government, never strong, has been further under- mined (see Chapter 9) and many of the public water utilities are now run by state boards. Potentially this has the advantage of a wider view being taken of the relation between supply and demand, but it also of course makes the utilities less responsive to specific local problems.

It is also possible to approach these problems from a very different statistical base. Statistical evidence from a variety of sources suggests that about 30–40 per cent of the urban population live in slums – whose inhabitants do not have access to flush sewage systems. Some of these may have pit latrine systems, and some have night-soil collection systems. It would appear that half the remaining population are not properly connected either, although they are more likely to have some partially adequate alternative disposal system.

The low levels of connection have two 'beneficial' effects: one is that current water demand levels are lower than they would otherwise be, and the second is that much of the potential sewage that could be discharged into the rivers is not. These benefits are, of course, bought at the cost of hazardous health conditions for the urban population.

The National Commission on Urbanization observes that 80 per cent of water supplied to urban areas passes through the urban area, ending as sullage, sewage or effluent of some kind. Virtually all is untreated: some is discharged simply to sink into the ground, and a lot goes into the drainage system (see Chapter 8). By the year 2001 Delhi alone will discharge about 4.1 billion litres a day, against its supply of 5.1 billion per day. The commission is at pains to point out that proper collection and treatment will not only provide a better habitat, but crucially, will also recycle the water. Indeed, it suggests that recycled water costs significantly less than developing new sources, at increasing depth or distance.

Future Demand

I am assuming that the current actual average water supply in urban areas for all inhabitants is at most 50 lpcd. Other estimates (but older) put it considerably lower. Using the projections for urban population to the year 2031 given in Table 1.1, if development were to mean water consumption for all inhabitants at 200 lpcd, then with the urban population quintupling the total urban water demand would rise 20 times in 35 years. Industry that accompanies industrialization will also in all likelihood increase its demand at a faster rate.

Urban demand is by its nature fairly constant throughout the year. The high levels of demand that can be foreseen will therefore operate on a fairly even basis throughout the year. The question is then whether the sources are equally able to face this demand throughout the year. The historical, cheapest and preferred source for most major cities has been surface flow, abstracted from the major rivers. We will look at this source first.

Surface flow is so seasonal that it can barely be considered adequate to meet existing levels of provision, let alone demand. Some idea of the seasonality can be judged by the discharge figures for the Ganges at Varanasi – a flow of 13 454 cumecs in the summer, and only 285 cumecs in the winter, when the river has the appearance of a sequence of languid connected pools – or by the figures of river flow by Messerli and Hofer in Chapter 4. Another way of looking at seasonality is to say that for most of this area the four monsoon months of June to September account for 85 per cent of total rainfall. Supposing that surface flow is split the same way, then the Yamuna at Delhi has a dry season flow of 8.5 million cumecs per day. This flow (probably an exaggeration of the lowest flows) would only just meet the water demand of 25 million people using 200 litres per day (5 million cumecs). Although clearly a substantial part of the consumption would be discharged, in effect it would be discharged with at least some level of contamination back into a near dry channel. Such a scenario is neither impossible, nor, on present trends, necessarily unlikely, although at present urban areas are minority users compared with agriculture. If enhanced dry season surface flow is seen as a solution, the finger will point towards building more dams in the Himalayas, and in the southbank Deccan hills.

The second source for urban areas is ground water. The sediments of the Ganges basin form a giant sponge, usually with a water table near the surface, and also many other aquifers in different deposits at increasing depths. The near-surface water levels do vary throughout the year, but not by as much as the seasonality of rainfall would lead one to suppose. Often the variation is measured only in a few metres. It would seem that there are adequate resources in most of the Ganges plains to meet the levels of demand envisaged from this source, but on three conditions: first, investment is provided for an adequate number of boreholes; second, there are adequate energy supplies for the extraction required; and third, the water is not contaminated, or only to the extent that modest treatment will render it potable. The finger again points towards the provision of more power supplies for the plains – and again towards dams in the hills as the best source of such power.

Logic says that any approach to the problems of water supply will involve storage in the hills and control of the river regimes. From the urban point of view the maximum power demands occur in the hot season (March–May), when river flows are least, so surface flow can be augmented and power provided for ground water extraction at the same time. On the other hand these patterns of water release do not match the demands of agriculture: the hot season is the low season for agriculture. Irrigation demand in agriculture usually peaks in the winter season, December to February.

Table 7.2 Water demand in selected global regions.

	Annual withdrawal m^3 per capita	Withdrawal as percentage available	Percentage domestic	Percentage industry	Percentage agriculture
Asia	526	15	6	8	86
Europe	726	15	3	54	33

Source: Chisholm in ODA (1992).

Irrigation and Agriculture

In India somewhere near 90 per cent of total human water demand is for agriculture (see Figure 1.6 for a diagrammatic illustration of water resources and use in India). This is near the average for Asia, but very substantially different from Europe (see Table 7.2), where industrial and urban development is greater (and of course the climate and terrain very different). Yet it would appear prima facie that economics do not justify such levels of use by agriculture. To quote Fauceys (1992):

> In a year, 1000 cum of water may be used either to provide water for 80 people, or to grow food for between 1.6 and 3 people. This imbalance suggests . . . domestic water should win every time. It is far more economic to move food from a rain-rich area to a dry area than it is to move water.

Although the disparity between the two figures suggests that overwhelmingly the equation will work out in favour of urban water use, the equation is, of course, never this simple. The level of agricultural water demand depends on a wide range of variables, most of which are liable to substantial change. At first sight there would appear to be a simple kind of climatic determinism at work in India – with the wetter eastern parts of this plains region being a traditional rice-growing area, and the drier western parts traditionally being more wheat orientated. But crop breeding during the Green Revolution has produced new breeds of rice which perform better in irrigated conditions in drier sunnier areas than in the moister and cloudier conditions of the east. Given also that there is a substantial demand for rice and a price margin in its favour, there has been a very substantial increase of rice growing in the western areas of the plains, in some cases rice becoming even more important than wheat. The difference in water demand between rice and wheat is substantial: therefore, for this reason amongst others, there has been a substantial increase in agricultural water demand in the western parts of the plains.

Variation in the preferred crop and the associated implicit water demands is therefore one reason why it is difficult simply to speak of areas as 'rain-rich' or 'rain-poor'. Another is the pattern of seasonality of rainfall. The maximum rainfall in the western wheat areas occurs during the Kharif (monsoon) season, when it is too hot and humid for wheat to grow; and the monsoon is too unreliable this far west for rain-fed rice to be a reliable staple crop. Thus the traditional farming pattern has been to grow wheat in the cooler Rabi (winter) months, using retained soil moisture from the monsoon, and irrigation from open wells where possible. The first of the major nineteenth century canal irrigation schemes, the Upper Ganges canal, started in the 1850s, used the low winter flow of the Ganges to provide protection and security for this winter wheat crop. The arable acreage could be expanded for a while by taking new land into cultivation, but ultimately further increases could only be accommodated by increasing the cropping index (gross cultivated area/net cultivated area: indicating the extent to which a piece of land is cropped more than once a year). This, of course, means growing more in the second season. After independence in 1947, the Upper Ganges canal was modified to provide for irrigation in the monsoon period and the growing of crops such as rice and sugar cane. There are technical, seasonal and geomorphological reasons, elaborated below, why water could not be provided in the wet season before extra investment was made – but to summarize here, the principal difference is that in the low season the river water carried little silt, but in the high season silt flows are very high and can choke a canal system fast.

In sum, the relationship between rainfall, agriculture and water demand is too complex for regions to be characterized in a static manner as rain-rich or rain-poor.

The Major Gravity Irrigation Systems: Design Principles

It will help in understanding some of the following if the general principles behind the design and construction of a major surface gravity irrigation canal system are understood (see also Chapman, 1983). At the headworks there is either a dam or a barrage. A dam is a storage device and can smooth flows between seasons and sometimes between years as well. A barrage is the diversion weir across the main river that lifts the water level so that water can pass down a side off-take to the canal. The barrages are designed so that they can abstract a quantity of water from the river which is related both to the command area and to the average water available. They are also designed to allow maximum floods to pass downstream without themselves as structures becoming undermined and broken. Of course, a dam can be built upstream of a barrage to further regulate flow to the barrage. The design of the barrage may be further complicated by taking account of the silt load carried by the river. Sometimes a ponding weir upstream of the main barrage traps silt, which is released through both weirs by bottom gates at appropriate intervals.

The canals then divide into a sequence of main canals, branch canals, distributaries and minor canals. The total length of these in an average Ganges system may be several thousand miles. The length of all canals on the biggest system in Uttar Pradesh, the Sarda Sahayak Canal, is 9 960 km. At each switching point there will be some kind of control device to switch quantities of water one way or the other. The quantities ought in theory to be accurately known, but often imperfect depth gauges are taken as substitutes – and their accuracy can be badly affected by silt and weeds. Between the minor and the field channels, there is an 'outlet', an important concept since it is often at this level that control is handed from the Irrigation Department to the farmers. From the field channels there are 'nakas' or the final field outlets. A system may supply up to 500 000 farmers; each outlet may cover from about 100 acres, with between 10 and 20 farmers, to hundreds of acres and hundreds of farmers.

Most of the early canals were unlined, and so are many elements of even recent systems. Though clay fraction and fine silt will slowly seal the beds to some degree, there are consistent transmission losses to ground water throughout the system, and typically a figure of 60 per cent will be quoted.

The calculation of the area to be irrigated depends on a number of assumptions. The different crop types have different water demands, but typically crops are classified as 'irrigated wet' – meaning paddy and sugar cane, and 'irrigated dry' – meaning the rest, such as wheat or cotton. Knowing what crops should be grown in which areas can give an indication of water demand. I will for the moment call the area which can be irrigated simultaneously the 'irrigated area' (not a usual term). The area to which water can be conveyed by the system is known as the command area (or the culturable command area if parts of the command area are not cultivable). The irrigated area could be the same as the command area, in which case all parts could receive water at all times (a situation which does prevail in some small paddy-field schemes). But usually the command area is much larger than the irrigated area, and so water is switched around the network. The schemes built by the British tended to maximize the difference – in other words, the water duty (the area to be irrigated by a given quantity of water) was increased. The reason for this was that a maximum number of farmers would receive some water, thereby receiving some famine protection. In addition, since water would be scarce, its use would be maximized, so the output per unit of water would be high rather than the output per unit of land. It would also reduce waterlogging in parts of the command, although the transmission losses must have also been increased (although I have never seen comparative transmission loss figures for a large high water duty and a small low water duty scheme in the same area from the same source).

System Design and Management in the Ganges Valley

Under the British there were two distinct approaches to the management of the Ganges schemes, and these differences have survived to the present – one approach derived from the North India Canal and Drainage Act 1873, and the other from the Bengal Act, covering both Bengal and Bihar (once part of Bengal). In our terms here, this means that the former act covers the drier western plains, and the latter the wetter eastern plains.

To take the former first, water duty was very high – meaning that there was little water in relation to the irrigable area – and crops were not zoned. This means that farmers had little water, but could choose what to do with it. Water allocation was by the famous 'warabandi' – literally meaning 'fixed turn'. In this system water leaves the minor to enter the field channels through outlets permanently open and of fixed size. These were calibrated so that when the minor was full to a bottom-end benchmark, then all outlets would be running at their design rate. They would stay switched on for a week at a time, with a known calendar of rotation – usually about one week in three. During the active week a farmer would have a fixed share of the total time to use his water, the share being in proportion to his landholding in the outlet command.

The Bengal Act schemes operated in a different and wetter region. Here it was assumed that there would be significant rainfall in many areas during the growing season. Irrigation would therefore be more supplemental, and rather than being scheduled in advance would be called for on demand. The assumption was that the cropping pattern would be known, and that a substantial proportion would consist of wet irrigated crops, principally paddy. In these schemes, therefore, there were variable gated structures all the way down to and including the outlet.

There are many ways to measure the performance of these schemes: whether the design water quantity reaches the design outlets at the design or requested time; whether the design improvements in crop yields occur; whether incomes and tax revenues rise as designed. By most accounts the performance of these systems has been highly variable, and in recent decades has tended to diminish, in both old and new schemes. The commonest faults are that farmers at the head of the schemes get as much water as they require, sometimes more than is good for them, while those at the tail-ends get an unreliable and small supply. Theft (by breaching canals) is quite common, and so is tampering with gates. Corruption is endemic.

Mostly the faults are exaggerated and accentuated in the Bengal Act schemes such as the Son and the Gandak, rather than in the North India Act Schemes such as the Ganges canal or the Sarda (see Figure 7.1 for the major systems). The usual explanation is that farmers in the wetter eastern areas do not rely on predicted irrigation flows to plan their crops: this is done on the assumption of adequate rainfall. But when drought occurs, the head farmers will resort to any practice to save their crops. These systems are subjected to much wider variations in demand than the 'warabandi' systems of western India.

Canal systems are obviously designed engineering features, but they are also clearly human political structures, redefining environmental resources in both good and bad ways. The systems the British designed worked better, but within a political hegemony in which the managerial class clearly held great power. In modern India the democratic tradition has shifted power away from the administrators and engineers, and simultaneously their economic position has deteriorated, since salaries in real terms are nowhere near the level, compared to the farmers, that the British enjoyed. A simple anecdote may illustrate some of the differences. When the British ran the Son system, only canal officers were allowed on the canal bank, which they patrolled on horseback. Farmers found on the bank were liable to a summary whipping. Now the farmers fear no such action, and probably see little of the officials on the banks (the horses have long gone, and the frequent requests for motorcycles as substitutes have not been funded). They therefore take buffalo to bathe, treading down the banks in the process, and hence encouraging weed growth. Buffalo can

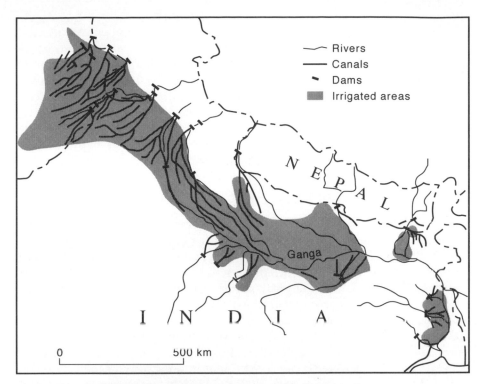

Figure 7.1 Major irrigation systems of the Ganges valley.

also be used as regulators, blocking the flow downstream, and raising the off-take to a farmer's fields.

There are other problems too. The canals cut across natural lines of drainage, and the irrigated areas rarely have enough new drainage lines developed. The result of both deficiencies can be an increase in water-logging – and incidentally a concomitant increase in malaria – leading often to increasing salinization, a condition which is hard and expensive to correct.

There is an endless argument waged about the value of these schemes. According to Seckler (1981) the return on capital is dismal, less even than that of other lowly performing public sector industries in India in the 1960s and 1970s. According to Chambers (1988), investment in making existing schemes work properly would be far more effective than investment in new schemes. A major deficiency he notes is in the lack of training of engineers (who like to design and build structures) as systems managers responsible for the farmer–system interface and the management of the main system itself. This problem is not restricted to India alone: under-performance has been widely recognized, and the new International Irrigation Management Institute has been founded in Sri Lanka to mitigate just such problems. We are therefore left with a question: why is there such a continuing effort in building new schemes of this sort? Partly the answer is because government sees in the provision of water the greatest guarantee against famine, and the best chance for matching food output with population growth rate: but also it has to be said that a very large part of the reason is the existence of a large canal-building lobby similar to the motorway lobby in the UK – a body of engineers and contractors who have profited and stand to profit further from building grandiose schemes. But the schemes are also tantalizingly related to storage dams in the hills, even if the main purpose of the latter might be power generation.

Agriculture, Ground Water and Tubewells

Ground water has been used since time immemorial to irrigate crops, from open wells, some kutcha (unlined) others pukka (bricklined and more stable). The number of such wells continues to increase, and these days they may be energized by a pumpset rather than by human or animal lift power. But undoubtedly the greatest increase in irrigation during the late 1970s and 1980s has been in tubewells. These are literally tubes which are drilled into the ground, perhaps with a diameter of 15 cm or less. They have a permeable membrane in the zone from which water is to be extracted, and a submerged or shaft-driven pump. Prima facie it would appear that such tubewells are most likely in areas not reached by canal water: but in practice they have diffused widely within canal command areas too. They can be costly for a farmer to install, and they are energetically expensive since they require either electrical or diesel power sets, and quite often both, since electrical power supplies are unreliable and intermittent.

The reasons for their adoption are as follows. First, they are under a farmer's control. In agriculture reliable and predictable water matters more than unreliable larger quantities. Second, they can have a beneficial effect in reducing local water tables, therefore reducing the risk of salinization and waterlogging. But in some areas the pumping has reached the stage where declining water tables spark a 'pumping competition' between farmers, with those affording bigger and deeper tubewells depriving neighbouring farmers with open wells of any water at all.

The interaction of surface systems and tubewells has led to the doctrine, somewhat after the event, of 'conjunctive use'. The conjunctive management obviously means the maximization of returns by simultaneous use of both resources: but this is harder to achieve than to outline, since one system is in the hands of one authority and the other is in the farmers' hands. In some areas the point has been reached where the canal system is not seen by the farmers as a delivery system for crops, but as a massive inland delta system whose purpose is to be leaky and to recharge local ground water: but at the moment in the Ganges plains, the more likely fear is still one of waterlogging rather than failing water tables.

Current Trends in Irrigated Agriculture, Flooding and Salinization

If the waterlogging of land is normal and results in overland flow (such as in natural marshy wetlands) the resultant ecosystem is usually healthy and biodiverse. Considerable areas of the Terai are naturally marshy, and in their own terms healthy (although from a human point of view often, in the past, lightly settled because of malarial problems). In India's monsoon tropical climate, for nine months of the year potential evapotranspiration (PET) considerably exceeds rainfall. If the water table rises close enough to the land surface in an area which was previously well enough drained, capillary action begins to take water up to the ground surface, where it evaporates and leaves a salt deposit. This is damaging waterlogging. In this case the movement of water in the upper soil horizon is upwards: by contrast in the previous healthy soil with a deeper water table or with rainfall exceeding PET the movement was downwards.

Canal irrigation schemes in India have been blamed for rising water tables and the extensive increase in salinization, which renders a soil sterile, and which is either impossible or very expensive to correct. Anecdotal evidence from satellites and from ground observation suggests that this is a real problem, particularly in Uttar Pradesh. In Pakistan it is known that 25 per cent of the area that has ever been provided with canal irrigation is now unproductive because of salinity – a massive waste of investment. But it is difficult to get any hard data on the scale of the problem in India. The Govind Ballabh Pant Institute's Atlas of Uttar Pradesh (Singh, 1987) suggests that there are 11.4 lakh ha of salt-affected land, and that this figure is not diminishing. A map (see Figure 7.2) shows in which areas this mostly occurs – in the lower doabs. But it also shows separate areas of waterlogging. These areas, predominantly in the Terai, are mostly outside of current canal irrigated areas, and as I have suggested may have 'healthy' wet conditions.

However, there is a local word frequently used to describe sterile salt-pan land – 'usar' land. The same atlas shows that the biggest increases in this usar land (see Figure 7.3) occured precisely in these Terai areas, and that elsewhere usar land diminished – although this contradicts the statement that salt-affected land has not diminished.

There is a further twist to this conundrum. Tubewells are frequently cited as being useful in reducing the chances of salinization (or reversing minor damage), because they lower water tables and provide a downward flow of water through the soil, reversing capillary action. Indeed the

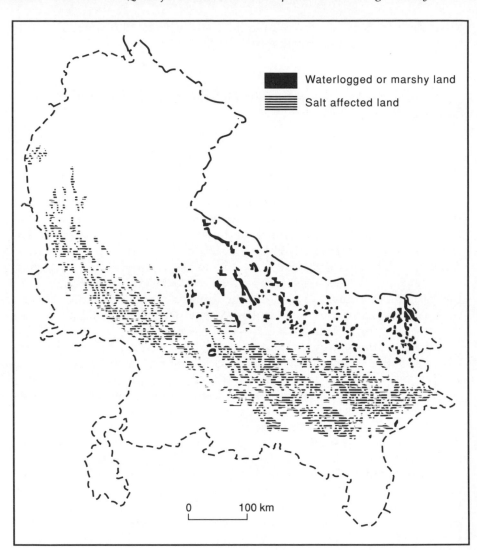

Figure 7.2 Salt-affected and water-logged areas of the Uttar Pradesh, 1980. *Source:* Singh (1987).

Table 7.3 Irrigated area in Uttar Pradesh.

| Year | Hectares (00 000) | | | |
	Canals	Tubewells	Other wells	Tanks and other sources
1950–51	18.5	2.8	19.1	8.1
1960–61	19.9	5.4	18.4	6.9
1970–71	25.0	23.3	17.0	6.7
1980–81	31.8	50.5	7.5	4.7
1983–84	33.4	54.7	6.2	4.7

Source: Singh (1987).

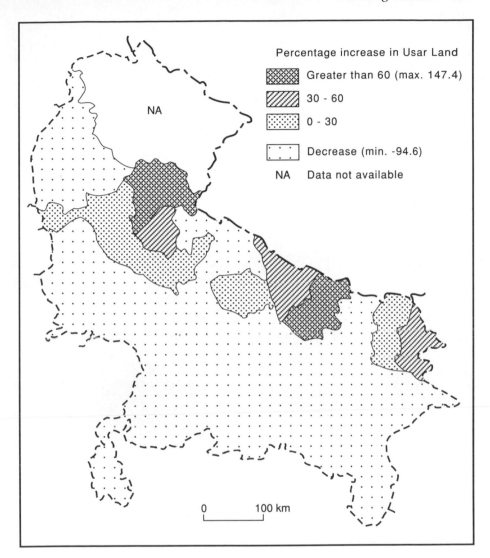

Figure 7.3 Increase in usar land in Uttar Pradesh, 1950–80. *Source:* Singh (1987).

increase in tubewells is welcomed officially for this reason. Table 7.3 shows how there has been a very rapid increase in tubewells in Uttar Pradesh over three decades. Figure 7.4 shows where the proportion is highest – not surprisingly where canal irrigation is least, but also in the area where usar land has increased most. The Terai area is therefore a conundrum on the basis of these data – on the one hand, it is naturally waterlogged and flood prone but not classified as salt-affected, and on the other hand it has had the greatest proportion of tubewell irrigation, which should be beneficial, yet it has the greatest increase in usar land.

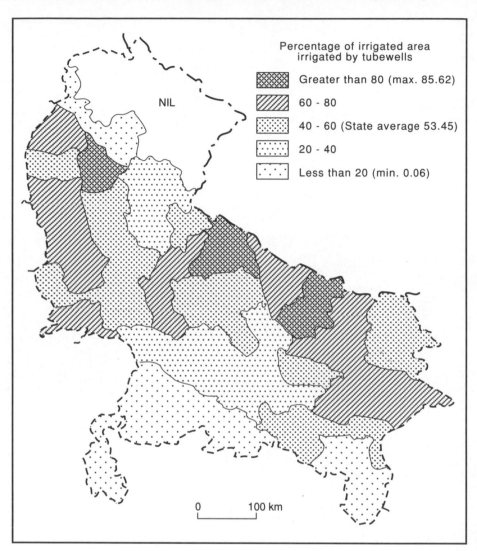

Figure 7.4 Proportion of irrigated land irrigated by tubewells in Uttar Pradesh, 1980. *Source:* Singh (1987).

Summary and Conclusions

Water demand in urban areas is bound to increase dramatically in the next few decades, and urban water may well outprice agricultural water. But agriculture is also set to increase its demands on current trends. Both sectors could substantially improve water efficiency – in the urban areas by proper treatment and recycling, and in rural areas by stemming the massive waste that occurs in large-scale surface systems, and adhering to different cropping regimes (easier said than enforced). Presently it seems as if irrigation has led to increases in salinization – although it is not easy to establish exactly how much and where – and to that extent a major cost of irrigation schemes is left out of calculations when new projects are appraised. If both urban demand and agriculture seek supplies from the rivers, shortages will grow imminently, particularly in the long dry seasons. However, the ground water reserves are plentiful, and recharged at any conceivable demand level. The major hindrance in developing this resource is the energetic cost – and again the finger points at hydropower in the hills (see Chapter 5).

References

Chambers, R. (1988) *Managing Canal Irrigation.* New Delhi: Oxford and IBH Publishing.

Chapman, G.P. (1983) Underperformance in Indian irrigation systems: the problems of diagnosis and prescription. *Geoforum,* **14**(3), 267–75.

Chisholm, M. (1992) Demographic Trends: Implications for the Use of Water. In ODA, *Proceedings of the Conference on Priorities for Water Resources Allocation and Management.* Natural Resource Engineering Advisors' Conference, Southampton, July 1992. London: Overseas Development Administration.

Fauceys, R. (1992) Domestic water use: engineering, effectiveness and sustainability. In *Proceedings of the Conference on Priorities for Water Resources Allocation and Management,* Natural Resource Engineering Advisors' Conference, Southampton, July 1992. London: Overseas Development Administration.

GOI (1988) Water and sanitation. In *Government of India: Report of the National Commission on Urbanization,* Vol. II. New Delhi, pp. 293–301.

ODA (1992) *Proceedings of the Conference on Priorities for Water Resources Allocation and Management.* Natural Resource Engineering Advisors' Conference, Southampton, July 1992. London: Overseas Development Administration.

Seckler, D. (1981) *The New Era of Irrigation Management in India.* Mimeo. New Delhi: Ford Foundation.

Shankar, U., Bahal, A. and Martin, M. (1994) 'The Drowning of a City' and other news stories. *Down to Earth,* **2**, No.21, 25–36. New Delhi: Centre for Science and Environment.

Singh, L.R. (1987) *A Planning Atlas of Uttar Pradesh.* G.o. Uttar Pradesh, Lucknow: Govind Ballabh Pant Social Science Institute, Allahabad and Planning Department.

8

Water Quality in the River Ganges

V.K. Kumra

Editors' Note

Dr Kumra makes reference here to the increased siltation load of the rivers in the plains because of deforestation in the hills. It is clear from earlier chapters that many experts would deny this anthropogenic causative link – but we have left the remark in place because it is symptomatic of the extent to which it has become an established 'fact' for workers in other disciplines. Dr Kumra provides some interesting data on pollution. There are many sources of data on pollution, but the material is not gathered centrally, and different experts refer to different sources with different conclusions – a point made by Dr Ahmed in the next chapter. We should also remember that pollution monitoring can be sensitive to very minor changes in the location of instruments, and that the situation may be worse or better than described here.

Introduction

The holy River Ganges is a life-line for millions of people in India. Through the ages it has had a major impact on the culture, civilization, health and well-being of the largest concentration of population in South Asia. But with the ever-increasing density of population, with increasing industrialization and intensifying agricultural practices and ever-increasing demands for irrigation, the Ganges basin is facing environmental problems of unprecedented magnitude. It is being used for disposal of effluents from domestic and industrial sources which has caused great damage to its water quality. In most cases the situation has been allowed to deteriorate; in others it is not neglect but ignorance that worsens the problems. If appropriate measures to maintain the age-long purity of the Ganges are not taken before it is too late, this, the holiest river of the world, will lose its grace and sanctity. Although the government of India launched the Ganga Action Plan (GAP) in June 1986 to restore the river's purity, the task has barely yet begun. This chapter is about the current levels of pollution, and about attempts to rectify the situation.

The Ganges Basin

The Ganges, originating in the central Himalayas at Gangotri, descends to the plains at Rishikesh. From there it flows more than 2000 km until it reaches the sea, building, eroding, and watering the plains that are home to so many millions of people. Along its course from Gangotri to Ganga Sagar, there are 29 major cities, more than 70 towns, and thousands of villages. Besides, there are 132 large industrial units in the Indian part of the basin, of which 86 are located in Uttar Pradesh, 43 in West Bengal and 3 in Bihar. Almost half of these (66) are located on the bank of the river at Kanpur alone, the industrial hub of Uttar Pradesh.

The worst culprits for degradation of the river water quality are community sewage, and partially cremated and unburnt human bodies 'buried' in the river. The share of industries to total pollution load is also significant (15–20 per cent). In addition, agricultural pollution is increasing. According to a report of the Central Water Pollution Prevention and Control Board, about 0.6 million tons of chemical fertilizers (34 per cent of the country's annual consumption) and 1300 tons of pesticides are being applied in the Ganges basin every year, which results in contamination of surface and ground water by toxic substances. All these demands have depleted the quality of the river, in which millions of Hindus regularly immerse themselves to wash away their sins. Therefore, it becomes imperative to analyse the pattern of pollution levels along its course so that long-term remedial measures can be adopted to alleviate pollution of the Ganges.

Pollution Levels Along the Ganges

According to one estimate the total urban domestic and industrial wastes generated in the Ganges basin carry about 2000 tons of biological oxygen demand (BOD) per day for final disposal either on land or in surface water. Out of the eight states, Uttar Pradesh contributes the maximum urban organic pollution load to the river, discharging about 1000 tons of BOD load per day. Besides, the river carries 340×10^6 metric tons of sediments per year (Valdia, 1985). Deforestation in the Himalayas greatly increases erosion and sedimentation. The estimated annual soil erosion rate from fields is also high (270 t/ha) in comparison to the Congo (3 t/ha), Amazon (13 t/ha) and Nile (8 t/ha) (Stocking, 1988). Partly this is due to the nature of the rainfall regime and the geology of the Himalayas, but it may also relate to the poor management of cultivated lands and overgrazing in parts of the basin. Because these sediments contain organic material, a high load also depletes dissolved oxygen (DO) in water and thus affects the self-purifying capacity of the river. Because of the high silt load and the seasonal nature of flow, the river constantly changes its bed configuration, and in the low season gives the appearance of a series of pools connected by a languid flow. Diversions of the flow in the low season for irrigation are decreasing the low season flow, causing a slower rate of dilution of pollutants (Table 8.1). It is unrealistic and detrimental to think that the natural system can any longer cope with these pollution loads, and it is, therefore, essential to plan and design and to raise funds for construction of municipal and industrial waste water treatment works.

Table 8.1 Low season flow of the Ganges at selected stations (cumecs).

Locations	Rate of flow
Narora	321
Kannauj	1542
Kanpur	1679
Fatehpur	1725
Allahabad	1870
Varanasi	4120
Patna	5693
Munghyr	7248

Source: Environmental Research Laboratory, ZHCET, Aligarh Muslim University, Uttar Pradesh, India.

Before it descends into the plains, the Ganges water is relatively clean. Disposal of sewage water starts mainly from Rishikesh. It has been observed in a recent visit to the area that in Rishikesh, near Triveni ghat, sewage is being discharged into the river. Hindustan Antibiotics Ltd discharges 9028 m^3/day of waste, containing highly toxic chemicals, into the river. Indian Drugs and Pharmaceutical Ltd (24 km upstream of Har-Ki-Pauri) and Bharat Heavy Electronics Ltd (9 km downstream of Har-Ki-Pauri) also discharge their effluents into the river. Overall, about 17.5 million litres per day (MLD) of waste water is discharged into the river at Haridwar. It has a population of 0.146 million and another 57 000 people visit the city every day. This number swells to 1.5 million on the auspicious days during Kumbha. Out of the total 24 km of sewer line, 14 km is clogged owing to continuous siltation received from the Mansa Devi hills. Table 8.2 shows that although the concentration of BOD (2.0 mg/l) is below the prescribed standards (3.0 mg/l), the DO content is not sufficiently high (5.7 mg/l) to restore the water quality of the Ganges at Haridwar.

Further downstream from Haridwar, at Narora and Kannauj, it is least polluted as the concentration of DO is significantly high (Narora, 8.7 mg/l;

Table 8.2 Biological oxygen demand and other indicators, River Ganges, at 12 selected locations.

Monitoring station	Ganges water quality				BOD generation in catchment area (kg/day)
	BOD (mg/l)	DO (mg/l)	COD (mg/l)	Total coliform (MPN/100 ml)	
Hardwar	2.0	5.7	8.6	2 400	100 430
Garmukteswar	5.1	6.8	11.4	1 430	195 599
Kannauj	7.3	6.2	13.4	NA	343 815
Kanpur	15.3	6.5	28.4	NA	171 440
Allahabad	9.3	7.4	22.0	31 250	105 923
Varanasi	9.3	6.4	20.0	12 075	111 963
Patna	1.3	7.4	16.2	125 500	354 926
Munger	2.2	6.4	22.3	24 200	179 386
Farakka	0.03	8.1	16.2	125 500	157 495
Nabadwip	0.6	7.5	14.4	58 500	58 194
Dakshineshwar	2.0	6.0	19.8	240 000	198 542
Diamond Harbour	8.0	7.1	185.4	8 250	74 207

Source: State Water Pollution Control and Prevention Boards of Uttar Pradesh, Bihar, and West Bengal.

Table 8.3 Seasonal variation in water quality in the Ganges.

Station	Index for bathing in different seasons		
	Summer (Apr.–Jun.)	Rainy season (July-Sept.)	Post-monsoon (Oct.-Nov.)
Hardwar	53	44	46
Kanpur	17	12	16
Varanasi	31	34	28
Patna	25	26	22

Source: Ganga Project Directorate, New Delhi.

Kannauj, 8.9 mg/l). These two towns do not contain any large-scale industry and the main source of pollution to the river is sewage discharge. As the river crosses the plains its flow is augmented at some times of the year both by surface drainage (during the monsoon) and by recharge from ground water (between the monsoon and the hot season). Thus the self-purifying capacity of the river is adequate for water quality at these two locations to be satisfactory. But at Kanpur the situation changes again for the worse. The total sewage generation is about 275 MLD (Kumra, 1981) and analysis of sewage water discharged revealed that the BOD is considerably (270 mg/l) above the prescribed limit. In addition, about 150 industrial units discharge their untreated toxic wastes into the river, resulting in severe damage to water quality. The mean recorded value of DO (3 mg/l) at Jajmau reflects gross levels of pollution. It is caused by discharge from 80 tanneries, containing high concentrations of chromium

(>30 mg/l) and with 3000 mg/l of BOD. A large number of dairies are responsible for disposal of animal excreta into the river through sewers and open drains, further adding to the organic pollution load of the river. A survey of fisherfolk reported their complaints that their daily fish catch has come down to 15 kg from 30–40 kg a few years before (Singh, 1988).

So far the State Water Pollution Prevention and Control Board has prosecuted only five tanneries. Recently the High Court of Allahabad, as a result of a citizens' action, has ordered the closure of 29 tanneries at Kanpur which were regularly discharging untreated toxic wastes into the river, causing considerable damage to aquatic life in the downstream areas.

The shifting course of the Ganges is also affecting Kanpur in another way. The main channel of the river has shifted some 7 km laterally towards Unnao and away from the city, between Gangpur and Bithoor, a distance of 25 km. The result is that the ancient bathing ghats receive just a trickle of highly contaminated water. Thousands of people bathe in this polluted backwater of the river and perform rituals for dead persons which result in harmful effects on their health. To maintain drinking water supplies and power generation, the old channel of the Ganges is dredged at an annual cost of £0.12–0.16 million by the state Jal Nigam and Kanpur Electric Supply Undertaking.

Table 8.4 Water quality indices for the Ganges at selected locations.

Location	Agriculture		Bathing, drinking without treatment		Industrial use with minimum treatment		Water supply		Overall WQI	
	S	W	S	W	S	W	S	W	S	W
Rishikesh U	95	94	51	89	51	94	64	100	70	95
Rishikesh D	96	94	54	90	52	92	46	97	63	94
Kanpur U	89	84	41	58	50	57	57	55	59	69
Kanpur D	86	81	11	60	49	53	20	70	38	69
Varanasi U	71	49	75	55	71	62	83	69	75	65
Varanasi D	70	46	33	42	72	60	47	50	55	64

S = summer, W = winter, U = upstream, D = downstream.
Source: Courtesy of Dr D.S. Bhargava.

During recent years popular agitation has reflected the fact that people are becoming aware of the increasing pollution levels of the Ganges at Kanpur. The Chitale Committee (Chairman, Central Water Commission) has advocated the construction of a pilot channel costing over £2.8 million, as a temporary measure. The dredged channel is supposed to be a makeshift measure until a barrage can be constructed on the Ganges, upstream of Bhairon ghat – but so far the problem of Kanpur still remains unsolved.

At Allahabad a similar story is repeated. The volume of the river flow at Allahabad is about 1.3×10^{11} m^3 per year (including 7.7×10^{11} m^3 of the river Yamuna). At Allahabad, unlike Kanpur, domestic wastes rather than industrial wastes are the major contributor to river pollution, since the city has little large-scale industry. (The Indian Farmers Fertilizer Corporation (IFFCO), 25 km upstream of Allahabad, discharging about 6500 m^3/day of effluents into the river, is the only significant source of industrial pollution to the river between Fatehpur and Allahabad.) There are 13 large sewer lines in the city pouring about 100 MLD of waste into the river. According to a recent study, a pH value of 8.43 is recorded at Allahabad, which is the second highest value after Kanpur. At the Sangam, the holy confluence of the Ganges and Yamuna, the water is slightly to moderately polluted. Bacterial counts are found to be high due to bathing. A sewage treatment plant is under construction at Naini with a capacity of 60 MLD but it will not solve the problem of the remaining 40 MLD of untreated effluents being discharged into the river every day. There is a need to install one more sewage treatment plant upstream of the Sangam so that the water quality of the Ganges can be maintained for bathing at Allahabad.

Likewise, at Varanasi, with its approximately 1 million population, 125 MLD of effluent is discharged into the river through sewers alone. In addition, the Assi nallah (drain) carrying municipal wastes also brings about 4 MLD of oily and chemical-ridden effluent from the Diesel Locomotive Works (DLW). The Banaras Hindu University has already installed a treatment plant for 1.85 MLD of waste water and its capacity has been raised to 8 MLD very recently. As much as 90 per cent of the total pollution of the river is caused by the nine drains which pour untreated wastes directly into the river. The River Varuna, which joins the Ganges after the Rajghat bridge, receives waste from seven open drains and a butchery, and has such a high BOD that it causes significant deterioration of the river water quality. Besides, on average 42 000 dead bodies are cremated on the left bank of the river by traditional methods, the ashes and remains being committed to the river, in addition to 3000 bodies of persons unknown and 9000 dead cattle which are thrown into the river every year. This has resulted in contamination by ash and biological pollutants. The State Pollution Prevention and Control Board has recently claimed that as a result of new measures the BOD concentration of the river has dropped from 8.0–15.0 mg/l to 3.8–6.9 mg/l over the last four years at different locations on the river front. This is partly due to diversion of Assi nallah by 1 km upstream and partly due to new diversions for sewage lines. A new treatment plant is also under construction.

A recent study made by the Thames Water Authority, UK revealed that apart from the problem associated with the Konia outfall, located downstream of the city, the major pollution problem at Varanasi is one of localized gross pollution coinciding with the most heavily used part of the

Ganges, including major bathing ghats and the city water intake point. Further, the polluting effect of the Konia sewer outfall and the River Varuna is again indicated by high bacterial counts (100 000 MPN counts/100 ml) downstream of these discharges. Treatment plants are being set up at Konia and on the Varuna at Dinapur which should have been commissioned by 1992. The Diesel Locomotive Works has already increased its capacity for waste water treatment to 8 MLD and is recovering toxic chemicals from effluents. An electric crematorium started functioning in 1989. Although the number of bodies cremated there has not been as great as hoped for, the increasing cost of traditional cremation (particularly if sandalwood is paid for) should mean an increase in cremations at the crematorium.

If all the above-mentioned plans at Varanasi are fully and properly implemented, about 80 per cent of all the pollution load of the Ganges at this city could be mitigated.

Eighty kilometres downstream of Varanasi, another public sector unit making morphine from opium at Ghazipur, a distillery and a sugar factory at Nandganj are also discharging untreated effluents into the Ganges, again causing significant deterioration of the water quality. Along the Ganges in Bihar a number of industries, including fertilizer, distilleries and light engineering, have developed particularly at Patna, Monghyr and Bhagalpur. At Patna, an estimated 200 MLD of waste water is discharged into the Ganges through seven outfalls along its 15-km stretch. The total BOD load generated by industries is calculated as 8000 kg/day which is much less than that of domestic wastes (25000 kg/day). Sewage water of the city contains very high bacterial counts (90 120 MPN count/100 ml) but it is only 11 000 in the midstream of the river. Other pollutants like phosphorous have been recorded as increasing 15-fold, nitrogen has doubled, sulphate has increased 3½-fold and silicate 2½-fold during the last 10 years.

The most important industry located on the bank of the Ganges in Bihar is the oil refinery at Barauni. Nearly a decade ago a stretch of about 2 km of the river at Barauni caught fire and burnt for almost 16 hours before dying down. Enquiries later revealed that effluents from the refinery were discharged untreated and made the river flammable. Further downstream at Mokamah, the multinational Bata Shoe Factory and McDowell distilleries discharge their effluents directly into the river. As a result the river water can no longer be used by the villagers for drinking and bathing purposes, and now they have become dependent on tubewell water supply.

At Calcutta the Bhagirathi–Hooghly river basin is moderately to grossly populated due to the concentration of innumerable industries in the belt. total volume of liquid waste discharged through outfalls is 252 MGD (million gallons per day), of which 77 MGD is contributed by the industries alone. There are over 150 industrial units on the river bank, of which 90 are jute mills. Pulp and paper industries alone discharge about 50 per cent of the total industrial effluent generated in the belt. Besides, discharge of toxic and oily effluents from Calcutta port have also contributed significantly to the pollution load of the river. The study made by Gopal Krishnan (1985) showed that fish caught in the Hooghly estuary were highly contaminated with heavy metals such as mercury and zinc, which can lead to disastrous consequences if consumed by human beings. Due to excessive discharge of industrial effluents, the temperature of the river water has increased considerably, resulting in the depletion of saturated oxygen in the water, thus harming aquatic life in the estuary. It has been found that Ganges water is not only unsuitable for human consumption, but has also to be classified as unfit to be treated for drinking water supply by a conventional treatment plant.

The aforementioned study testifies that the Ganges and major tributaries carry a wanton discharge of untreated sewage and industrial effluents from various polluting sources spread all along its course in the plains. From the moment the sacred river touches the plains at Rishikesh it is desecrated with pollutants of varying toxicity, with Uttar Pradesh contributing the major share (50 per cent) of the total urban–industrial pollution load. The river is highly polluted at Kanpur, Allahabad, Varanasi and Diamond Harbour, moderately polluted at Fatepur, Patna and Monghyr, and less polluted at Kannauj and Narora as far as organic pollution load is concerned. The Ganges becomes seriously overloaded between Kanpur and Allahabad, particularly in the hot summer months when stream flow and turbulence are low and the effects of dilution and oxygen transfer from the air are reduced, so that the BOD of introduced wastes exceeds available oxygen. DO levels are also reduced because warm water holds less oxygen and speeds up bacterial decay (Miller, 1988). A number of irrigation projects have been undertaken in this stretch of the river which have resulted in withdrawal of excessive water, affecting stream flow and turbulence.

In order to assess the status of the water quality of the Ganges, Agrawal and Bhargava (1977) developed a composite water quality index according to water uses. Tables 8.3 and 8.4 reveal that the water quality of the Ganges at selected locations was found to be poorer in summer than in winter. For bathing, the desirable index number is fixed at 50. Except at Haridwar, the river water quality is too poor for bathing at all locations along the Ganges. To restore the pristine purity of the Ganges, a number of schemes are presently in operation under the Central Ganga Authority (CGA), but efforts still have a long way to go to make an impact. Therefore it is imperative to examine the progress of the GAP.

Cleaning the Ganges

Although the government of India has initiated action for cleaning the Ganges from Haridwar to Diamond Harbour under the CGA, the latest reports say that little has been achieved. By the end of 1989 only 50 schemes with a cost of Rs 160.39 millions were completed, but it was hoped that by the end of 1990 all such schemes related to the construction of the sewage systems, pumping stations and treatment plants will be completed (CGA, 1989). The immediate dual objective of the CGA is to reduce the pollution load of the river, and to establish self-sustaining city authorities with the capacity to install and maintain new treatment plants. The first phase of the CGA envisaged major works such as renovation of sewage pumping and treatment plants, setting up of new treatment plants to produce energy, manure and biogas and laying down sewage disposal systems where they do not exist at present. According to the report of the CGA, all the sewage pumping stations in Rishikesh and Haridwar are in order and pollution of the river has been checked to some extent. Similarly, at Kanpur for cleansing the main stream a detailed project costing £310 000 has been sanctioned for the renovation and restoration of the existing sewage pumping station and treatment plant. In Varanasi, Allahabad and Patna, the treatment plants should have started functioning by the end of 1990. Recovery of biogas and its conversion into electricity is to be undertaken at Haridwar, Kanpur, Allahabad, Patna, Varanasi and a few units at Calcutta. It is expected that sewage treatment plants will be self-sustaining as regards their power.

The CGA has used the model of the Thames Water Authority (TWA) for cleaning the Ganges, unmindful of the dissimilarities in the situation. (The Thames is much too small a river for comparison with the Ganges. It does not arise from a tropical ecosystem, which is highly productive and yet highly sensitive to human interference. The rate of sedimentation is also very low in the Thames. Further, it is very near to the sea and open to tidal waves, resulting in easier cleaning as a result of a high rate of dilution.) The TWA has developed a computerized freshwater river quality model for the Ganges suitable for analysis of critical stations along the river, introducing various new concepts in river quality simulation, of which the most far-reaching is that of temporal correlations. This enables the model to take advantage of any seasonal and diurnal effects which are present in quality and flow data and then reproduce these effects in simulated output. Associated time-of-travel effects are also modelled (Brown, 1986). It will be useful in studying seasonal and spatial variation of water quality in the Ganges as well as alleviating pollution.

Mr Griffith, Pollution Control Manager, Thames Region, NRA, presently working for CGA in India said (in a personal communication) that 'We hope to control pollution of the Ganges but it will take time. There is a need to create awareness among the people and industrialists of India of the problem of pollution'. Mr Triggs, also of TWA, commented (personal communication) that standards set for restoring the quality of the river based on coliform counts may never be achieved. These are based on European and American standards, where people do not bathe in rivers as in India. The coliforms are not derived from faeces alone; they also come off the skin surface. The government proposes to bring the count down to 500 MPN/100 ml at bathing ghats, a standard set by WHO. According to Trigg, meeting these standards is not essential: rather, the most important aims are to reduce BOD and raise DO.

Operation Ganga will face difficulties regarding the maintenance of a minimum flow in the river, since the pollution level largely depends upon the velocity of water flow, particularly at critical points along the river, where large industrial units and urban agglomerations are located. In addition, although new effluent cleansing plants may be built, there is no guarantee that they will be maintained – and maintenance may turn out to be the weakest link in the chain. The success of the plan will largely depend upon the co-ordinated efforts of all the agencies involved in it. The concept of integrated pollution control (IPC) should be adopted by the CGA; this will also include preparation of new legislation so that a wider collection of scheduled works would be subject to a new integrated licensing regime. The IPC approach is significant in that it would allow the Central Water Pollution Prevention and Control Board to regulate waste and water emissions even where other regulatory agencies covering these discharges already exist (O'Riordan and Weale, 1989). It is not reasonable to construct waste water treatment plant for reducing organic pollutants separately for every individual industry, particularly the smaller ones. Joint treatment of industrial effluent with domestic waste is usually more economical and easier to operate so long as the pretreatment regulations for discharging industrial effluents into public sewers are established and followed strictly. In Kanpur such a scheme is being implemented so that toxic wastes from tanneries can be jointly treated. Greater involvement of indigenous industry could possibly help in working out methods more suited to local conditions. Other tributaries of the Ganges should also be given emphasis as regards disposal of effluents from industries and domestic sources.

The main hindrance in the implementation of the GAP seems to be the lack of public awareness. Although we cannot stop people bathing in the Ganges because of religious sentiments, it is better to inculcate in people an awareness of the problems and to provoke their active participation in pollution control programmes. A number of non-governmental organizations have come forward, such as 'Swatcha Ganga Abhiyan' (Clean Ganges Campaign) at Varanasi to create awareness among the people of India, and their efforts should be encouraged. It is important that both experts and the public participate in both recognizing and curing the ills that have befallen our holy river.

Acknowledgements

I am grateful to Professor M.D.I. Chisholm, University of Cambridge, for his hospitality and encouragement and to the Association of Commonwealth Universities for the award of a Commonwealth Academic Staff Fellowship. The author also wishes to thank Mr Onkar Dikshit and Mr Amitabh for their help.

References

Agrawal, G.D. and Bhargava, D.S. (1977) Accounting for microbial populations in mathematical models for self-purification in streams. *Journal of Institute Public Health Engineers, India*, 1, 7–10.

Ahmed, S. (1988) The gutter and its ghats. *The Times of India*, 26 June, 4.

Banerjee, B.N. (1989) *Can the Ganga be Cleaned?* New Delhi: BR Publishing Corporation, pp. 30–40.

Brown, S.R. (1986) 'TOMCAT: A computer model designed specifically for catchment quality planning within water industry'. Paper presented in *International Conference on Water Quality Modelling in the Inland Water Environments*, Bournemouth, England, 10–13 June, p. 38.

CGA (1989) Report. New Delhi: Government of India.

Gopal Krishnan, K. (1985) Effluents poison fish in Hooghly. *The Hindustan Times*, 5 April.

Goudie, A. (1986) *The Human Impact on the Natural Environment*, 2nd ed. Oxford: Basil Blackwell.

Kumra, V.K. (1981) *Kanpur City: A Study in Environmental Pollution*. Varanasi: Tara Book Agency, p. 67.

Miller, G. Jr, Tyler, G. (1988) *Living in the Environment*. California: Wadsworth Publishing Co., pp. 461–5.

O'Riordan, T. and Weale, A. (1989) Administrative reorganisation and policy of change: the case of Her Majesty's inspectorate of pollution. *Public Administration*, 67(3), 291–2.

Singh, O. (1988) *India's Urban Environment: Pollution, Perception and Management*. Varanasi: Tara Book Agency, p. 99.

Stocking, M. (1988) Recognising environmental crisis in Africa. In P. Blaikie and T. Unwin (eds), *Environmental Crisis in Developing Countries*. Monograph No. 5, Developing Areas Research Group. London: Institute of British Geographers, p. 189.

Valdia, K.S. (1985) Accelerated erosion and landslide prone zones in the central Himalaya. In J.S. Singh *et al.* (eds), *Environmental Regeneration in Himalaya*, Nainital: CHEA and Gyanodaya Prakashan, p. 24.

9

Whose Concept of Participation? State–Society Dynamics in the Cleaning of the Ganges at Varanasi

Sarah Ahmed

Editors' Note
India has a union or central government presiding over a federation of devolved states, each with its own parliament (legislative assembly). In political economy the word 'state' is often used to mean the coalition between the formal and informal structures of public control and authority and those elite classes and bureaucrats who dominate them. Dr Ahmed refers to such a State quite often, and for that meaning the initial letter is always a capital 'S'. When she means central government we also use an initial capital 'S'. Whenever she means simply a constituent state of the federation, such as Uttar Pradesh, we use state with a small initial 's'. Remember that the State as we have defined it can include both central and state politicians and bureaucrats, working as part of the same coalition of authority but at different levels.

Pandit think
before you drink
that water.
The house of clay you are sitting in –
all creation is pouring through it.
Fifty-five million Yadavs soaked there,
and eighty-eight thousand sages.
At every step a prophet is buried.
All their clay has rotted.
Fish, turtles and crocodiles
hatched there. The water is thick
with blood. Hell flows
along that river, with
rotten men and beasts.
(Kabir[1])

Introduction

In February 1985 the Indian government launched the Ganga Action Plan (GAP), its first major attempt to systematically control and monitor the pollution of a significant river in the country. Not only is the Ganges important in physical and economic terms – it drains 26 per cent of India's land area and carries a quarter of its water resources – but it has immense symbolic value for the millions of Hindus who bathe in it every day and who use its waters for washing, drinking and ritual purposes.

Thus in June 1986, the then Indian prime minister, Rajiv Gandhi, officially inaugurated the GAP as a 'people's programme' at the ancient and holy city of Varanasi, Uttar Pradesh.

> The Ganga Action Plan is not just a government plan. It has not been prepared for the PWD (Public Works Department) or government officials alone. It is a plan for all the people of India; one in which they can come forward to participate. It is up to us to clean the whole of the Ganga and refrain from polluting it.[2]

Such a statement implies that participation of 'the people' is not only necessary to achieve programme objectives, but that it can be secured provided the right approach has been adopted. This chapter seeks to examine the rhetoric and reality of participation in the implementation of the GAP at Varanasi. It provides an insight into a specific set of micro-relationships – those between programme administrators and the local community – and the consequences of these interactions for the management of a public 'commons' resource such as the Ganges.

Although participation is often seen as a *sine qua non* for the success and sustainability of development projects (Cernea, 1985; Lisk, 1985; Korten, 1986; Montgomery, 1988), it raises a number of questions: who is the public? why is their participation sought? and how and at what level is such participation desired? Varanasi is indicative of these issues as it has a plurality of interacting rationalities, which suggests that questions of pollution control and participation cannot be isolated from the nature and distribution of power in society.

Figure 9.1 schematically illustrates the various interests involved in or impacted by pollution and its control at Varanasi. Beginning with the State, this paper looks at how some groups at the different levels (1) define and approach participation in the framework of the GAP, while others (2) are affected by the *lack of* any attempt to have a participatory dialogue. That is to say, there is little communication between the micro- and macro-levels in Figure 9.1; on the contrary the GAP does not challenge the existing institutional order, but reflects and reinforces poor top-to-bottom com- munication. Thus, the dilemma of pollution control at Varanasi is indicative of the larger discourse on State–society relations in India (Nandy, 1989; Khan, 1989; Lele, 1990; Patnaik, 1990). This discussion is based

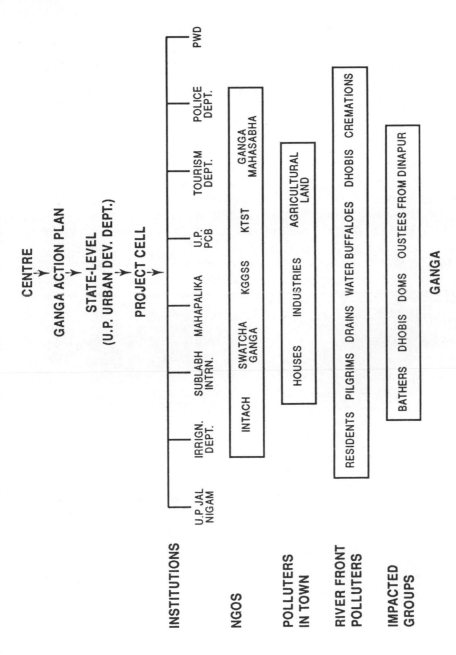

Figure 9.1 Pollution at Varanarc: original, impacts, and organizational responses.

on two research visits to Varanasi, the first in 1988 and the second in 1990.

The State and Participation: Myth and Reality

The GAP is the first time the centre has intervened at the local level through local state governments, to control water pollution, water being a state subject in India.[3] The centre can do so because environmental protection is enshrined in the Indian Constitution as a fundamental duty of the State. Article 48A added under the 42nd Amendment (1976) says that: 'The State shall endeavour to protect or improve the environment and to safeguard the forests and wildlife of the country' (in Jariwala, 1990, p.1).

Moreover, Article 47 directs the State to improve the health of its people as one of its primary duties. Although the GAP is the first politico-administrative effort to control water pollution with the implied objective of improving the health of the nation and the environment, it has been preceded by numerous judicial judgements which have invoked the rights and duties of the state (see Gaur, 1987; Hayward, 1990; Singh, 1986).

Thus, in launching the GAP the then Congress (I) government at the centre sought to legitimize the role of the State as guardian of the natural environment and protector of the national psyche (Walker, 1989; O'Connor, 1989). This point was clearly evident in the promise (to clean the Ganges) made to the electorate during Rajiv Gandhi's election campaign in December 1984 and the subsequent official announcement of the programme in February 1985 to coincide with his inaugural speech as prime minister, despite the fact that the GAP was finalized well before Mrs Gandhi's assassination.

The official GAP ceremony at Varanasi (June 1986), where the waters of the Ganges were symbolically mixed with that of seven other rivers in the country, further cemented this socio-ecological concern of the State. The corporate magazine (*Business India*) then commented on the unmistakeable political overtones of the inaugural function:

> . . . when the Prime Minister described the Ganga as the greatest symbol of national unity and likened its pollution to the emergence of divisive forces, the metamorphosis of the environmental project into a political programme was complete. Scientific credibility was decisively shoved into the back seat to make room for political expediency. (Muralidharan, 1986, p.80)

According to Midgley (1986a, pp.38–44), there are four forms of State responses to participation:

1   the anti-participatory mode;
2   the manipulative participatory mode;
3   the incremental mode of participation;
4   the participatory state.

These categories are not necessarily definitive and it may be possible that a

State falls between one or more classifications, combining elements of both. Using Midgley's framework, I would argue that the response of the Indian State to participation in the context of the GAP has been both manipulative and incremental. By manipulative, I mean that the State has supported participation when it chooses to do so, largely in its own interests, to gain votes and political support. Not only, as already mentioned, was the official announcement of the GAP timed to coincide with Rajiv Gandhi's inaugural speech, but moreover some of the State-directed forms of participation at Varanasi simply involve using people as cheap labour without giving them power in decision-making processes or any role in the monitoring of the various pollution control schemes. For example, after one recent monsoon the government organized national social service (NSS) camps, where students from all parts of the country came to clean the silt from the ghats (large steps leading down to the Ganges), plant trees, interact with the public and so on. While these are important awareness-raising measures, the point to be stressed is that they were undertaken by volunteers who were in Varanasi for a short, fixed period of time who did not see their responsibilities as a chore, and who would not be involved in any long-term local presence to back up the initial action. In addition, the camp was combined with fun and cultural activities, and recognized and duly acknowledged by local bureaucrats and prominent citizens for its social significance. But the work more consistently put in by NGOs and local individuals (see below) is hardly recognized by the government, which means they have less incentive to continue (Centre for Science and Environment, 1985, p.330).

The State's support for participation is incremental insofar as it has a *laissez-faire* or ambivalent approach to implementation which fails to encourage local efforts or to ensure the effective functioning of (theoretically) participatory institutions such as local government. Midgley maintains that such an incrementalist approach to social development can usually be associated with pluralist political ideas and a strong centralized government. Coalition politics in India, it can be argued, has needed and received a form of value consensus that could keep aspirations alive (through their articulation in images and programmes such as community development) without actually fulfilling them (Lele, 1990, p.23).

Thus, the only way for the State to strike a balance between planning and public participation is by increasing *bureaucratic sprawl*: 'Allowing a highly differentiated public to get involved in the design and management of projects requires *more* rather than less control, uniform decision-making bodies and a strong administrative hierarchy' (Robertson, 1984, p.130).

At the next level there are a plethora of hierarchical agencies and decision-making committees to execute, manage and monitor the GAP. In the following section I look at the top-down mindset within the most important of these implementing bodies, the Uttar Pradesh Jal Nigam.

The Uttar Pradesh Jal Nigam: Institutional Constraints

The UP Jal Nigam (UP Water Supply and Sewerage Board), with an annual budget exceeding Rs 1500 million and about 10 000 full-time engineers, is one of the largest public sector undertakings in the world. Established in 1975 under the UP Water Supply and Sewerage Act, it replaced the Local Self-Government Engineering Department (Zaheer and Gupta, 1970, pp. 653–66) with the responsibility for the overall planning, developing and financing of water supply and sanitation in the state. The chairman, managing director, financial director and other members of the board of directors are appointed by the state government. Five elected heads of local bodies are also nominated by the state government to sit on the board. Apart from state-level financing, the Jal Nigam is also funded by the centre and institutions such as the LIC (Life Insurance Corporation), World Bank and UNDP, but nevertheless it still faces resource constraints.

Varanasi generates about 125 million litres per day (MLD) of waste water, only 16 per cent of which (20 MLD) is treated by the sewage treatment plants at Benares Hindu University (BHU) and the Diesel Locomotive Works before being discharged into the Ganges. The main treatment at Konia (80 MLD) was to be commissioned in spring 1992. The Jal Nigam is responsible for the construction of sewage treatment facilities and responds to GAP proposals. In the original GAP document the project advisors calculated, on the basis of costs and benefits (water for irrigation, residue sludge as fertilizer and biogas for energy), that these treatment plants would not only be self-sustaining, but also profitable. However, there is very little resource recovery at this stage, and to quote D.G. Jamieson from Thames Water Plc: 'I do not know of any sewage treatment plant which makes a profit, let alone breaks even – reducing costs is more important' (Field Interview, Reading 1989).[4]

Part of the reason that there is, for example, little or no gas being generated by these plants is that the BOD of the incoming waste water is rather low. Academics at BHU, where one such plant has been built, maintain that the raw waste water was not properly analysed by the Jal Nigam before it designed the plant so that the BOD quoted was higher than it actually was: they took a 'grab' sample, rather than an average. Thus, when making a bid for the tender they could say we will charge Rs x for every mg/l of BOD removed or treated. If the actual BOD is 100 mg/l, but they quote it as 200 mg/l, then the 'costs' (payment to them) will increase from $100x$ to $200x$ (Informants Varanasi, 1990).

Moreover, the BOD of the sample varies with the time at which it is taken – during the peak discharge periods the BOD could be 300 mg/l while on average it may be just 50 mg/l. On the whole, however, Indian sewage is 'weaker' (in terms of gas potential) compared to Western sewage, as the diet is largely vegetarian. As Jamieson explains, it is the fat content which generates methane – at least 20 per cent of the sewage content in the UK is fat (solid).

The BHU academics were not consulted in the design of the treatment facility on their campus. Although they offered to build it they received no reply or encouragement from higher authorities – a case of 'foiled participation' or, as Robertson asserts, the public are simply 'not expected to offer significant *technical emendations*' (Robertson, 1984, p. 137). They maintain that there are other and cheaper alternatives to the present treatment plant, such as waste stabilization ponds, which are being used at the Indian Institute of Technology, Kanpur and could have been replicated at BHU for the treatment of wastes being generated on campus.[5]

But the faith of the bureaucracy in their own rational, technocentric knowledge (O'Riordan, 1989, p. 86) serves to exclude others while reinforcing institutional identity (Douglas, 1987, p. 59). Thus, understanding how senior natural resource professionals perceive environmental problems, their causes and solutions is one step towards understanding how certain policies are decided and implemented given that one has little access to the decision-making processes themselves (Caldwell, 1970; Craik, 1970; Sewell, 1971).

Although I was able to conduct fairly long interviews with the chief engineer (CE) and general manager (GM) of the Jal Nigam, I did not have the same kind of luck with others, who were conveniently 'unavailable'.[6] What follows is their perception of participation and the GAP – it is not necessarily representative of the Jal Nigam, but the views of these technocrats are significant given that they are the two most important individuals within the Jal Nigam at Varanasi and, therefore, wield considerable decision-making power.

Public health engineers by training, they have both been associated with the GAP since its inception. They feel satisfied with the work of their own agency, but admit, reluctantly, that there are inter-agency problems in terms of co-ordination: 'Too many agencies involved each working in their own field' (CE).

On public participation in the technical aspects of the GAP (e.g. by the BHU academics) the GM is quite definitive about the expertise and knowledge of the Jal Nigam professionals: 'People have little to contribute to the technical aspects of the GAP – they will only confuse the issue. If you open the plans for discussion it will take longer to achieve results as they (referring to the NGO representatives) will discuss it for years and not do anything.'

As Ingram (1976, p.70) maintains, participation increases the 'costs' of receiving and assimilating information, as not only does it lengthen decision-making processes, but it also questions agency goals and values.

On the other hand, the GM is critical of the obsession that bureaucrats and engineers have with meeting targets (project deadlines) rather than basic objectives – keeping the Ganges clean: 'Targets cannot become objectives, they are simply a means of achieving a particular objective'. In this respect, i.e. the 'objective' side of the programme, he feels that there is a role for the public to play: 'The public must be associated with the monitoring of the pumping stations (to check that there is no waste water leakage). I have brought this up at several Task Force (local coordinating body, headed by the Divisional Commissioner) meetings, but I am a single person and cannot guarantee this happening.'

Such a statement reflects the 'prisoner of bureaucracy' dilemma within which the GM finds himself, literally, trapped, i.e. loyalty to the bureaucratic agency or mission devotion overrides flexibility and innovativeness (Schaffer, 1969, p.190).

Both the CE and GM are very clear about what public participation means in practice and what are the most appropriate mechanisms for encouraging it. According to the GM, such participation involves feelings, emotions and the like: 'It cannot be encouraged by the administration issuing orders or slogans alone. It has to come from the people . . .' The CE believes that the river police and home-guards (next section) are not the most appropriate mechanisms for stopping people from using soap, throwing unburnt bodies or defaecating along the banks of the river. He calls for public education and awareness programmes: 'Until people themselves are prepared to clean or keep clean their river, we will not be able to do so. No one can be stopped by the use of force; public and social sanctions are necessary.'

This discussion illustrates not only the faith the Jal Nigam has in its technical capabilities in terms of pollution control, but also its awareness of the social aspects of such technology, given the nature of the resource it is dealing with and the particular sociocultural context in which the technology is being implemented. However, its conception of public participation is limited to 'soft' options like educating the masses so that they do not pollute the Ganges, which assumes that people are the problem rather than institutions and structures. For example, although it acknowledges that the main source of pollution is sewage and sullage followed by industrial effluents, the CE feels that unless the 'human' sources of pollution (bathing, washing clothes, offering flowers to Ganga, the Goddess, dumping of the dead bodies and carcasses) are stopped, the water quality will not improve. Moreover, the discussion on participation does not consider the mechanics of how some sections of the public can be involved in, for example, monitoring of the pumping stations or in the development of low-cost alternatives such as waste stabilization ponds. In the next part, I look at the river police force as an institutionalized response to the non-technical aspects of water pollution control.

Patrolling the Ganges and the Ghats: For Whom?

In July 1988 the government of Uttar Pradesh installed a river police force at Varanasi, inducted from the cadres of the Special Flood Fight Force of the Provisional Armed Constabulary. Its duties include the checking of drug trafficking and public nuisances such as hooliganism, the cheating of pilgrims and tourists; and preventing people from throwing rubbish or unburnt bodies and animal carcasses into the Ganges or washing clothes or defaecating along the ghats. Moreover, according to the city plan document they are meant to: . . ."*educate, train and mobilize* public opinion against various forms of pollution . . . to provide round the clock rescue and other facilities at festival time, to register and regulate river transportation under safety limits . . .' (GAP, 1987, p.21).

Most people interviewed in Varanasi clearly did not like the police force, as it had failed to build any rapport with them and, it seemed, was only out to harass them. Having a police force has not yet changed anything (least of all, the quality of the Ganges water) it just means that there are more officials to be bribed by the public, by those that can afford to do so.

Pandit Tiwari explains that sometimes when the police find a dead body floating down the river in their vicinity, they simply push it along to the next outpost where it becomes someone else's responsibility. Furthermore, they take money from the municipal corporation to cremate unidentified dead bodies, but then throw them, unburnt, into the river.[7] According to Amarnath Yadav, a BJP MLA: 'When the protectors have become the eaters, then what is the point of protection? At least 90 per cent of the unburnt bodies thrown into the Ganga are done so by the police or with their prior consent' (Field Interview, Varanasi 1990).

The Superintendent of Police (SSP), though he denies knowledge of this practice, admits that there is probably some corruption in the force as there is with any government service because of the poor conditions of pay and service. They have no proper quarters: they live in a large makeshift tent out on the steps of the main bathing ghat and in similar tents at other outposts.

The point is not whether there should or should not be a pollution control or monitoring mechanism, but whether it should be state-imposed and, more specifically, whether it should be seen as the task of the police (who have a bad reputation nationwide) to enforce this mechanism, however defined.

'We don't need a police force to keep the Ganga clean – the impetus should come from the people,' said Dr Anand Krishnan, Dean of the Fine Arts Faculty at BHU (Field Interview, 1988). There are many who agree with this viewpoint, for the river police have little, if any, community education or extension work practice, they do not know how to communicate with the people in a language that they understand, and nor do they respect their customs, or their knowledge of their environment.

Failure to regulate means that the very reason for regulation becomes discredited. But it also necessitates a search for alternative and hopefully more effective means of regulation which include local water users (Uphoff, 1989). Since the State and the bureaucracy have been ineffective at mobilizing public support for the GAP we have, as the next section considers, a third factor, namely the NGO. My discussion will be focused on the Sankat Mochan Foundation, the largest of the NGOs in Varanasi.[8]

The Sarkat Morchan Foundation – People or Power Centred?

NGOs can be defined as formalized institutions, i.e. 'sets of structured relationships with legally determined boundaries and functions' (Shepherd *et al.*, 1986, p.iv). This does not imply that they all necessarily function as such: some are more structured than others and have the resource to technically 'operate'. In the Indian context, NGOs have largely been appreciated for their ability to respond to locally perceived needs using innovative and flexible methodologies, to try and ensure that development not only meets the needs of those it is seeking to develop, but does so in a just and equitable framework, in terms of both people and the environment (Shiva and Bandyopadhyay, 1988; Shah, 1989; Sethi, 1989).

However, any discourse on NGOs must look at both their relationship with the State and at who constitutes and runs these organizations, for all too often attempts to strengthen these institutions as part of the drive to 'restructure decentralization' only serve to increase the power of those already in power. While there is a growing body of writing on the former interaction (Fernandez, 1987; Tandon, 1989; Omvedt, 1989), there is little work on the patterns of power and participation within NGOs (Farrington and Biggs, 1990, p. 7), partly because of the nature and process of such information collection. To understand how NGOs function, one has to be a participant observer. In doing so, relationships are built and it becomes very hard to take an objective stand. Moreover, NGOs work with little formal administration, and there is little by way of records etc.

The Sankat Mochan Foundation (SMF) was established in July 1982 to raise public awareness of the pollution of the Ganges and the growing deterioration of Varanasi (Sankat Mochan Foundation, 1983). In Sanskrit, *sankat mochan* means the removal of all sufferings and hardships of the people. It is the name of the second most popular temple in Varanasi, whose 'mahant' (hereditary head) Veer Bhadra Mishra (from now on referred to as Mahantji) is also Professor of Hydraulic Engineering at BHU. He is especially suited as a leader (President of the SMF) as he embodies the confrontation of religion and science surrounding efforts to clean the Ganges (Wilson, 1986):

> One day (1975) I had to choose a spot where I could take a dip in Gangaji. It was a very painful realization, but not a difficult one to make for I saw raw

sewage floating on the surface of the river and dead bodies etc. I started talking and writing articles in newspapers describing the increasing levels of pollution of the Ganga and their effects on Banaras and Banarasis. At first, people thought I was crazy – didn't I have enough work to do at the temple and at BHU they asked, besides, how could Gangaji be polluted? . . . But gradually, they began to listen. (Field Interview, Varanasi 1990)

The initial planning phase of the SMF was supported by an endowment of Rs 200 000 from the temple and private contributions from concerned individuals. Professional expertise was sought from interested persons in the country and abroad. In autumn 1982, Mahantji visited the USA at the invitation of environmentalists there, particularly Pete Seeger, who started the Hudson River Clearwater Campaign (Ahmed, 1989), looking for some way to connect the work of the SMF with friends in North America. As a result of discussions with various members of the Tides Foundation, San Francisco, the 'Friends of the Ganges Fund' was established to:

1 support the work of the SMF by providing technical and financial assistance, albeit limited; and
2 foster global awareness of the significance of health problems caused by water pollution in India and elsewhere.

In November 1982, Mahantji, along with the support of academics, religious leaders and politicians amongst others, launched the Swatcha Ganga Abhiyan (Clean Ganga Campaign), a public education programme to make people aware of the plight of the Ganges and to formulate a people's approach to the issues and problems at hand. Today the campaign organizes, on a relatively periodic basis, a children's painting competition on the theme of river pollution, a Kavi Sammelan (three-day poetry festival) and a Log Sangit Sammelan (three-day folk music festival) where poems and songs in praise of the Ganges are united with a more important environmental message.

In addition, there is an environmental education programme in some of the larger and better endowed schools such as the Tulsi Vidya Niketan and the Besant schools.[9] However, because of the sporadic nature of such efforts and the fact that awareness and knowledge are but the first steps in any environmental education programme (Balasubramaniam, 1984), it is too early to judge how far such action has or can be translated into the development of attitudes, values and skills which will help towards participation in environmental decision-making or in work at the community level outside the formal education system.

The SMF also collects and analyses water samples from the main bathing ghats at its small laboratory. It feels that data generated by the government agencies on the quality of the Ganges are unreliable, when it is available, and that there is a need for an independent 'watchdog body' to check their results by undertaking their own assessments. But the problem for the SMF is that they do not have the technical, human and financial resources to disseminate their data and so, as an ex-bureaucrat remarked recently, 'it is redundant.'[10]

Swatcha Ganga began by capitalizing on people's traditional love for Mother Ganga, by asking them the simple rhetorical question: 'Would you do this to your *Mother?*' 'I say to them, "Isn't the pollution a disrespect to your mother? Is it not spitting over your mother?" That disturbs people and they are ready to do anything if you put the problem in this way.' (Mahantji, quoted in Berwick, 1990, p.29).

Although Baranasis have a living relationship with the Ganges which the campaign has used to its advantage, the traditions which hold the Ganges sacred do not always contribute to her preservation. As Peavey (1986, p. 106) comments: 'People's relationship to the Ganga is born of habit. It hasn't been rethought for many generations.' It is for the SMF to question and encourage others to question those religious practices, such as the dumping of unburnt bodies into the Ganges which, given increases in population and demand for water supply, should, arguably, not be allowed to continue.[11]

At another level, the momentum which is generated at public events organized by the SMF is not channelled into constructive activity. There is simply no structure for people to get involved in the activities of the SMF, as the office-cum-information centre maintained by the SMF is only open in the late evenings, i.e. after 7 p.m. This means that women and children crucial to Swatcha Ganga's objectives are unlikely to visit it unless accompanied by a male or older member of the family. Moreover, as all the executives hold full-time jobs elsewhere (mostly as lecturers at BHU), any action taken by them is difficult to sustain (Ahmed, 1990).

Thus, much of the public relations work rests on the charisma of one person – Mahantji. Effective leadership demands patience, flexibility and the ability to communicate in a language which the community can understand. As the leader, both of Swatcha Ganga and the Sankat Mochan Temple, Mahantji is bound by religious norms. He continues to bathe in the Ganges (partly for his own personal contentment) but he has stopped sipping the water three times while bathing (a practice called *achamaan*) for he knows it can be dangerous.

Mahantji has a certain aura which has helped to attract not only some local people to the campaign, but also numerous national and international visitors wanting to make videos, films, write articles, etc. Mahantji speaks gently, yet his graceful demeanour can be both angry and passionate when deliberating the injustice to the Ganges being perpetrated by the human race. It is easy to become mesmerized when listening to him and to understand why he is called the River Man.

The SMF's concern for the Ganges is not far from the ecocentrism preached by the American trancendentalists (O'Riordan, 1981, p. 3) – it is born out of a sense of responsibility for the earth and a plea for a basic ecological understanding of the intimate human–nature relationship also elaborated in the sacred Hindu texts (see Dwivedi, 1988). Such an approach allows the SMF to consider the local community as a homogenous, culturally monolithic unity rather than assess how different groups of people (class and caste-based) are impacted by both pollution and the GAP. Thus, participation is simply equated with the numbers of people who are present at the various cultural events and meetings, who listen passively to the songs, poems and speeches, but have little opportunity to respond (Eldridge, 1984, p. 422). In that respect, it is not dissimilar from the official discourse on participation which, in turn, allows the various NGO leaders to attend, for example, the GAP Task Force meetings, but is reluctant to share information or decision-making power with them (Robertson, 1984, p.137).

The last section examines how one of the micro-level groups, who are both a cause of river-front pollution and who are affected by the GAP, is being excluded from the concept of participation as defined by the State, the bureaucracy and NGOs.

Besides, Whose Clothes are We Washing? The Dhobis of Varanasi

There are about 15 000 dhobi (washermen) households in Varanasi who use the river-front for washing clothes. Theirs is a hereditary occupation and the dhobis are one of the lowest scheduled castes in the country, with little access to education or alternative sources of income (partly because of the nature of their work, which in a ritual sense is deemed polluting, since they handle the dirty clothing, including menstrual clothing, of other persons of other castes).

The colonial powers attempted to restrict the washing of clothes along certain stretches of the Ganges, for it was feared that the dirt from these garments would contaminate the water for people bathing downstream and the use of soap and detergents was also considered unsound.[12] Likewise, under the GAP, periodic attempts have been made to prohibit the washing of clothes in the Ganges, for not only do the authorities believe that it contaminates the river (despite the absence of any scientific data to support this contention), but perhaps more significantly, for them that is, it spoils the panoramic view of the ghats.

In 1986 the dhobis formed a union when it became clear that their occupational livelihood was being threatened by the GAP. Their leader, Laxman Prasad Kanujia, is literate and has some organizing experience as he has been in politics for the past 10 years, originally with the Socialist Party and now with the BJP. He is helped by an executive committee and ward representatives who inform the dhobis about meetings through word of mouth.

On 28 March 1988, 11 dhobis were arrested by the river police force for allegedly violating the pollution control measures under the GAP. Their arrest immediately sparked off a demonstration outside the main city centre police station and the dhobis were released later that day on personal bonds. However, the next morning none of the dhobis went to work. Instead, they walked with their donkeys and banners to the administrator's house, where they sat in protest against the so-called ban on washing clothes in the Ganges. They complained about the way they were being constantly harassed by the police when the local administration had failed to provide them with alternative washing arrangements: 'What pollution will they (the government) stop when they are so corrupt themselves? The government is trying to move the poor, but though they are powerless they will not move; they will only get poorer if they do so' (Field Interview with Kanujia, 1988).

By spring 1990 the government had built two large dhobi ghats downstream of the main sewage pumping station at Konia. Not only are these facilities too far away for them to walk to on a daily basis when their only means of transport are their old and slow donkeys, but they were not designed in consultation with them so that the structure is totally inappropriate for their needs.[13]

Between 1988 and 1990 the dhobi leaders had held extensive discussions with the city administration. Moreover, they had shown them various tanks and ponds within the city which could be developed as washing places, accessible to the majority of dhobis (e.g. one water tank could serve dhobis from 10 neighbouring wards). The fact that this local knowledge was never incorporated into the formal plans, let alone considered until after money was sanctioned, is a clear indication of the faith the GAP authorities have in their own professional expertise, even if it proves to be ineffective or useless (Redclift, 1987, p. 151).

Popular support for the dhobis' cause exists only at a verbal level – there is little media coverage of their actions. Kanujia did not want to involve local politicians, whom he felt had a habit of appearing at public meetings to dominate the podium, usually in an effort to gain votes, doing very little active work the rest of the time. As for the NGO leaders like Mahantji, he felt that they did not think about the poor but were happy to make grandiose speeches about the need to clean the Ganges.

Kanujia also thought it unfair that other economic groups such as the milkmen, whose water buffaloes were contributing to the pollution of the Ganges when they bathed, were not being asked to move. The Yadav (milkmen caste) were economically and politically strong (at that time) in the UP and local government and, therefore, he maintained no one could (physically) touch them.

It is clear that the administration in their efforts to achieve the goals of the GAP (or at least being seen to be trying to) have decided to pick on a weak and poor community. There are other more critical sources of pollution (sewage and industrial waste water) at Varanasi but because it takes time to build a treatment plant the local authorities have decided that there must be something they can do which will meet the approval of the central and state-level GAP monitoring bodies, who have been fairly critical of their slow progress to date. According to the mayor, the orders to stop using soap in the Ganges emanate from Delhi, which feels the pinch, as it were, from major funding agencies who constantly want to see quick results. He blames the bureaucrats for their lack of foresight in the implementation of the GAP – projects are drawn up in Delhi with little knowledge of grassroot realities.

The divisional commissioner (a top-ranking IAS bureaucrat) on the other hand, was quite unsympathetic: 'No one wants to shift, but sometimes you have to impose your force of will on people in the national interest' (Field Interview, Varanasi 1991).

But, as Kanujia explains:

> Washing my clothes is my business, what else can I do – steal? All the Hindus think that the Ganga is their Mother – I have no disagreement with the efforts to clean the river, though they are just eating the money. But what are you doing for my family? If we don't wash clothes, we don't get food and we are not so literate that we can find other jobs. And if we do, then who will wash the clothes? . . . I am fighting for my future and that of my children – this is not just a problem for me . . . but a question of survival for the community . . . I have to continue to struggle. (Field Interview, 1990).

The dhobi leader's remarks suggest that the control of pollution through the application of technology is not by itself a sufficient solution in terms of sustainable water management. That is, the quantitative and qualitative aspects of environmental damage or the remedies suggested can no longer be separated, if 'sustainability' is a desired long-term objective (Barbier, 1987, p. 103). As Tulsidas Mishra, a Varanasi journalist, remarks: 'If development is hurting the *rights* of the poor and weaker people, then it is not *development*' (Field Interview, Varanasi 1990).

Participation and Power: Readdressing the Dilemma

> The more the economics and politics of development are kept out of reach of the masses, the more they (the masses) are asked to 'participate' in them. For they are told that it is for them that 'development' takes place. (Kothari in Escobar, 1984, p. 399)

Participation, unlike salt, is not a missing ingredient which can simply be sprinkled on to enhance flavour or obtain a specific result. The GAP was not designed as a participatory environmental project (Drijver, 1989, p. 3) despite politically sanguine claims about it being a 'people's programme'. On the contrary, it reflects poor top-to-bottom communication, it is acceptable precisely because it does not challenge the existing institutional order, and its participatory content is symbolic rather than substantive. As Panna Lal Yadav, a local councillor, puts it: 'In my opinion, they (the GAP) forgot to include the people' (Field Interview, Varanasi 1990).

The technological dichotomy of the rational decision-making process – 'professionalism' – creates uncoordinated, fragmented and eventually expensive 'knowledge' (systems of expertise) which renders invisible the knowledge and lives of the people whose daily means of subsidence is intricately interwoven with the resource base at which development is directed. Further, bureaucratic politics, what Schaffer calls 'bureaucratics' (Schaffer, 1980, p. 189), maintains a cult of insideness or incorporation, based on institutionalized patterns of procedure, privileges, favoured conditions and a language of authority.

Not only do bureaucratic institutions create, classify and control information, but they also distort information flows to both the public and political leadership. Limited data are made available to the public at the best of times (and that too with much manipulation) while project progress is often not correctly 'signalled' (Hart, 1988, p. 26) to senior bureaucrats if it is felt that such information may penalize lower-level bureaucrats. Thus, institutional legitimacy (Douglas, 1987, p. 92) is maintained despite visible inefficiency and ineffectiveness.

Moreover, the NGOs in Varanasi, at least, work within the socio-economic and politico-administrative framework of the city and do not pose a significant threat to either the hegemony of the State or dominant social groups. They are run by individuals '. . . whose views are liberal and paternalistic rather than radically egalitarian' (Midgley, 1986b, p. 155). In the case of the SMF, the so-called charismatic leadership, while important for organizational building, is rigid and hierarchical and does not provide for a second echelon of leadership. In addition, it has made the NGO something of an international showpiece, '. . . a place of pilgrimage for international development tourists' (Midgley, 1986b, p. 157).

Their 'participatory' efforts (and that of the State) are based on the religious and cultural symbolism associated with the Ganges which, although it '. . . represents an environment of trust for the believer' (Giddens, 1990, p. 103), does not question the nature and distribution of the power in society. Thus, they are more concerned in saving the Ganges rather than the lives of the people who are dependent on it as an economic resource and who are being impacted by the GAP.

The discourse of participation needs to recognize and accommodate a realistic assessment of the possible. That is, some measure of State intervention, with respect to water pollution control, cannot be avoided because of the State's traditional role as the provider of the common good and its access to resources to do so. Given the inability of NGOs in Varanasi to complement this activity on a sizeable scale, such intervention, whatever the misgivings and costs, is likely to continue, slowly but unhindered. Those at the top will, in the absence of middle-level pressure, extract their dues; those at the bottom will suffer social and economic exploitation quietly and the Ganges will inevitably never be as clean as it should and could be.

Participation must be based on recognition that the public is not a homogenous entity with a clearly articulated sense of the 'common good'. Rather it must begin from the bottom as a process of empowerment, building upon the general desire for a cleaner Ganges, but not overlooking the specific demands of those who are being affected by such efforts. Egalitarian, co-operative and flexible leadership is necessary, for community-building is a slow and painful process at the best of times and in the climate of distrust which is the political reality of much of India today, it will require great courage to rebuild trust in the interest of their environment and their future.

Notes

1 In Hess and Singh (1986, p. 57). Kabir was a fifteenth century saint-cum-poet who lived in Varanasi. He ridiculed all formalized religions, though each claimed him as its disciple.
2 Rajiv Gandhi in *The Gangu Action Plan – An Exhibition* (n.d.), p. 3.
3 Although state-level governments are responsible for the development and management of water resources, according to the constitution, the centre reserves the power to regulate and develop inter-state rivers and river valleys. Conflict is inevitable – between Union and state governments, between upstream and downstream users and between local people and the State over the definition of national interest and public good. See Shiva (1991, pp. 183–329).
4 Dr Jamieson is the Director of Thames Water International operations in India, responsible for the technological assistance being rendered to the GAP.
5 Waste stabilization ponds are basically large shallow ponds in which organic wastes are decomposed by micro-organisms in a combination of natural processes involving both bacteria and algae. They have simple maintenance requirements and lower costs than conventional sewage treatment and ensure better pathogen removal. But care needs to be taken to keep the area around the pond free of vegetation as they become breeding sites for mosquitoes.
6 Both the CE and GM did not want me to interview middle-level engineers. They thoroughly enforced their positions as 'gatekeepers' in this context, restricting access to others.
7 In 1989 the crematorium at Harishcandra ghat, one of the traditional cremating ghats at Varanasi, began operating. It costs Rs 50 to cremate a body in the crematorium as opposed to more than Rs 400 on a fuelwood pyre. The municipal corporation meets the cremation expenses of unidentified bodies in the crematorium.
8 Although other groups have been identified as NGOs at this level, they have little in the way of infrastructure or resources compared to the SMF with whom I stayed during my research visits.
9 This environmental education programme is usually activated by a group of Swedish teachers who visit Varanasi every winter, bringing with them teaching resources which are then locked away till they return next year.

10 Martand Singh, then Secretary of the Indian National Trust for Art and Cultural Heritage (INTACH, Delhi) at a heated discussion at Mahantji's residence, Varanasi, 1990.
11 This is easier said than done, since it involves a number of interests: religious believers who maintain that the bodies of sadhus (saints), children under the age of 12 and those who die of infectious diseases should not be burnt; poor people who simply cannot afford the facilities of the crematorium; and the river police, who comply with the system by allegedly allowing some bodies to be dumped into the Ganges.
12 Suggestions were continuously being made to relocate the dhobis either to the opposite bank of the Ganges or further downstream. Not until 1935 was the first bye-law passed to regulate the washing of clothes away from the main bathing ghats.
13 The dhobis took me to see these ghats – not only is there no space for them to dry clothes, but the design consists of little cubicles having an inlet and outlet for water, in which they are meant to stand knee-deep. They felt that they would end up splashing each other with water and that this would lead to needless fighting.

References

Agarwal,'S.L. (ed.) (1980) *Legal Control of Environmental Pollution*. New Delhi: Indian Law Institute.

Ahmed, S. (1989) The Clearwater Runs Deep. *The Times of India*, Bombay, 26 June, p. 4 (Sunday Review).

Ahmed, S. (1990) Cleaning the Ganga: rhetoric and reality. *Ambio*, **19**(1), 42–5.

Balasubramaniam, A. (1984) *Ecodevelopment – Towards a Philosophy of Environmental Education*. Bonn: Friederich Naumann Stuftung.

Barbier, E.B. (1987) The concept of sustainable economic development. *Environmental Conservation*, **1**(2), 101–10.

Berwick, D. (1990) Sacred and Profane. *The Sunday Times*, London, 1 July, pp. 23–30 (Sunday Magazine).

Caldwell, L.K. (1970) Authority and responsibility for environmental administration. *Annals of the American Academy of Political and Social Science*, **389**, 107–15.

Centre for Science and Environment (1985) *The State of India's Environment 1984–85: A Citizen's Report*. New Delhi: Centre for Science and Environment.

Cernea, M.M. (ed.) (1985) *Putting People First – Sociological Variables in Rural Development*. Oxford: Oxford University Press.

Craik, K.H. (1970) The environmental dispositions of environmental decision makers. *Annals of the American Academy of Political and Social Science*, **389**, 87–94.

Diwan, P. (ed.) (1987) *Environment Protection – Problems, Policy Administration and Law*. New Delhi: Deep and Deep.

Douglas, M. (1966) *Purity and Danger – An Analysis of Concepts of Pollution and Taboo*. London: Ark.

Douglas, M. (1987) *How Institutions Think*. London: Routledge.

Douglas, M. and Wildavsky, A. (1983) *Risk and Culture – An Essay on the Selection of Technical and Environmental Dangers*. Berkely: University of California Press.

Drijver, C.A. (1989) *People's Participation in Environmental Projects in Developing Countries*. Leiden University: Papers on Environments and Development, no. 10.

Dwivedi, O.P. (1988) Man and Nature: an holistic approach to a theory of ecology. *The Environmental Professional*, **10**(1), 8–15.

Eck, D.L. (1982) *Banares – City of Light*. New York: Alfred A. Kropf.

Eldridge, P. (1984) The political role of community action groups in India and Indonesia: in search of a general theory. *Alternatives*, **10**(3), 401–34.

Escobar, A. (1984) Discourse and power in development: Michel Foucault and the relevance of his work to the Third World. *Alternatives*, **10**(3), 377–400.

Farrington, J. and Biggs, S.D. (1990) NGOs, agricultural technology and the rural poor. *Food Policy*, **15**(6), 39–49.

Fernandez, A.P. (1987) NGOs in South Asia: People's Participation and Partnership. *World Development* **15**, 39–49.

GAP (Central Ganga Authority) (1987) *Ganga Action Plan*. New Delhi: CGA.

Gaur, K.D. (1987) Judicial approach to environmental laws. In P. Diwan (ed.) *Environment Protection*, pp. 465–75.

Giddens, A. (1990) *The Consequences of Modernity*. Cambridge: Polity Press.

Hart, H.C. (1988) Political leadership in India: dimensions and limits. In A. Kohli (ed.) *India's Democracy*, pp. 18–61.

Hasan, Z., Jha, S.N. and Khan, R. (eds) (1989) *The State, Political Processes and Identity – Reflections on Modern India*. New Delhi: Sage.

Hayward, T. (1990) Ecosocialism – Utopian and Scientific. *Radical Philosophy*, no. 56, 2–14.

Hess, L. and Singh, S. (1986) *The Bijak of Kabir*. New Delhi: Motilal Banarsidass.

Holloway, R. (ed.) (1989) *Doing Development: Government, NGOs and the Rural Poor in South Asia*. London: Earthscan.

Ingram, H. (1976) The politics of information: constraints on new sources. In J.C. Pierce and H.R. Doerksen (eds) *Water Politics and Public Involvement*, pp. 63–73.

Jariwala, C.M. (1980) The Constitution 42nd Amendment Act and the environment. In S.L. Agarwal (ed.) *Legal Control of Environmental Pollution*, pp. 1–7.

Khan, R. (1989) The total state: the concept and its manifestation in the Indian political system. In Z. Hasan, S.N. Jha and R. Khan (eds) *The State, Political Processes and Identity*, pp. 33–72. New Delhi: Sage.

Kohli, A. (ed.) (1988) *India's Democracy: An Analysis of Changing State–Society Relations*. Princeton: Princeton University Press.

Korten, D. (ed.) (1986) *Community Management: Asian Experiences and Perspectives*. Connecticut: Kumarian.

Lele, J.K. (1990) The legitimacy question. *Seminar*, no. 367, 21–5.

Leys, C. (ed.) (1969) *Politics and Change in Developing Countries*. Cambridge: Cambridge University Press.

Lisk, F. (ed.) (1985) *Popular Participation in Planning for Development Needs*. Hampshire: Gower.

McGregor, A. (1990) Culture, Blindness, Institutions and the Analysis of Policy in Developing Countries. Paper presented at Development Studies Association Annual Conference, Glasgow.

Midgley, J. (1986a) Community participation: history, concepts and controversies. In Midgley, J., Hall, A., Hardiman, M. and Narine, D. (eds) *Community Participation, Social Development and the State*, pp. 13–44. London: Methuen.

Midgley, J. (1986b) Community participation, the state and social policy. In Midgley, J., Hall, A., Hardiman, M. and Narine, D. (eds) *Community Participation, Social Development and the State*, pp. 145–60.

Midgley, J., Hall, A., Hardiman, M. and Narine, D. (1986) *Community Participation, Social Development and the State*. London: Methuen.

Ministry for Environment and Forests (1985) *An Action Plan for Prevention of Pollution of the Ganga*. New Delhi: Ministry for Environment and Forests.

Ministry for Environment and Forests (1987) *The Ganga Action Plan – Varanasi Chapter: An Introduction*.

Ministry for Environment and Forests (n.d.) *The Ganga Action Plan – An Exhibition*.

Montgomery, J.D. (1988) *Bureaucrats and People – Grassroots Participation in Third World Development*. London: John Hopkins.

Muralidharan, S. (1986) The Ganga clean-up: consequences of politics. *Business India*, 8–21 September, 80–3.

Nandy, A. (1989) The political culture of the Indian state. *Daedalus*, **118**(4), 1–26.

O'Connor, J. (1989) Uneven and combined development and ecological crises: a theoretical introduction. *Race and Class*, **30**(3), 1–11.

Omvedt, G. (1989) Ecology and social movements. In H. Alavi and J. Harriss (eds) *South Asia*, pp. 288–96. Basingstoke: Macmillan.

O'Riordan, T. (1981) *Environmentalism*. London: Pion Ltd.

O'Riordan, T. (1989) The challenge for environmentalism. In R. Peet and N. Thrift (eds), *New Models in Geography*, Vol. 1, pp. 77–102.

Patnaik, A.K. (1990) Relative autonomy. *Seminar*, no. 367, 26–30.

Peavey, F. (1986) *Heart Politics*. Philadelphia: New Society Publications.

Peet, R. and Thrift, N. (eds) (1989) *New Models in Geography*, Vol. 1. London: Unwin Hyman.

Pierce, J.C. and Doerksen, H.R. (eds) (1976) *Water Politics and Public Involvement*, Man, the Community and Natural Resources Series, no. 4. Ann Arbor Science. Ann Arbor: Michigan.

Redclift, M. (1987) *Sustainable Development: Exploring the Contradictions*. London: Methuen.

Robertson, A.F. (1984) *People and the State – An Anthropology of Planned Development*. Cambridge: Cambridge University Press.

Sankat Mochan Foundation (1983) *Ganga*. A Newsletter, Varanasi.

Schaffer, B. (1969) The Deadlock in development administration. In C. Leys (ed.), *Politics and Change in Developing Countries*, pp. 177–211.

Schaffer, B. (1980) Insiders and outsiders: insideness, incorporation and bureaucratic politics. *Development and Change*, **11**, 187–210.

Sethi, H. (1989) Resource conflicts: recent trends in policy and struggle. *Social Action*, **39**(2), 191–7.

Sewell, W.R.D. (1971) Environmental perceptions and attitudes of engineers and public health officials. *Environment and Behaviour*, **3**(1), 23–59.

Shah, G. (1989) Grassroots mobilization in Indian politics. In A. Kohli (ed.), *India's Democracy*, pp. 262–304. Oxford: Princeton University Press.

Shepherd, A., Fraser, C. and Kalimullah, N.A. (1986) *NGOs in India – Aspects of the Current Debate*. Papers in the Administration of Development no. 25. Birmingham: Institute of Local Government.

Shiva, V. (1991) *Ecology and the Politics of Survival – Conflicts Over Natural Resources in India*. New Delhi: Sage.

Shiva, V. and Bandyopadhyay, J. (1988) Political economy of ecology movements. *Economic and Political Weekly*, **23**(24), 1223–32.

Singh, C. (1986) *Common Property, Common Poverty*. New Delhi: Oxford University Press.

Slater, D. (1989) Territorial power and the peripheral state: the issue of decentralization. *Development and Change*, **20**, 501–31.

Tandon, R. (1989) The state and voluntary agencies in India. In R. Holloway (ed.), *Doing Development*, pp. 12–29. London: Earthscan.

Uphoff, N. (ed.), *Improving International Irrigation Management with Farmer Participation: Getting the Process Right*. Studies in Water Policy and Management no. 11. Boulder: Westview.

Walker, K.J. (1989) The state in environmental management: the ecological dimension. *Political Studies*, **37**(3), 25–38.

Wilson, R.T. (1986) Along the Ganga – Environmental Consciousness and Cultural Performance. Unpublished dissertation, University of Wisconsin, Maddison.

Zaheer, M. and Gupta, J. (1970) *The Organization of the Government of Uttar Pradesh*. New Delhi: S. Chard.

PART IV

Downstream

10

Environmental Myth as International Politics: the Problems of the Bengal Delta

Graham P. Chapman

Popular Explanation and Recent Floods in Bengal

In 1987 and 1988 Bangladesh suffered from two widespread and damaging floods, some of the worst of those for which reasonable records exist. The popular press was quick to build on anxiety (expressed in such publications as Eckholm's (1976) book *Losing Ground*) about deforestation in the Himalayas because of fuelwood scarcity and the farmers' land hunger, consequent excessive run-off and high silt loads leading to deposition on the plains and increased flooding. That such a simplistic view could cause great damage by warping political relations and changing development priorities was noted by Ives (1989) and by Ives and Messerli (1989), and yet it is still widely current.

In a recent paper entitled 'Indo-Bangladesh common rivers: the impact on Bangladesh', published in a new and serious journal *Contemporary South Asia*, Islam (1992) has highlighted what he perceives as the deleterious consequences that follow from the fact that India and Bangladesh share so many rivers (57 are recognized). The list of evils which he notes is widened as follows (p. 215):

> The consequences of hydrological change [note: on which of the shared rivers is not specified] because of upstream diversion are as follows:
> 1) siltation and rise of river beds leading to flood, demolition of river embankment and changed river course: 2) decreased soil moisture and increased salinity leading to desertification; 3) decreased water level leading to problems in agriculture, industry, navigation, fishery and domestic use; 4) decreasing upstream flow leading to saline intrusion in the coastal area and damage to mangrove forest. (Islam, 1992).

As if that was not enough, Islam also notes armed clashes between Indian and Bangladesh border forces over border demarcation in areas where the rivers are shifting their courses. This generalized list includes charges relating to floods and also to the lack of water and desertification. It is a list which has been derived from observation of present problems only, with no sense of the history of environmental change in Bengal. Further, the culprit is seen in singular terms as upstream management – meaning in this context India. Now, there are indeed many environmental problems in Bangladesh, many of which have upstream elements within their complex set of causes, most of these elements being natural and a few artificial. But to group all these problems together, and then attribute them in such a singular way without a proper investigation of their causes, is not intellectually sound.

Why should this happen? At one level it is easy to say that there is a simple political motivation to embarrass India: but I do not doubt the sincerity of the authors who write like this, and such an answer does not really address the issue that the claims are seen to be real by the people that make them. The problem is partly that it is in the nature of the human–environment interface that there are many complex causes, and many resultant effects, making it difficult to disentangle natural from anthropogenic changes. But it is also more than that: our ideas of cause and effect in science are heavily biased towards experiment and replication, and the derivation of general principles, which are valid for all places and all times. Such an approach undercuts the value of historical and uniquist explanation.

One strand of this chapter is therefore to consider some of the environmental problems of Bangladesh. But another and equally important strand is a consideration of environmental claims making.

Environmental Claims Making

This is the subject of research in Europe by Burgess and Harrison (1993). From this work it is quite clear that there is a relationship between popular understanding of the environment, the media's need to process these issues as news stories, and wider political responses. Given the limited factual basis to knowledge of most environmental issues, and given the enormous scope for collision between conflicting value systems, such as conservation versus development, it is often not the issue itself which steers the debate, but the preconceptions that proponents bring to it. This has, of course, been well highlighted in Chapter 2 of this book.

I wish next to introduce a separate idea (but not yet properly researched), namely the expectation that 'urban Western man' has of the concept of 'knowledge'. Because of the legacy of Baconian science, knowledge is intimately tied up with the idea of controlled experiment, of management, and of technical hardware solutions. In such an approach knowledge derived from experiment can be replicated. It is thus essentially an *ahistorical* approach to knowing, since laws are held to be universal in time and space. It is also an approach which tends to trivialize the complex specificities of place – whether in ecological or cultural terms. This approach to the definition of knowledge is worldwide – it has also been implanted in most officials and educationalists of the developing countries, and its consequences are clearly seen. At the 1992 United Nations Conference on Environment and Development at Rio, academics and politicians were alerted to possible long-term feedback relationships such as those underlying the thesis of global warming. But these concerns are now projected on a public whose understanding *and expectation* of 'knowing' lacks historical depth. The result is somewhat perverse. A single year of drought in Britain is evidence in the newspapers of global warming: a single cold wet winter, evidence that the thesis is a sham. With respect to Bengal, undoubtedly there are many changes occurring now in the delta. But there always have been. Thus what perhaps is different now is the perception of those changes, that they necessarily have an anthropogenic cause – implying that humans have caused a disruption of a natural equilibrium.

Thus, to summarize, what distresses me about Islam's paper on the common rivers is both the lack of any (geo)historical depth and the willingness to appeal to pseudo-universals (i.e. 'desertification'). The next section of this chapter therefore tries cursorily to fill in some of the geo-historical background to Bengal's problems, and, for reasons which will become apparent later, to include some recorded details of the impacts of seismic forces on the delta.

Formation of the Bengal Delta

The way in which our understanding of plate tectonics has in turn explained the raising of the Himalayas has been spelt out in Chapter 1. The process has resulted in a dramatic landscape – of the highest mountains on earth in one of the highest rainfall/precipitation areas, many rocks of recent origin and low resistance, leading to massive rates of erosion and sedimentation, both on the plains of India and in the delta of Bangladesh. The rates of erosion and deposition have varied as the climate has changed – and, of course, at some times the rivers have incised themselves even into their recent deposits as sea levels have fallen. During the height of the last pleistocene glaciation, sea level was much lower than it is now. The rivers (proto-Ganges–Brahmaputra) incised their courses into whatever form the proto-delta took. During the retreat of the ice-caps and the rapid rise in sea levels, the river discharges from the Himalayas were presumably much higher than now, and the sediment certainly of a different nature,

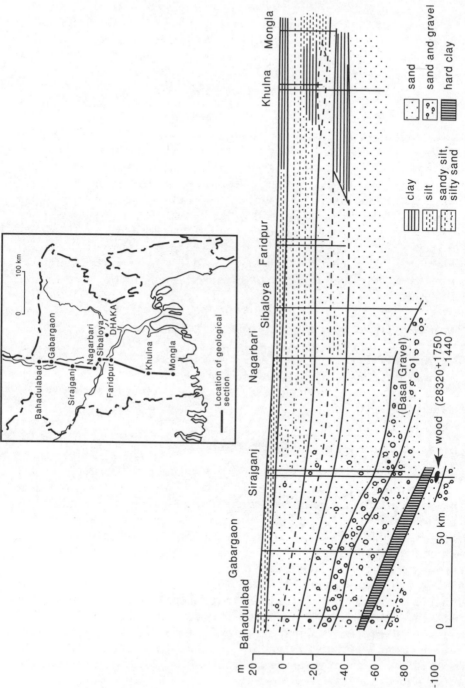

Figure 10.1 Cross-section of deposits in Bengal delta. *Source:* Umitsu (1987).

being more sandy/gravelly and less silty. The cross-section of the lower delta in Figure 10.1 shows a mixture of gravels, sands and clays, which is partly a function of distance from main channels, since floods deposit fine alluvium far from the river channels, whereas bedloads are coarser sands.

The relative sea level is thus a function of several variables, including the eustatic post-glacial changes (accounting for much of the change in Figure 10.2), tectonic uplift or depression of different areas, rates of silt deposition, and rates of silt compaction. Figure 10.2 suggests that there is no reason to expect complete stability in an indefinite future.

The landforms of the whole Ganges–Brahmaputra plains are still highly dynamic. The inland equivalents of the delta are the alluvial fans at the foot of the mountains, across which the rivers migrate as they drop their loads. The Kosi has migrated 100 km west in 250 years (see Figure 4.7), and the Tista has behaved similarly (see below); the Beas (Indus basin) was captured by the Chenab in 1790 (Buckley, quoted in Michel, 1967, p. 48). Below, further information is given on the movement of rivers within Bangladesh. Figure 10.3 summarizes the landforms of the delta; the movement of the Ganges across its successive levees is quite clear. Since the British arrived and founded Calcutta (1670s), it has become evident that there is a long-term shift of the discharge from the western to the eastern distributaries. The Hooghly has accordingly lost discharge and become more heavily silted. Sarma (1986) reproduces a series of older accounts of the problems of the rivers of Bengal. One of these is a proposal by Franklin in 1861 for a new canal from the Bagirathi/Hooghly to the Matabanga (a distributary parallel to and to the east of the Hooghly). He says (Franklin, in Sarma, 1986, p. 21):

> Now the result of the rivers to the south-east having their greatest velocities towards the end of the floods instead of the beginning, is that they scour out for themselves and carry into Soonderbunds the greater portion of their deposit that is brought into them by the Ganges waters, and in addition to this they deepen and widen their channels. Whilst, owing to the Matabanga and other rivers to the southwest becoming sluggish and gorged towards the end of each season's floods, the deposit which is brought into them by the Ganges is to a great extent left in them, and they are gradually silting up and becoming mere overflows to the Ganges during the floods.

From this and a myriad of carefully surveyed water heights, it is clear that the regional scale of change was well understood by some engineers a long time ago.

One can add current process accounts. Coleman in 1969 (quoted in Brammer, 1990b), has recorded lateral erosion of 860 m by the Jamuna in a single year, and bed formations 15 m high by 1000 m long, moving 600 m in a 24-hour period during flood. The Meghna scoured a new channel 45 m deep and half a mile from its previous main channel in a matter of days in 1988 (Rogers, quoted in Brammer, 1990b).

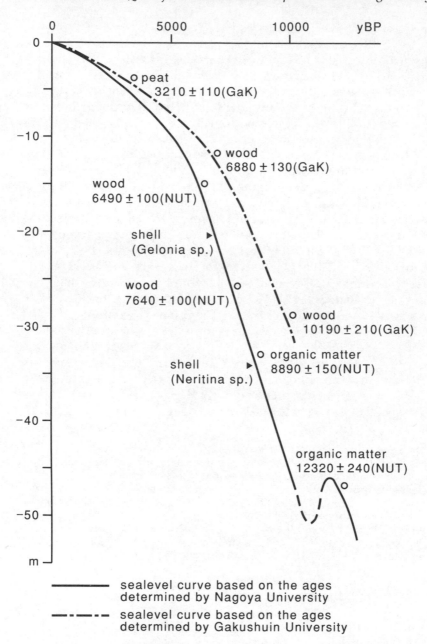

Figure 10.2 Sea-level change in Bengal. *Source:* Umitsu (1987).

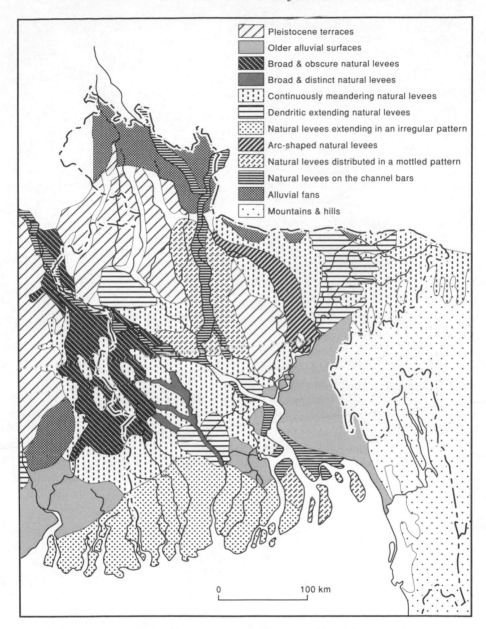

Figure 10.3 Land-forms of the Bengal delta. *Source:* Umitsu (1985).

Seismic Impacts on the Geomorphology of Bengal

The following are extracts from two accounts of the 1887 earthquake which shook the whole of Bengal (and parts of Bihar and Orissa):

The alluvial plain is studded with clusters of hills called Tilas by the inhabitants. A Tila may be only 2 or 3 ft out of the plain; on the other hand, some attain a general altitude of 50 feet. They generally consist of moorum covered by sand, and are used as homestead land . . . The land between the tilas is cultivated except where it consists of bog, often of great depth. Crossing these bogs constituted the chief difficulty in constructing this portion of the railway . . .

The earthquake . . . occurred at 4.30 pm Madras time in the afternoon of the 12th June 1897. It lasted almost 3½ minutes, the oscillations being from east to west at the rate of ten a second. Speaking generally, the earthquake did little or no damage to the railway where it runs through the hills and tilas . . . On the plain however, and between the tilas the damage was enormous . . . At one place where the line crosses a bog known as the Dulcherra, the earthquake shook the bank down into the bog, and left it with almost as much to fill again as when work on it was begun . . .

Near the Khawai [river] the bank opened out in great fissures . . . on the ordinary ground level mud and sand welled out of the fissures and did much damage to the crops. One of the most extraordinary effects of the earthquake occurred at a point 1½ miles east of the Khawai. Here the whole road, bank, rails and bridges for a length of over a mile was shifted about 6 to 8 feet northwards. At Daragaon 5 miles east of Shaistaganj, the west end of the station yard, for its whole width of 4 chains, sank 2 to three feet into the ground; as the ground sank, water welled up, and nothing could be more terrifying to behold than the manner in which the very ground seemed to dissolve in welling water . . .

To restore the line to a condition fit for running would have been easier had the earthquake occurred in any of the earlier months of the year: the ordinary labour in Sylhet, the district through which this part of the railway runs, is all imported from countries west of Calcutta, and it is the custom of the labourers to return to their homes at the beginning of the rains. (Anderson, 1900)

The second account is from the Rangpur District Gazateer (from current northwest Bangladesh). It observes that the earthquake:

was heralded by a loud rumbling noise from the east, followed by instantly yawning fissures, east to west in direction, from which torrents of sand and water poured over the surrounding country . . . Large tracts of cultivated land were covered with a thick layer of sand, causing much damage to cultivated crops and rendering many lands unculturable. The earthquake wrecked or damaged most of the public and private masonry buildings, the railways, all sources of water supply, and almost all the roads and bridges.

. . . The earthquake made great changes in the drainage of the country. The beds of many rivers were upheaved and also contracted by the slipping of their banks . . . Both the Tista and the Ghaghat were reported to have suddenly become fordable in places. The latter river, an important drainage channel in the district was since 1897 a shallow sluggish stream with a weak current and a strong tendency to silt and be choked with aquatic vegetation.

Upheaval in some places was accompanied by subsidence in others. On the whole, the effect of the earthquake was to raise the level of the district. The conversion of considerable arable areas, especially in the Gaibanda sub-division, into uncultivable marshes and swamps would seem to indicate the contrary. This is accounted for by the fact that, in the process of upheaval the country had assumed in places a cup-shaped formation, allowing little or no outlet for accumulated rainfall. Vast new *beels* formed, and the rivers became marshes.

It is suspected that seismic activity played a large part in the change of the Brahmaputra's course (Figure 10.4) from the east side of the Madhopur

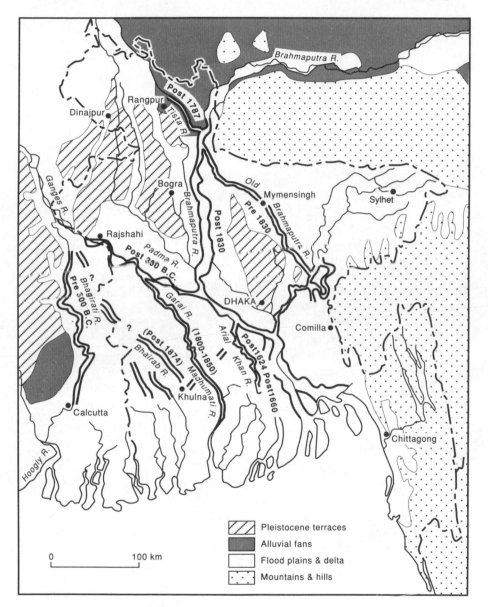

Figure 10.4 Changes in river courses in Bengal. *Source:* Umitsu (1985).

tract to the west side starting in 1830 (Umitsu, 1985, p. 157). The earthquakes of Assam between 1951 and 1956 have been attributed with releasing greatly increased sediment loads (Ives and Messerli, 1989, p. 137) that have contributed to the formation of new islands at the river mouths. Much of the delta itself is sinking, as the sediments compress. The Tista (also noted above) shifted its course suddenly in 1787 during an exceptional flood, only to change it again after the earthquake in 1897 (Johnson, 1975, p. 10).

Hazards in Bengal

Cyclones at the Land–Sea Interface

On 5 October 1864 a massive cyclone struck West Bengal, causing death and destruction far inland. The number of dead from the initial storm damage is unknown, but certainly many more died in the outbreak of disease and starvation that followed. In Calcutta itself there was extensive damage to buildings, and two steamers, the leviathans of the age, were among the 200 boats reported sunk. More recently the parts of Bengal that lie in Bangladesh have been subjected to the terrible storms of November 1970 which probably killed as many as half a million people, and the recent disaster of May 1991 near Chittagong.

These storms are a part of the 'normal hazards' of the Bay of Bengal as a whole – Andhra Pradesh in India has suffered badly in recent years too. But they have a particular impact on the northern coast of the bay, because the tidal waves are here funnelled towards that small part of the delta (iceberg like, much of it is under water) which creeps imperceptibly out of the sea, offering no natural barriers to stem the onrush of the waves.

But also, as with the floods described in the next section, escalating population pressure plays its part in turning adverse conditions into disaster. The population doubling time in Bangladesh is now only 32 years. More people now live in highly exposed coastal sites than ever before.

Floods in Bengal

There are three types of flooding in Bengal, which can happen independently, or (a true calamity) simultaneously. First are flash-floods from adjacent higher ground, usually around the edges of some of the Pleistocene terraces. They come fast and go fast. The second type, rare and mostly confined to the Jamuna, is river flooding, when the major exotic rivers over-top their banks. The third type is rainwater flooding, common everywhere, when the monsoon rains fall faster than they can be drained. This is usual in most of the bhils (beels) and other back-swamps, and the whole of the Meghna/Sylhet depression routinely turns into a lake during the monsoon.

This does not mean that there is necessarily too much water. The impact of the floods depends on the extent to which there is a 'normal' expectation of them and adjustment to them. Agriculture is finely tuned: flooded swamp land is planted as waters recede. In deep-water areas (predominantly in Bangladesh) there are long-strawed rice types that can grow up to 12 inches in 24 hours (Farmer, 1979), and ultimately to 12 feet high, to keep abreast of rising flood waters. But throughout history there have been major floods, often when rainfall floods are backed up by coincident river floods, which have caused major damage. On these occasions crops may be inundated long enough (total submergence for more than 4 days is usually fatal) to be killed off; human lives may be lost; draught animals may be lost with consequent impacts on subsequent land preparation; capital equipment (ploughs, byres, houses) may be lost. In addition, roads and railways may be damaged.

Flood protection levées have therefore been built in various places, some big, some small, some totally enclosing polders, to give some insurance against such losses. The problem is that the rivers shift their courses, and barriers built far back may even find themselves under attack. If such barriers work for some years, and then are breached, the result can be worse than if they had never been built. Given the staggering and ever-increasing population pressure in Bangladesh, people start to live in lower areas which appear safer after a barrier has been built, and hence these people are, almost literally, sitting ducks in the event of a breach of the defences.

The 1987 floods (Figure 10.5) (a map of the actual floods is not possible since there were no cloud-free days for satellite or aerial photography) were predominantly local flash-floods and rainfall floods, whose drainage was impeded by exceptionally high river levels, particularly in the Ganges. The floods of 1988 were predominantly river floods caused by exceptionally heavy rainfall in the Himalayas and the Shillong block. The Brahmaputra (Jumna in Bangladesh) effectively became a river 50 km wide (Brammer, 1990).

Production losses due to the floods in addition to capital losses were very high (see Table 10.1). But the actual yearly production totals were not so bad (Table 10.2). Some farmers were able to resow after the floods subsided, but in general greater emphasis was put on the second season (the rabi) crop, when soil moisture was much higher than usual, and the farmers' efforts were rewarded by higher prices.

Partly this also reflects the growing emphasis on rabi wheat crops and on irrigated boro rice (both outside the monsoon season) which is happening anyway, as cropping intensity rises. Indeed, controlled water from pumpsets in the dry season (from tubewells or rivers) is also seen as offering the best support to new seed types of both wheat and rice.

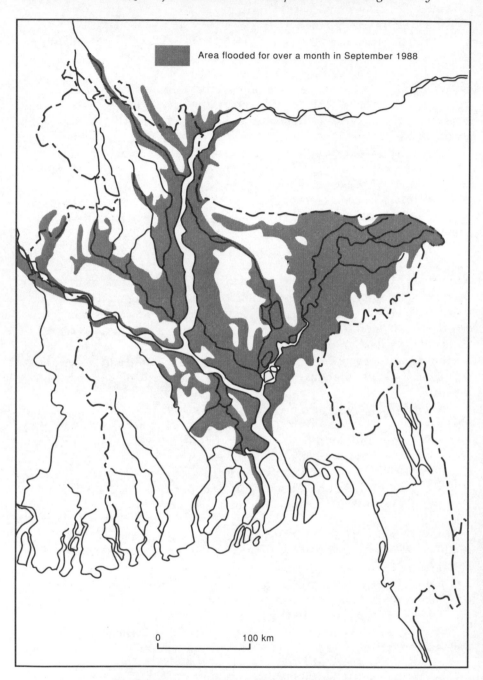

Area flooded for over a month in September 1988

0   100 km

Figure 10.5 Area flooded for over one month, September 1988. *Source:* Brammer (1990).

Table 10.1 Losses due to flooding in Bangladesh, 1987 and 1988.

	1987	1988
Area flooded	57 000 km^2	82 000 km^2
Cattle, goats lost	64 700	172 000
Rice production lost	3.5 million tonnes	2 million tonnes
Trunk roads damaged	1523 km	3000 km
Rural hand tubewells flooded	NA	240 000

Source: Brammer (1990).

Table 10.2 Cereal production in Bangladesh, 1986–1988.

Year	Production (million tonnes)				
	Aus	Aman	Boro	Wheat	Total cereals
1986–1987	3.13	8.27	4.01	1.09	16.50
1987–1988	2.99	7.69	4.73	1.05	16.46
1988–1989	2.86	6.86	5.80	1.02	16.54

Source: Brammer (1990).

The Problem of Too Little Water in the Dry Season

Bengal is home to India's largest city, the ex-imperial capital of Calcutta (population in 1981, 9.2 million), for long India's largest and most important port and manufacturing centre. It is still overwhelmingly the most important port for the whole of eastern and northeastern India. But the Hooghly River, besides which Calcutta lies, 100 miles upstream from the sea, is silting up, as the flow in the delta has shifted more and more to the east. Calcutta has also had problems with land communications. The main train line between India and Assam ran through East Pakistan, and after 1949 India became locked in a trade war and embargo with Pakistan.

In the 1950s India therefore conceived of the Farakka barrage, just upstream from the international border, which would divert water from the Ganges into the Bagirathi, an upstream branch of the Hooghly, thereby, it was hoped, flushing out the silt, easing navigation, providing more water for the city, and also some for irrigation. In addition it would carry a new rail link over the Ganges to northern West Bengal and on to Assam.

From the Bangladesh viewpoint the diversion of water in the dry (low) season has a number of deleterious effects. Those most commonly cited are a loss of water for irrigation and urban use. In the mouths of the Ganges the reduced flow also allows saline bores to penetrate much further upstream than hitherto (Figure 10.7), again reducing irrigation potential, and also possibly harming ground water. Table 10.3 shows the figures given by Abbas (1982), to demonstrate that there is already a deficit in the

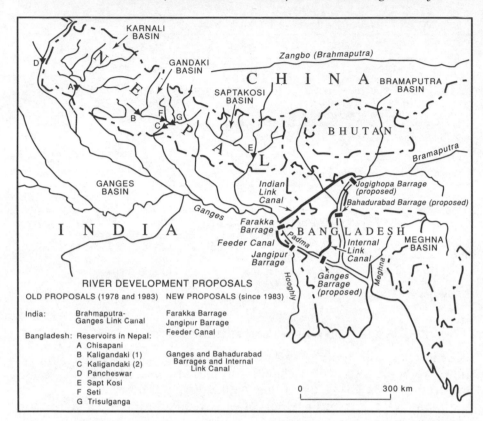

Figure 10.6 The location of Farakka barrage. *Source:* Crow and Lundquist (1990).

dry season, without counting on the future needs as population increases and development occurs in the region, in particular increasing demands for irrigation water upstream in the Ganges plains.

India's attitude to Bangladesh's protests has given the impression that, as the upstream state, she is inclined to believe she has prior rights to do with the water as she wishes. This attitude, if correctly identified, can be linked conceptually to the dispute between India and Pakistan over the sharing of the Indus waters – a difficult issue which was resolved in the Indus Waters Treaty of 1960 only with the help of massive investment from the World Bank underwritten by the USA. This treaty allocated all the water of the three eastern rivers of the Punjab to India, and the waters of the western rivers to Pakistan. This meant that Pakistan had to resupply canals cut off from their original source (Michel, 1967). In 1956, during the confrontation between the two states, India unilaterally abrogated her adherence to the Barcelona Convention to which she had been a signatory in 1921, which forbade a state to alter natural conditions to the detriment of neighbouring states.

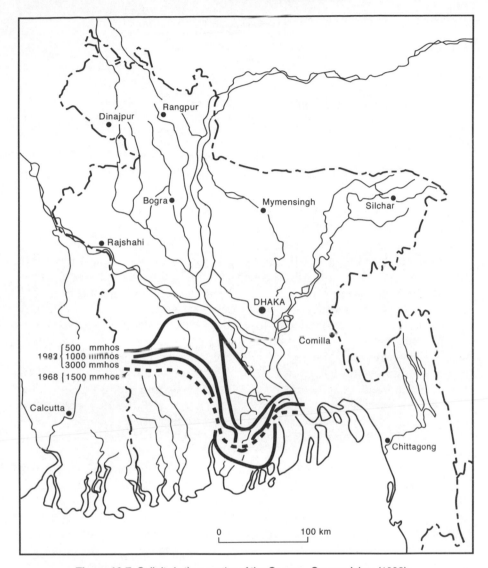

Figure 10.7 Salinity in the mouths of the Ganges. *Source:* Islam (1992).

The Farakka dispute postdates the Indus dispute: and it can be said that India has proved a tough negotiator in this case too, though some of the arguments, such as the fact that very little of the flow into Bengal originated in Bangladesh, are not normal grounds for indifference to a downstream state. But it is also true that to some extent history caught out, in that the building of Farakka began in the Pakistan days, and India did have at that time serious foreign policy problems in relation to Pakistan as a whole – most notably over Kashmir. But now sovereign Bangladesh

Table 10.3 Use of Ganges water: flow at Farakka (in millions cubic metres).

	Dry season (November to May)	Wet season	Total
	61 674	397 181	458 855
Requirements			
Bangladesh	51 806	7 400	59 207
India	20 969	14 801	37 004
Nepal	Not calculated	Not calculated	37 000
Excess/deficit	−11 101	374 978	325 639

Source: Recalculated from figures in Abbas (1982).

has inherited the problem over Farakka, despite the fact that she is now much more of a candidate for Indian co-operation and concern, and is less linked to extraneous foreign policy complications.

Crow and Lundquist (1990) divide the history of negotiation into four phases. From 1951 to 1971 the project was discussed and planned. From 1971 to 1977 the barrage was built and implemented, without international agreement. In 1977 a short-term agreement was signed between India and Bangladesh over the allocation of low season flows, running for five years. During this time it was imagined that the negotiation of a full-scale treaty settling the principles for the development of the Ganges–Brahmaputra basin would be completed, and implementation would follow in 1982. In the event there has been serious difficulty in reaching an agreement, and hence there have been a number of *ad hoc* extensions of the 1977 agreement in the form of a Memorandum of Understanding (MOU) pending a new 'final' solution. But now (1994) even the last MOU has lapsed, and there is a total foreign policy void.

Part of the problem is that there is an ever changing and more complex understanding of what exactly constitutes 'the problem'. Initial concern focused on the division of the available dry season flow at Farakka. But increasingly other issues have grown in significance. First, there is the possibility of augmenting the dry season flow by upstream storage dams. Next there are many other shared rivers which should also be the subject of agreement – for example, there are new Indian barrages on the Teesta and Gumti. So should there not be a regional rather than individual river approach? Next, whereas there is a high demand for Ganges water, but not enough of it, there is little demand for Brahmaputra water, and much of it. (This is a mirror image of the Indus/Punjab situation, in which the eastern areas of greatest demand were supplied by the smallest rivers – so in the end a regional water transfer was devised, followed by a myriad of subsequent developments.)

In the early 1980s India and Bangladesh suggested conflicting solutions. Bangladesh wanted many storage dams in the Ganges, the biggest on the

Nepalese border, to augment the low season flow. (It would also allow a new navigation canal to link the new port of Mongla with Nepal, though crossing a neck of Indian land.) At various stages Bangladesh attempted to initiate trilateral talks with all three countries, although India resisted, insisting that it would be the vehicle through which the downstream–upstream issues could be discussed (Crow and Lindquist, 1990). Effectively the suggestion has been subjected to diplomatic strangulation.

The Indian proposal was to augment the flow at Farakka by diverting flow from the Brahmaputra. This would involve a canal half a mile wide right across Bangladeshi territory, with both of the significant control points in Indian hands (Figure 10.6).

Because these two approaches are clearly radically different, one can imagine how the talks could drag on without resolution.

The current situation is that Bangladesh seems to be developing a 'new line', something akin to the original Indian proposal and close to a variant of it proposed by India, but with different political implications. The engineering basis is for a Brahmaputra–Ganges link, but wholly within Bangladeshi territory. But Bangladesh not unnaturally does not wish to commit itself to such a solution without an agreement on the actual figures for sharing of the waters both in the Brahmaputra and the Ganges. This is extremely difficult to achieve, not least because there is major disagreement between the two sides over what are the correct figures for the Brahmaputra's discharge.

The essence of the dispute at the moment has been summarized by Crow and Lindquist (1990) as: India will not consider sharing (of the Ganges and others) without augmentation from the Brahmaputra, and Bangladesh will not consider augmentation from the Brahmaputra without a guaranteed share of the principal joint rivers.

The irony is that in the end it might be possible to allocate all (low season) discharge of the Brahmaputra to Bangladesh, and all (low season) discharge of the Ganges to India, compensating for the division by engineering works – all highly reminiscent of the vivisection achieved in Punjab. But it should also be noted that there the absolute division of the rivers in Punjab required a detailed 10-year transition with allocation of water flows season by season, and very considerable argument over costs – who was going to pay for replacement and facilitating works in whose territory? Would India pay for Bangladesh's engineering works to get more Ganges low season flow? It should also be remembered that the engineering could be different from that in Punjab in that it could involve the co-operative management of a canal for the delivery of water across a sovereign territory to another.

Towards the end Crow and Lundquist's (1990) account mentions that the floods of 1987 and 1988 have had a very limited impact on the progress of the negotiations. The floods are seen as a separate issue, because the only major works upstream that could mitigate them (and then only some of them) would be the colossal storage dams which would have to be managed trilaterally by India, Nepal and Bangladesh (and conceivably by China and Bhutan too). And the reason why Bangladesh has recently begun to shift its negotiating stance is that it is beginning to concede that the dams might be too big, too costly, too far off in the future, and too unreliable in terms of operational performance (much of the rainfall that causes flooding would occur downstream of the storage sites anyway). Some agreement has been reached between India and Bangladesh about levées on smaller rivers which cross the border.

One aspect of the new link canal that I have not seen discussed is its possible impact on flooding. Such canals impede drainage, not only by seepage loss and changing local ground water levels, but also because their embankments impede drainage lines, and borrow pits become new swamps. The railways of Bangladesh and the Ganges plains had such an impact that they were attributed by some with aiding an increase in malaria. Consider the position of the link canal (Figure 10.6) in relation to the area flooded in 1988 (Figure 10.5).

The Human Response to Floods

There has always been a human response and adaptation to the vagaries of this environment. Historically this has been smale-scale, but in recent decades the proposed responses have escalated, as international involve-ment in 'development' has escalated, and the assumption that governments can effect changes at larger scales has grown stronger in the public mind. Governments have sought refuge in part in the seductive promises of modern earth-moving machinery and modern engineering methods.

Several countries and country groups became involved in planning to obviate as far as possible repeats of Bangladesh's flood disasters, or at least to alleviate their worst effects. The G7 group of developed industrial countries have involved themselves in attempting to devise 'a solution' to the floods problem (Brammer, 1990b), and French and Japanese proposals were also forthcoming for different embankment schemes. The World Bank then became involved in producing a co-ordinated Flood Action Plan with the Government of Bangladesh, publishing the first overview and proposals in late 1989 (World Bank, 1989).

The proposals cover many different aspects of the problem. They include studies of the engineering and siting of embankments, the development of compartmentalized polders, river training, and approaches to improving the management of water control, flood warning and flood preparedness, and enhancing flood refuges. The compartmentalized polders would allow selective flooding of land in the event of extreme flood events. Who would choose which land to flood and which to 'save'? And how would compartmentalization affect the drainage of rainwater?

All the components also include studies on environmental impact assessment, particularly on aspects such as the ecology of local fisheries which could be disrupted. The country has been split into different regions, and there should be a phased attempt at investigating results from schemes in the upstream areas before continuing with schemes lower down stream – though the phasing is over a short period.

The published report does not address itself to the international problem of water sharing and water transfer, and if implemented in full would presumably pre-empt any international link canals, which would have to cross some of the protected regions. It is also unclear how it would even relate to water transfer from the Brahmaputra to the Ganges via a link canal inside Bangladesh.

The tenor of the report at face value seems cautious, acknowledging the possibility of failure in river training, the likelihood of having to retire embankments away from the river, the possibility of breaches and the difficulties of draining polders which have become flooded. But it does not question its basic assumption that there will have to be major engineering works, and these works will be manageable and to the advantage of the economy and the environment. It acknowledges that the works themselves will dispossess thousands of farmers, but probably underestimates the actual and human costs involved. 'Soft' responses such as crop insurance schemes and 'soft and hard' responses for better flood protection for selected settlement sites (analogous to cyclone shelters) get only brief and ancillary comment.

In one critical sense the dynamism of the environment may be overlooked. The report gives evidence of the variability of rainfall and river discharges, and of the different damage inflicted by floods of return periods of between 2 and 500 years. It states that there is no evidence of any long-term secular change in the probabilities involved. *But it does not mention earthquakes, which can liquify embankments and sink them in matters of minutes, and initiate large-scale shifts in drainage patterns.*

But the proposals for more embankments on the main rivers are now increasingly unlikely to be accepted. Recently the World Bank's stance has begun to change, its own environmental advisors believing that long-term engineered taming of the rivers is not possible, and that alternative strategies should be adopted.

The flooding in Bangladesh has so far been identified as being of three types: flash, river and rainfall. But there are many who believe the major cause is the aggrading of the river beds, which has been caused by excessive silt deposition, and which becomes part of a positive feedback system, since aggrading river beds will drop more load, causing further aggradation. This line of argument then leads to popular concern over deforestation in the Himalayas and increased erosion and deposition. Ives and Messerli (1989) show that there is very little evidence that there is currently extensive deforestation, that there is no evidence of increasing flood frequencies, that there is no evidence of enhanced erosion rates caused by human activity (natural processes seem quite capable of producing the current effects), and that in any event if there is increased erosion the most likely immediate impact is in Nepal at border dams, or on the Indian plains.

From a more local viewpoint, Farakka is somehow supposedly implicated in both increasing siltation in the lower Ganges, and also in causing flood releases. Islam several times mentions that India takes only silt-free water and pushes the silt into Bangladesh. Several mass marches across the border by thousands of Bangladeshis have been planned from time to time – a convenient way of externalizing internal discontent. But, according to Crow and Lindquist (1990), these views should not be given much credence.

Conclusions

Simplistically, one normally proceeds on the basis that there is a problem, that one can find a set of solutions, and that one can choose and implement the best solution.

In practice, problem-solving is an iterative process that can involve at the least the following three steps, starting at any one of them, and then progressing through the whole loop more than once. After a few iterations, the problem(s) might not be the problem one first thought one had.

1 Finding the solution to a problem depends in the first place on agreement on the nature of the problem.
2 Finding the solution depends upon a proper assessment of the causes, even when 'proper' means confessing to a present and likely continuing state of ignorance or uncertainty. Lack of proof to the contrary should not be a licence for a half-baked theory to masquerade as fact.
3 Solutions have to be tested for feasibility, which means testing the assumptions on which they lie. There is no point in pursuing impossible solutions, feasible only in an ideal world (usually that of physical engineering bereft of political and social engineering).

My starting point is that the problem of Bengal is development: how to improve the lives of the rapidly increasing millions in the population. (In this light, perhaps the best anti-flood device would be an immediate halt to all population growth. But that has to be dismissed as an unreal-world engineering scenario.) The biggest problem the population faces is that of uncertainty – over the timing and extent of possible losses to crops, property and even land.

The backdrop to this is continents in collision, and the dynamic and ever-changing delta region, the most active surface reminder of the activity of the plates beneath. The active superficial geomorphology is a major source of uncertainty on a subcontinental scale. This uncertainty is not subject to elimination. (It may get worse because of climatic change. Interestingly, Brammer (1989a) considers the possible effects of sea-level change, and considers that deposition – often deliberately 'harvested' – may match sea-level rise; there could also be reductions or increases in rainfall, which would of course lead to major changes in sedimentation in the lower basin.)

The major constraint on action at larger scales is the difficulty of co-ordinating governments which are individually responsible to their own citizens, not to the population of the basin. Crow and Lindquist (1990) begin their illuminating report with the observations that 500 million people live in the Ganges–Brahmaputra basins, and that 30 per cent of the world's 800 million poorest people live here. But the most significant fact is concealed by these aggregated figures – that they are partitioned into separate sovereign states. To relax this constraint the concepts of respons-ibility and sovereignty would have to be modified by a basin-wide common environment. Not only is this unlikely in the short term, but the very fact that there have been and may be major political realignments suggests that no long-term and expensive technological fix should presume continuity of current political form. (The British assumption of a continuing hegemony in the Indus led to the development of an integrated scheme which was dis-integrated after 1947 at great cost.)

An idiosyncratic and unconventional proposal is to presume that the problem is not one of drought or floods or cyclones. It is of risk which small farmers and the poor face at the micro-scale, such that for many there are inducements to have large families (although there are also strong cultural impulsions as well). Interestingly, in a way, most of the current agricultural improvements are occurring at the micro-scale, through the use of small-scale irrigation in the dry season. The link between micro- and macro-scale does not have to be through embankments and river training. And there are strong suspicions that many of these schemes will be costly, transitory and ecologically disruptive.

Brammer (1990) has shown that at the national scale, even in bad years, Bangladesh has not done as badly as at first feared (Table 10.2). If, at the macro-scale, risk even in bad years is not so high, there could theoretically be a means to redistribute risk. (This was one of the benefits that the railways are thought to have brought to India in the nineteenth century.) Therefore, as a thought experiment, let us assume that there are donors around who might be prepared to sink billions of dollars into vast engineering schemes, but then ask them to reconsider, and instead to lend the same money to an institutional innovation – a national crop insurance scheme run at local levels (and an urban–regional plan to concentrate the more expensive capital investments of urbanization on Pleistocene terraces, or other sites selected by astute geomorphologists). This means doing what the local farmers have done for millenia – accepting the vagaries of the environment and having a flexible response – but this time with an added institutional extra layer, meaning that the flexible response is local but plugged into a national framework. Bangladesh is probing this path: by building village safety mounds – local earth encampments surrounded by borrow pits – and by trial crop insurance schemes (Bangladesh Minister for Information, personal communication). Such a proposal is actually presaged now by the volte-face which has occurred in the UK this year over the management of coastal erosion. The south of Britain is sinking, and major amounts of money have been poured into coastal defences, often of land of lowish value. Sometimes defences in one place change the movement of sediment, and result in erosion in other places. The defences have continually been damaged and breached. Now the government has decided that managed retreat is better: the sea should be allowed to have its own way, and new salt marshes encouraged to develop, and for farmers and other land users suitable economic help should be provided for the adjustments they make. This is a historically sensitive and place-specific approach. But such a soft approach is not yet part of the paradigm of Bengali Development International Ltd.

I do not pretend that such a soft approach will answer all the problems. Farakka still exists; the investment in Calcutta is fixed in a way that the rivers are not, since ironically in Bengal the speed of economic and social locational change is slower than that of environmental change; the demands on the Ganges low season flow will escalate. With hindsight, it might have been best if this flow had not been interfered with at all, and all upstream development made dependent on extraction from the massive ground water reserves (which, however, is energetically expensive). But, of course, the current state of affairs has to be accepted as the reality, and hence, in this respect at least, if Bangladesh does want to augment the Ganges low season flow, then a physical link with the Brahmaputra seems likely. However, even here there is a caveat. Looking at the current proposal it seems that a great deal of digging will shift the confluence (for some of the waters) only a small way upstream, so that a new Ganges barrage will become necessary as well. One wonders how long a life such a project would have.

My final conclusion is that simplified myth propagation will not help anyone. That India and Bangladesh have a problem over Farakka and that this barrage affects dry season flows cannot be denied. But to generalize from the one tangible case to make India a scapegoat for all other environmental ills is not useful. Quite clearly, the manifold problems of Bengal cannot be blamed simply and only on India's and Nepal's upstream behaviour.

Acknowledgement

I would like to thank Hugh Brammer for his comments on an earlier draft of this paper. The faults remain mine.

References

Abbas, B.M. (1982) *The Ganges Water Dispute*. New Delhi: Vikas.

Anderson, F.P. (1990) The effects of the earthquake in 1897 on the Shaistaganj Division of the Assam–Bengal railway. *Proceedings of the Institute of Civil Engineers*, **141**(3), 258–61.

Brammer, H. (1989a) Monitoring the evidence of the greenhouse effect and its impact on Bangladesh. Paper presented at The International Conference on the Greenhouse Effect and Coastal Area of Bangladesh. Coastal Area Resource Development Management Association (CARDMA), Dhaka.

Brammer, H. (1989b) Floods in the agro-ecology of Bangladesh. Paper presented at the International Seminar on Bangladesh Floods: Regional and Global Environmental Perspectives, Dhaka.

Brammer,H. (1990a) Floods in Bangladesh. 1. Geographical background to the 1987 and 1988 floods. *Geographical Journal*, **156** (1), 12–22.

Brammer, H. (1990b) Floods in Bangladesh. 2. Flood mitigation and environmental aspects. *Geographical Journal*.

Burgess, J. (1985) News from nowhere: the press, the riots, and the myth of the inner city. In J. Burgess and J. Gold (eds), *Geography, the Media and Popular Culture*. London: Croom Helm.

Burgess, J. and Harrison, C. (1993) The circulation of claims in the cultural politics of environmental change. In A. Hansen (ed.), *Environmental Issues and the Mass Media*, Leicester: Leicester University Press.

Chapman, G.P. (forthcoming) *One into Three: the Geopolitics of South Asia from British Raj to India, Pakistan and Bangladesh*.

Crow, B. and Lundquist, A. (1990) Development of the Rivers Ganges and Brahmaputra: the Difficulty of Developing a New Line. *Development Policy and Practice Working Paper* No. 19, The Open University, Walton Hall, Milton Keynes.

Eckholm, E. (1976) *Losing Ground*. Washington D.C.: Worldwatch Institute.

Farmer, B.H. (1979) The 'Green Revolution' in South Asian ricefields: environment and production. *Journal of Development Studies*, **15**, 304–19.

Islam, N. (1992) Indo-Bangladesh common rivers: the impact on Bangladesh. *Contemporary South Asia*, **1** (2), 203–25.

Ives, J.D. (1989) Deforestation in the Himalayas: the cause of increased flooding in Bangladesh and northern India? *Land Use Policy*, **6**(3), 187–93.

Ives, J.D. and Messerli, B. (1989) *The Himalayan Dilemma: Reconciling Development and Conservation*. London and New York: The United Nations University and Routledge.

Johnson, B.L.C. (1975) *Bangladesh*. London: Heinemann.

King, L.C. (1983) *Wandering Continents and Spreading Sea Floors on an Expanding Earth*. Chichester: John Wiley.

Michel, A.A. (1967) *The Indus Rivers: a Study in the Effects of Partition*. New Haven and London: Yale University Press.

Sarma, S.S. (ed.) (1986) *Farakka – a Gordian Knot*. Calcutta: Asit Sen.

Schwarz, M. and Thompson, M. (1990) *Divided We Stand: Redefining Politics, Technology and Social Choice*. New York: Harvester Wheatsheaf.

Tapponier, P., Peltser, G. and Armijo, R. (1986) On the mechanics of the collision between India and Asia. In M.P. Coward and A.C. Ries (eds), *Collision Tectonics* (Geological Society Special Publication No. 19). Oxford: Blackwell Scientific, pp. 115–57.

World Bank (1989) *Bangladesh Action Plan for Flood Control*. Washington, DC: World Bank.

Umitsu, M. (1985) Natural Levées and landform evolution in the Bengal lowland. *Geographical Review of Japan*, **58** (Ser. B), No. 2, 149–64.

Umitsu, M. (1987) Late Quaternary sedimentary environment and landform evolution in the Bengal lowland. *Geographical Review of Japan*, **60** (Ser. B), No. 2, 164–78.

11

The Human Response to Environmental Dynamics in Bangladesh

Shahnaz Huq-Hussain

Editors' Note
Very few writers in Bangladesh are able to refer to Farakka barrage without repeating the same list of allegations of its impacts on the country. This list includes impacts such as 'desertification', a phrase not normally used apart from increases in desert margins, clearly something not happening here. We do not agree with all of what Hussain says about Farakka, and Chapman in the previous chapter specifically rebuts some of the allegations about adverse environmental impacts, but it is important to realize the depth of feeling in Bangladesh over this issue, and the currency of these views.

Introduction

The major part of the Ganges–Jamuna–Meghna delta falls within the territory of Bangladesh, and supports a large population, nearly 80 per cent of whom depend on the fertile alluvial soil for agriculture for their livelihood. The country is encompassed by a network of rivers vital for its agriculture and transport system. As many as 230 rivers, their tributaries and distributaries criss-cross the country, totalling 24 140 km in length (BBS, 1991). This network of rivers has created the landforms and topography of the country, and also provides its cultural motif. More than three-quarters of the country is less than 10 m above sea level and active flood plains comprise 80 per cent of the total area (Food and Agriculture Organization, 1988). The country comprises as little as 7 per cent of the catchment area of the Ganges–Brahmaputra basins. 93 per cent of the water it transports comes from upstream countries. The high density of population along the major rivers and the coast makes them vulnerable to natural hazards, which involve the risk of loss of life and/or damage to property. Floods, river bank erosion and cyclonic storms are common. Excessive rainfall during the monsoon along with deforestation in the upstream areas of the Ganges and Jamuna rivers generates huge volumes of water which it is difficult for the rivers and their tributaries to drain. The shifting rivers erode their banks in one place, wiping out villages and their lands, while throwing up newer land elsewhere, although the newer land is usually very sandy and takes years to make productive, adding an organic fraction to the soil.

Again, the unilateral withdrawal of water by India at Farakka upstream of Bangladesh has adversely affected agriculture in one-third of the country. Along with this, industry, fishing and the availability of drinking water have been affected. The northern and northwestern regions of the country are faced with desertification, while the tributaries of the Ganges have been excessively silted, causing increasing salinity in the southern and southwestern regions of the country. All these factors have affected densely populated areas of the country.

Thus, environmental disasters, part natural and part induced by people, severely affect the economy and social organization of the country. This chapter analyses the behavioural pattern and adjustment strategies of the population displaced as a result of natural calamities with special reference to river bank erosion in the Ganges (known as Padma in Bangladesh), Jamuna and Meghna basin.

Displacement and Human Response to Floods and River Bank Erosion

Flooding in Bangladesh is of three types, which can mutually reinforce each other. If the great rivers over-top their banks, then silt waters can flood the land; excessive rainfall on a flat land can also cause flooding – but this time, seen from the air, it is clearly not silty water; and there can be flash-floods at the foot of the small Pleistocene terraces, and the hills of northern Sylhet District. The chances of rainfall floods increase if the rivers are high and drainage poor. The worst floods will occur when both the Ganges and the Brahmaputra peak at the same time, and there is heavy local rainfall. Bangladesh receives 80 per cent of its annual rainfall during the monsoon season.

There is, however, a problem with defining the concept of flood. Since fluctuating water levels are normal and farming for centuries has been adapted to this, most monsoon increases in water levels cannot be called floods. The definition has to be anthropocentric, and it depends upon prior expectation and behaviour. If water kills a crop which can normally be grown at a certain time of year by drowning it, there is a flood. If water destroys a homestead which is normally high enough to be safe, there is a flood. For centuries farmers have obviously adapted their cropping calendar and their house sites so that normally they suffer neither privation. In recent years it has become more common to build embankments to stop 'flooding'. When this happens the density of population induces people to settle in the protected area. Then at some stage the embankment may fail, and there is a damaging 'flood', where previously such a rise in water level would have been thought normal. The behaviour of the river has not changed, whereas human behaviour and perception has.

During 1989–1990, 76 per cent of households were subject to at least one environmental hazard (Rahman and Sen, 1992). One of the worst, because it is most final in its impact on the family, is erosion. The Jamuna (Brahmaputra) river, which has a long history of channel changes, may shift its course by over 300 m horizontally in any one season, with catastrophic local effects. In the devastating floods of 1987, 1988 and 1990, the embankments were vulnerable to bank erosion, and on some occasions parts of the embankment collapsed as a result of bank erosion and pressure of water. One such example is the partial collapse of the Meghna–Dhanagoda irrigation project during the flood of 1988. Chandpur, a well-known river port of the confluence of Padma and Meghna, had to shift its ferry station frequently during the 1980s and this has become a norm at this place. It is important to note here that the river at this point had shifted its course by 500 m or more and cut a new channel of 45 m depth within a few days in 1988. Sirajganj, the twelfth-ranking town in the national urban hierarchy, located on the western bank of the River Jamuna, has been subjected to constant risk of river erosion. The municipal area of the town was reduced from 11 square miles in 1860 to 8.5 square miles in 1920 and subsequently to 4.2 square miles in 1981 due to bank erosion (Hossain and Roopnarine, 1992). Rajshahi, Sardah, Godagari etc. are other urban centres parts of which are under constant erosion threat from the Ganges–Padma rivers.

On average, nearly 18 per cent of the country is submerged every year (Master Plan Organization, 1986) but the intensity of 'flooding' may vary from year to year. During the massive floods of 1974, 80 per cent of the country was under water. While 40 per cent of the total area was submerged during the flood of 1987, more than three-quarters of the land was inundated in the catastrophic flood of 1988. According to the report of the Joint Task Force of the Government of Bangladesh and the UN (1988), 53 districts out of a total of 64 and about 30 million people were affected by the 1988 flood. The number of deaths were reported as 1410 persons, with crop damage of 10 million acres. The total loss during the floods of 1988 was estimated as US $425 million. It may be noted that the damage caused by the 1987 flood was much less, estimated as US $90 million. The reported number of deaths were 1700 and the crop loss was 5.5 million acres. It is, however, extremely difficult to find out the exact nature and number of people affected by floods and river erosion because of the lack of proper social impact study. Although river erosion and flooding generated massive loss of property, land and physical infrastructure, the affected people pursued a variety of survival strategies even under conditions of extreme distress. These involved shifts of occupation and joining the out-migration stream in search of a job, shelter and security in urban as well as other rural areas.

Human Adjustment in the Erosion-prone and Flood-affected Rural Areas

Although floods displace more people annually than river bank erosion, the displacement is temporary. In contrast, displacement by bank erosion is mostly long distance and permanent (Elahi, 1991). About a million people are directly affected every year by river bank erosion in Bangladesh. An estimate of the Bangladesh Water Development Board (BRDB) shows that at least 77 points along the banks of the Padma, Jamuna and Meghna rivers are under constant erosion threat. River erosion has also affected the land ownership pattern of many rural households. According to one study (Nazem and Elahi, 1990), more than 35 per cent of the displaced people belonged to the category 'absolute landless' on account of bank erosion in one of the northwestern upazilas (subdistricts).

People in the erosion-prone and flood-affected areas do not want to leave their native area unless they are desperate. As a choice of adjustment they tend to live in temporary or makeshift arrangements, particularly in the embankment areas closest to their homes. This may be explained by the fact that the displaced people still have the hope of recovering their lost land or desire to claim the emerging new 'char land' and remain within their native environment. These 'char lands' are used for growing different types of paddy round the year as well as groundnuts, sweet potatoes and vegetables, and building homesteads, which are crucial for destitute peasants. However, it is very difficult for the poor to reclaim this land, since the local landlords, known as 'jotdars', are too powerful, and drive them away. The landlords maintain their own force of 'lathials' (muscle-men) to grab the 'char land' by force, thus increasing their landholdings and enhancing their power. Such 'char fights' are a common phenomenon in many parts of the erosion-prone areas. Based on research into reports in one local daily newspaper, Baqee (1989) reported 134 incidents of 'char fights' during the period 1971–1980. It has been noted that the intensity of 'char fights' varies seasonally. During the monsoon when the 'char lands' are inundated, the incidence of fights is less than during the dry winter season. It should be mentioned here that although the government of Bangladesh has a defined 'char land' law, it is rather complex and not easy for the poor people to access. The presidential order of 1972 (Order No. 135) has indicated that all new lands in the form of accretion or in the form of reformation after flood will be vested with the government and not with the original owner. The government would lease out such lands, preferably to persons who have become landless through fluvial processes and to those possessing less than 3.3 ha of land. The purpose of this order was to reclaim all 'char lands' from local powerful landlords, prevent land consolidation and distribute something to landless families, who constitute 50 per cent of all rural households (Bangladesh Bureau of Statistics, 1981). However, very few poor families have secured such lands. Researchers (Baqee, 1989; Nazem and Elahi, 1990) have pointed out the flaws and deficiencies of this law and its consequences. These include lack of knowledge of the operation of 'char land' laws by the poor peasants, lengthy and difficult processes in implementing such laws on behalf of illiterate peasants in remote parts of the country because of the corruption of revenue officials, delays in surveys by the Land Revenue Department, and the slow accretion of viable agricultural land. The social consequences include deprivation, murder, burglary and the looting of crops.

The erosion-affected people attempt to make various adjustments on the basis of their own perception of the hazard. Initially, the displaced people tend to resettle in neighbouring villages because they cannot finance migration to a distant location. They also undergo fundamental changes in their occupation – from agriculture to fishing, various forms of manual labour, rowing small ferry boats or any informal activities like petty business, street hawking etc. Many of the marginal farmers whose land has been eroded by the river take up work as agricultural labourers in large land-holding households. In some of the northern districts along the Jamuna river, displacees have taken refuge on the nearby embankments of the Bangladesh Water Development Board and on abandoned railway tracks, leading to the development of rural squatters and slums. Elahi (1989) indicated that within the length of 248 km of the BWDB embankment stretching between Rangpur and Pabna, nearly 70 000 households have taken refuge. Gradually these sites become a permanent feature and eviction is rather difficult. The displacees, however, are not much welcomed at their new place because the local people feel threatened due to limited resources and opportunities available in the area. Many of the unfortunate victims of river bank erosion become fatalistic, perceiving their predicament as 'the will of God'. There is a long social memory of many major losses, which may lead to an expectation of such a fate.

Human Adjustment in Urban Areas

A government report (Government of Bangladesh, 1989) claims that nearly one-fifth of the squatter population of the cities of Bangladesh have

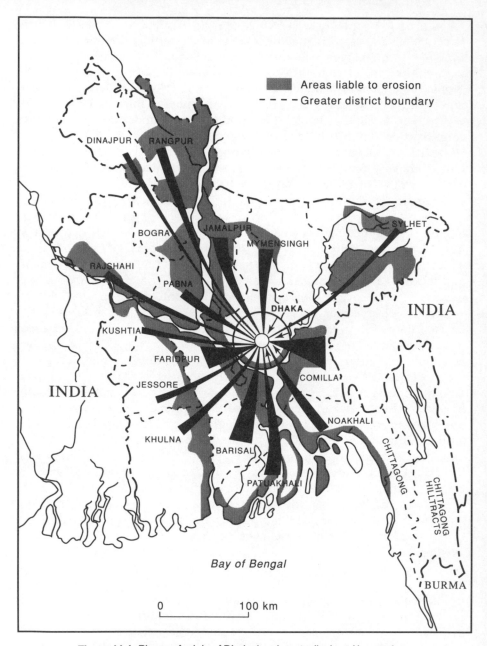

Figure 11.1 Places of origin of Dhaka immigrants displaced by erosion.

migrated as a result of river erosion. Although the consequences of displacement are difficult to measure, evaluation of the magnitude of the problem of displaced people is important in understanding their adjustment strategies in different settings. Various studies (Huq-Hussain, 1992; Mortuza, 1992) have indicated that substantial numbers of the poor rural families have become landless on account of river bank erosion, and more and more rural poor families are migrating to the cities, especially to the capital city, to escape from this adversity. This group of people are undergoing major changes in their way of life, especially in terms of their shelter and employment. Their occupational pattern not only alters in the city, but the domestic group also undergoes transformation. Households with greater numbers of earning members may be in a better position to fight the crisis than those with fewer earning members.

Adjustment Strategy of the Displaced Rural People in Dhaka City – an Example

River bank erosion leaves people not only helpless but also hopeless. Since poor people do not own any hut or property of any kind, they tend to move to the city permanently with their entire family. Several studies (Mahbub and Islam, 1991; Huq-Hussain, 1992; Mortuza, 1992) have mentioned that a large majority of migrants in Dhaka have originated from places close by, located along the banks of Padma–Meghna and Jamuna rivers, which are liable to floods and river erosion (Figure 11.1). These areas have a well-developed river transport system. River transport is the easiest and cheapest means of communication for the poor, and a study noted that out of 399 migrant households more than half used river ways to move to Dhaka (Huq-Hussain, 1992). For many, the river washes both the land and the people downstream. Table 11.1 based on different studies, illustrates the importance of river erosion in landlessness and in rural–urban migration of poor people.

Survival of the migrants in the city primarily depends on their employment position. The sluggish formal sector in the city is already saturated in terms of any kind of job. Hence, the only hope for the majority of the migrants, possessing little or no formal education, is to involve themselves in the informal sector work. The informal sector has been expanding fast in Dhaka since the late 1970s, absorbing the bulk of the rural migrants. According to one definition (Amin, 1981), in Dhaka the sector comprises

Table 11.1 Landless categories of river-erosion-prone migrants from different studies.

Study	Year	Total households	Percentage
Government of Bangladesh	1989	49 995	19
Majumder *et al.*	1989	299	9
Mahbub and Islam	1991	5 191	44
Huq-Hussain	1992	399	6
Mortuza	1992	341	5

enterprises employing less than 10 people, including the owner, and meeting one or more of such conditions as: operating in open premises or housed in a temporary or semi-permanent structure; not using any designated government space; functioning from a residence or backyard; and not being registered. There are many informal activities to which the migrants get access; however, the main concentration of male migrants has been observed in transport categories like rickshaw and cart pullers. The main concentration of females has been noted in the household sector, namely housemaids or servants. Manual and construction labour, hawking and vendoring are other occupations for both men and women.

The public transport system has not kept pace with the ever-increasing population of the fast-expanding city. As a consequence a large section of the middle-income-class people is heavily dependent on the cycle rickshaws. Rickshaw pulling does not involve much training and skill, and so it has become a lucrative sector for the migrants to be employed in. It does not involve any initial cost, since the rickshaw can be hired by paying a fixed amount of money to the rickshaw owner on a full- or half-day basis. Of course, the person has to be introduced to the rickshaw owner by a guarantor. Migrant females are also active participants in the fast-expanding construction industry. Here they work as brick crushers and load carriers. Women are also actively engaged in many other home-based informal activities, although they do not take much part in the marketing process. In most of the formal and informal sector work, personal introductions are important, for both women and men. The household members capitalize on any source of income. It has been observed (Huq-Hussain, 1992; Mortuza, 1992) that if the husband or father is a rickshaw puller, the wife and children are engaged as part-time domestic help, which also helps them to get left-over food and used clothing from the employer family. The family earnings are then just enough to live a life in the city.

For women there has been a recent increase in employment in the formal sector, as the ready-made garment industry has gone through a major export boom. Domestic work offers women an opportunity to be introduced to many modern technologies, and is a kind of skill training. Recent migrants will probably not have used appliances such as electric irons, gas stoves and telephones before. Housemaids who have learnt about these things are better equipped to compete in the garment industry. Many migrant women obtained work in the garment industries through the introduction of their employers (Huq-Hussain, 1992).

Migrants' Perception

It has been claimed by various surveys (Majumder *et al.*, 1989; Huq-Hussain, 1992; Mortuza, 1992) that the migrants have benefited from city life with respect to accommodation, employment and income. The migrants perceived that migrating to the city was a positive decision, and they have at least survived in the city, something which was no longer possible in their native rural place. Many of the migrant families are of the opinion that their overall economic condition has changed positively and they would not wish to go back to the villages.

Conclusion

In Bangladesh, rivers have been viewed as the main arteries of the country for centuries. Millions of people are dependent on the rivers for their livelihood. They support vast amounts of agriculture, fisheries, flora, fauna and transport, and provide drinking water. The rivers also prevent the impingement of saline water from the sea along the coastal belt. Therefore, the rivers play a vital role in maintaining the ecological harmony of the environment. The rivers also have a profound effect on the cultural life of the people of the Padma–Jamuna–Meghna basin. People develop their own mechanisms to withstand the hardships in their native place, but ultimately many are forced out by river erosion, since local social conditions will not permit them to regain access to new land. For many the move to the city proves to be a viable and permanent alternative, even if living conditions remain very poor.

Quite clearly, any plan for the sustainable development of the Padma–Jamuna–Meghna basin which takes into account people as well as environmental factors must also consider the social adjustment mechanisms locally and nationally which assist those persons inevitably overwhelmed by rapid environmental change.

References

Amin, A.T.M. (1981) Marginalization vs Dynamism: a study of informal sector in Dhaka. *Journal of the Institute of Development Studies*, 9(4).

Bangladesh Bureau of Statistics (1988) *Report on the Slum Area Census, 1986*. Dhaka: Government of Bangladesh, BBS.

Bangladesh Bureau of Statistics (1991) *Statistical year Book of Bangladesh*. Dhaka: Government of Bangladesh.

Baqee, M.A. (1989) Violence and agricultural seasonality in char-lands of Bangladesh. *Oriental Geographer*, **XXIX–XXX**, 25–36.

BWDB (1987) *Flood in Bangladesh*. Dhaka: Bangladesh Water Development Board.

Elahi, K.M. (1987) *Rural Bastees and the Phenomenon of Rural Squatting Due to River Bank Erosion in Bangladesh*. Seminar on Shelter for Homeless. Dhaka: Urban Development Directorate, Government of Bangladesh.

Elahi, K.M. (1989) Population displacement due to riverbank erosion of the Jamuna in Bangladesh. In J.I. Clarke and S.C. Kayastha (eds), *Disaster and Population*. London: Basil Blackwell.

Elahi, K.M. (1991) River bank erosion, flood hazard and population displacement in Bangladesh: an overview. In K.M. Elahi, K.S. Ahmed and M. Mafizuddin (eds), *River Bank Erosion, Flood and Population Displacement in Bangladesh*. River Bank Erosion Impact Study (REIS). Bangladesh: Jahangirnagar University, Savar, Dhaka.

Food and Agricultural Organization (1988) *Land Resources Appraisal of Bangladesh for Agricultural Development: Hydro-Climatic Resources: Inundation Resources Inventory*, 2. Dhaka: UNDP.

Government of Bangladesh (1989) *Bustee Niroshon Committer Protibedon*. Report of the Squatter Resettlement in Bangla. Dhaka: Ministry of Workers.

Hossain, Z. and Roopnarine, J.L. (1992) On the fringes: urban living among squatters of Sirajganj Town in Bangladesh. *Urban Anthropology*, 2(1), 45–65.

Huq-Hussain, S. (1992) Female migrants' adaptation in Dhaka: a case study of the processes of urban socio-economic change. PhD dissertation, Department of Geography, School of Oriental and African Studies, University of London.

Joint Task Force of the Government of Bangladesh and the UN (1988) *The 1988 Floods*, Dhaka: Government of Bangladesh.

Mahbub, A.Q.M. and Islam, N. (1991) Urban adjustment by erosion induced migrants to Dhaka. In K.M. Elahi, K.S. Ahmed, and M. Matizuddii (eds), *Riverbank Erosion, Flood and Population Displacement in Bangladesh*. Savar, Dhaka: REIS.

Majumder, P.P., Mahmud, S. and Afsar, R. (1989) *Squatter Life in the Agargaon area*. Report of the Bangladesh Institute of Development Studies, Dhaka.

Master Plan Organization (1986) *Water Resources and Water Demand, Irrigation, Water Development and Flood Control*, Vol. 2. Dhaka: Government of Bangladesh in Cooperation with UNDP and the World Bank.

Mortuza, S.A. (1992) Rural–Urban migration in Bangladesh. PhD Dissertation, Institute for Geographische Wissenschaften, Freie Universitat Berlin, Dietrich Reimer Verlag.

Nazem, N.I. and Elahi, K.M. (1990) Impact of river bank erosion on land and settlements in Bangladesh. In A.Q.M. Mahabub (ed.), *Proceedings of the Seminar on People and Environment in Bangladesh*. Organized by the UNDP and UNFPA, Dhaka, Bangladesh.

Rahman, Z. and Sen, B. (1992) *Rethinking Rural Poverty: A Case for Bangladesh*. Dhaka: Bangladesh Institute of Development Studies.

PART V

Conclusions

12

Conclusions

G.P. Chapman and M. Thompson

The most basic facts of this region are that its human population, already large, will increase substantially over the next few decades, and that the population will become increasingly urban and reliant on increasing industrial employment, and the logistics of urban support. This will mean an increasing demand for resources, and in particular an increasing competition between urban and rural areas, between industry and agriculture, for water. The combination of increasing resource demands and increasing technology with increasing risks of pollution could be taken to suggest that an environment whose carrying capacity may already be strained is destined for unbearable strains in the future – strains which would in fact be unsustainable.

Whether or not one takes this view partly depends upon one's presuppositions about the fragility of nature, the scale of human impact, and the meaning of sustainability. If nature is seen as inherently fragile, then the current situation may be that we are already too late, that breakdown has started and cannot be stopped: current practices are already unsustainable. On the other hand, it seems to us that sustainability is a poor concept – it seems tied somehow to notions of equilibrium, to notions of stasis, to a perpetual recycling and reproduction of the status quo.

If there is one conclusion that stands out immediately from this book it is that this region is so dynamic that it would be hard to define an equilibrium anywhere. Whether one is talking about the uplift of the mountains, or sedimentation in the plains, or changing river courses, or growing city populations, or developing irrigation and hydropower technologies, nothing is static – and perhaps the real issue is the extent to which the different rates of change are harmonious. In the days before sustainability became a *mantra*, geomorphologists used to talk of 'accelerated erosion', meaning that people could amplify an existing trend, but the trend was there already. With respect to erosion, most of the evidence of human intervention in this book points to an opposite dynamic – 'decelerated erosion'. Such an idea would not be alien to the authors of 'More people: less erosion' (Tiffen *et al.*, 1994). Indeed, it would be entirely possible to construct, though we have not done so here, a diagram of the theory of Himalayan environmental conservation which would have at least as much scientific foundation as the theory of Himalayan environmental degradation summarized, and largely dismissed, in the early chapters of this book.

Are people therefore nothing but a benign influence on these river basins – and the more people the better? Do we dare relax and take a Bauer-like view that the self-seeking behaviour of myriad economic agents will move everything to a welfare-maximizing state? Clearly the answer is no. Urban water use is polluting the Ganges to an alarming extent, the profit of some individuals being obtained by externalizing costs, literally dumping them in the river. This is damaging for all other river users, including aquatic life as well as human beings, and whether or not that aquatic life is seen as a human resource. That controlling pollution is not simply a matter of technology and money has been well illustrated in this book. The ritual significance of the Ganges for millions of pilgrims who bathe in its waters, and for the disposal of the dead, suggests that cultural attitudes will have to change substantially for the sake of the sanctity of that which is already deemed holy. It is also clear that the actual structure of political decision-making has a major impact on the way that pollution is acknowledged, and the extent to which its sources are tackled.

It might seem as if we are drifting towards a hierarchical consensus, in which some degree of regulatory control is necessary, and that such control will enable environmentally sympathetic development to proceed. Indeed that could be the case in terms of some aspects of pollution abatement. But that cannot be the only conclusion, since we have also seen that the scales and types of flooding and the scales and kinds of erosion that occur in Bangladesh are almost certainly beyond human control, and certainly so at any cost which is likely to be properly funded. The same has to be acknowledged for tropical cyclones. The strategy has therefore to be the same as that for cyclones: accept that the forces of nature cannot be brought entirely within control, and opt for adaptation. Adaptive strategies must be flexible, and one feature of that flexibility should be a pragmatic and easily rearranged mix of 'hard' and 'soft' solutions: for instance, survival refuges for people and their animals conjoined with social policies that harness and nurture the resilience that is already built into the lives of the people who have long coped with these prodigious natural forces. This is not to say that such solutions will be easily found or funded.

The problem of water stortages is most acutely spelt out in the case of dry season Ganges flows to Bangladesh, and the diversion at Farakka by 'the upper riparian' (Bangladeshi documents usually refer to India obliquely in this manner) manifestly makes things worse. Farakka is of course a political phenomenon, in the sense that any structure built anywhere reflects the policy that decided on its construction. That the sovereign polity occupies only part of the delta, and that a separate sovereign polity occupies the other part of the delta, is the basic social fact around which all else revolves. That it ought to be possible technically to find a solution is manifestly obvious, particularly when one realizes the extent to which high season flows are lost to the sea. The technical solutions depend on negotiated settlements and an agreed sharing of the costs and benefits – where many of the costs will probably be borne by external assistance.

The reason why the 'upper riparian' might not to be too co-operative in the short term is that, quite simply, charity begins at home, and it has enough of a large and burgeoning population that its first thoughts are to command resources at its disposal for their benefit. But in this case the benefit of the 'upper riparian' itself could be helped by the provision of more power from its own 'upper riparian', Nepal. There seems little doubt that the power potential of the Himalayas could make a very significant contribution to the development of the plains below. And as surface water becomes increasingly inadequate in the dry season for the combined and growing needs of urban areas and agriculture, the energy to develop ground water will be commensurately necessary. There is enough ground water that future demands can be met if it is properly developed. The surface rivers will then benefit by the continued discharge in the dry season, and the problems of Bangladesh and Farakka could in some measure be mitigated.

The *sine qua non* for the solution to both India's and Bangladesh's problems is energy: the ground water is 'down there' and it will have to be brought 'up here'. Humans and their domestic animals can and do lift water, and so can fossil fuels, indirectly as electricity, or directly in internal combustion engines. Alternatively, the sun's energy can be harnessed to do the job, either by generating electricity from the water that tumbles from the Himalayas to the plains, or by gassifying quick-growing woody species, or directly from the sunshine that falls copiously on the plains. Possibilities like hot fusion may yet deliver their promise. Other, as yet undreamt of, possibilities may emerge in the distant future.

Some of these energy sources (solar, for instance, both direct and via hydro-power) lend themselves to either centralized or decentralized production units. Others (nuclear, for instance, and coal) cannot be scaled down so that each village can have its own power plant. However, even within the limits imposed by these energy sources and their inherent physical properties, there exists a wide range of possible mixes and a wide range of options along the large/small, centralized/decentralized and capital intensive/labour intensive scales. We have already seen (Chapters 5 and 6) how two very different scenarios can be fleshed out for the development of Nepal's water resources, and much the same is true for the other energy sources that are (or may be) available.

In other words, the situation with regard to energy in the Ganges valley is much the same as it is anywhere else in the world. There are 'hard' paths and there are 'soft' paths; there are energy-guzzling futures and there are energy-frugal futures; there are managed, controlled and planned scenarios and there are unmanaged, piecemeal and self-organized scenarios. The viable path, if there is one, will thread its way through all these proclaimed solutions, and the lesson that can be drawn from this is that those who, in advocating any single one of these solutions, insist that 'there is no alternative' must be wrong.

The facts that would decide the issue, this way or that, will always remain smeared out, telling those people that gather them together in this way that this is the answer, and those people who gather them together in that way, that that is the answer. The resulting plurality of problem definitions is not some ghastly mess that will first of all have to be cleared out of the way. For one thing, you cannot get rid of it, it springs eternal. For another, you would not want to get rid of it even if you could, because it is precisely in the dynamic interplay of these contending visions of the future that our best chances lie. Divided we stand, united we fall (possibly after a spectacular short-term success).[1] Not all readers will agree with these views. But we hope that we have given enough material here for them to develop other thoughts of their own, which they will contribute to the ongoing debate.

The challenge, though it contains much that is technical, and much that can and should be reduced to economic calculation, is essentially institutional: encouraging the sorts of set-ups that thrive on this plurality and discouraging those that can perpetuate themselves only by excluding others. That the World Bank's support for the Narmada Valley Development Project has been humbled by a ramshackle coalition of environmental activists and illiterate tribals is not a disaster: it is wisdom asserting itself. And wisdom is possibly the most vital and least easily conjured up of all resources.

Notes

1 The full argument for this plural approach to technological decision-making is set out in Schwarz and Thompson (1990). For its empirical basis in the nuts and bolts of energy policy, see Keepin *et al.* (1984). A similar line of argument runs through Collingridge (1980).

References

BBS (Bangladesh Bureau of Statistics) (1981) *Population Census: Analytical Findings and National Tables.* Dhaka: Government of Bangladesh.

Collingridge, D. (1980) *The Social Control of Technology.* Milton Keynes: Open University Press.

Keepin, B., Wynne, B. and Thompson, M. (1984) Special Issue *The IIASA Energy Models.* Policy Sciences, **17**, 3.

Schwarz, M. and Thompson, M. (1990) *Divided We Stand: Redefining Politics, Technology and Social Choice.* London: Harvester Wheatsheaf, and Philadelphia: University of Pennsylvania Press.

Tiffen, M., Mortimore, M. and Gichuki, F. (1994) *More People, Less Erosion: Environmental Recovery in Kenya.* New York: Wiley.

Index